From the Walls In

Also by Charles Wing

FROM THE GROUND UP (with John N. Cole)

From the Walls In

CHARLES WING

Illustrations by Tom Paiement

An Atlantic Monthly Press Book
Little, Brown and Company   Boston Toronto

FIRST EDITION

The drawings on pages 4, 5, 6, 7, 8, 9, 10, 11 and 12 and those
between pages 20 and 21 were made possible through the
generosity of Greater Portland Landmarks, whose "Primer of
Architectural Styles" in *Living with Old Houses* is a practical
resource for those interested in housing, both old and new.

Figure 52 is taken from Strock & Koral: *Handbook of Air
Conditioning, Heating and Ventilating,* 2nd ed. Published and
copyright © 1965 by Industrial Press Inc. Reprinted with
permission.

Library of Congress Cataloging in Publication Data

Wing, Charles, 1939–
  From the walls in.

  "An Atlantic Monthly Press book."
  Bibliography: p.
  Includes index.
  1. Dwellings—Remodeling—Amateurs' manuals.
2. Dwellings—Energy conservation. 3. Solar
heating. I. Title.
TH4815.W56   643.7   78-26354
ISBN 0-316-94740-7

ALTANTIC-LITTLE, BROWN BOOKS
ARE PUBLISHED BY
LITTLE, BROWN AND COMPANY
IN ASSOCIATION WITH
THE ATLANTIC MONTHLY PRESS

Designed by Susan Windheim

*Published simultaneously in Canada
by Little, Brown & Company (Canada) Limited*

PRINTED IN THE UNITED STATES OF AMERICA

During one of the Cornerstones summer sessions one of the students' dogs began to feel poorly. In the course of conversation, the student told the local veterinarian that he was a participant in the Cornerstones program. "No horsefeathers over there" was the reply. This book is dedicated to Susan Black Wing, who keeps the horsefeathers out.

Contents

My Love Affair with Houses

Some five years ago I was living with my family as a refugee from the city on an old no-horse farm in Maine. I had left my job as lunar experimenter at MIT to return to the landscape of my childhood—the rolling, pine-tree pastureland of southern Maine. Like so many of my Woodstock contemporaries, I was drawn to the romantic image of life on a farm.

After a year of searching we found the place of our dreams in Woolwich—a collection of seven buildings in various stages of decay, but commanding a 360° view of the surrounding countryside. We congratulated ourselves on our good fortune. Later we heard that the property had been on the market for three years at the same price. Only we had been myopic enough not to see it for the disaster it was.

After returning the U-Haul truck, waving our city helpers off on the bus, and distributing the boxes to likely locations, we settled down to assess our future. I, as is my wont, began by scientifically compiling in an old laboratory notebook a list of tasks to be accomplished. I listed each task, the number of man-hours required for their accomplishment and the estimated cost. Susan, able to summarize a situation at an intuitive glance, began to cry; she cried for two weeks; she cried until the notebook was filled with four hundred entries adding up to three man-years, at which point I announced we were returning to the city.

Then a miracle happened. At the end of moving day we had planted a row of peas as a sort of toast to the land and our new life. The very day after I had given up, a single pea shoved a lump of clay aside and toasted us in return. Susan never cried again that summer.

We started working on the old farm. We cut down three huge dead elms (and the electric service and part of the ell in the process). We destroyed one of the outbuildings in trying to move it with our tractor. (It had no sills and its studs stuck in the ground like golf cleats.) We watered the garden and discovered that both of our dug wells were nothing more than large holes in the clay, filled once a year by the annual runoff. Fearful that the barn would succumb to the stresses of children swinging from 8″ X 8″ oak timbers, we engaged a bulldozer to bring it down. Like an aging warrior, the barn proved in its fight to death that we were wrong. In short, the scientist from MIT largely confirmed the natives' suspicions that people from Boston were fools.

But things began to get better. Soon, for every

project that proved a disaster, another proved a success. In spite of the abrasions, black and blue bumps, and purple thumbnails, the place began to pick up. Friends from the city couldn't believe we were doing it; even the neighbors had kind words (as well as occasional homemade doughnuts and advice on chicken plucking). Not that it would have made any difference; I was into this project to the end!

I was all the while paying the bills by teaching physics at Bowdoin College in Brunswick. I don't ordinarily hold much truck with astrology, but for want of a better explanation: some planets got together in 1973; Bowdoin offered me the opportunity to teach a course in any field outside my expertise. Their theory, to which I heartily subscribe, is that the best teacher is also a student. Boy, did I have a subject! "House Construction" seemed a little heavy for the ivy-covered halls of Bowdoin, so I camouflaged it under the title "The Art of the House." I was given a paid semester in which to investigate, read, argue, write, and reflect about that human construct we call the house. My experiences with carpentry had thus far left me with the distinct impression that some, at least, of the practices of the housing industry were without foundation. My position at Bowdoin left me in the rather strange position of being disdained by architects for having no formal training, looked upon by academic colleagues as lacking in intellectual prowess, and ignored at the local lumber yard as a pathetic dilettante. But it provided the perfect medium for the growth of a new way of thinking about houses.

The course was oversubscribed. It was immensely popular with the students who, like me, were fond of questioning the practices of their parents' generation. At first it was fun to ask, "Why this way? What are the functions we expect of a wall? How well does the conventional wall perform? Why is a basement necessary if all we expect of it is to house the furnace and laundry machines? Why does the government require a separate bedroom for each child when the only

alternative for many is no house at all?" At first it was fun, then it was serious. The back of the room began filling with "listeners" from outside the college. Slowly the tone of the course shifted. At the end of each ninety-minute class the college students left, the listeners moved down front, and education began in earnest.

Who were these people, the listeners? They were people like you. People in their twenties, thirties, forties, and fifties; people with children; people with dreams, but, above all, dreams for a conventional home built in the conventional way. If these people wanted a house, they themselves would have to build it. They would have to become owner-builders.

The owner-builder movement has had its ups and downs. The owner-builder marches forth, as I had, armed with ignorance. It is this ignorance that is both his salvation and his downfall. He doesn't "know" that all windows have to open, and by building fixed windows saves himself thousands of dollars. He doesn't "know" that a house has to face the street and, turning instinctively toward the south, he builds a passive solar house. On the other hand, he doesn't understand flashing, and his house leaks.

Clearly what was needed was a school for owner-builders. Not a vocational school where carpenters drill would-be carpenters on the hows but not the whys, but a school where ordinary people learn to think about their houses and find the answers to their questions. I left Bowdoin the following semester to turn the course into a school for owner-builders. Two years later, in order to develop further my interests, I left the Shelter Institute and started Cornerstones Building School with my wife, Susan. After teaching some five hundred students (or was it the other way around?), I took a break, sat down, and with coauthor, romantic postindustrialist, and recent owner-builder John Cole, committed my lectures to book form in *From the Ground Up*.

Meanwhile, back at the farm, I had fallen victim to my own preachings. It became increasingly difficult to deal with that out-of-square, off-center heap of dry rot called a house. From the ground up, from the ground up; clean, fresh, level and square; passive solar, optimum insulation, no maintenance. So down the road we went to the lower fifty acres, possessions piled in a trailer following tractor, followed by the two biggest and best Bowdoin students, to build the new vision. Quite a crew we were! For me, a fresh start as carpenter/architect. For them, the ultimate laboratory experiment. And the house was beautiful. It looked good; it smelled good and it was good. Its strong frame looked like the bleached ribs of a beached whale, the wood smelled like pine incense, and the house was pure Wings.

We lived in that house for two years and it worked. All of the conclusions we had drawn in the Socratic dialogue of the classes proved correct. It *was* possible to start fresh, examine the assumptions, and draw logical conclusions. The 1,729-square-foot house sailed through the Maine winters on pure sunshine and three cords of maple. People began to sit up and take notice.

But at the same time another notion was growing. There are 80,000,000 existing dwellings in this country, as some of their occupants increasingly reminded me. From the ground up is fine for those who wish to move, to buy land, to build a new home. But what about the overwhelming majority, who will for various reasons continue to live in existing housing? The real energy problem lies with these houses, and a solution to the energy crisis must include their rehabilitation.

Cannot the same analysis, the same questioning, the same spirit be brought to bear upon the *re*-building of houses? "Cannot we have *From the Walls in*?" asked my publisher. "Cannot we have a course for owner-rebuilders?" asked the students. Perhaps I hadn't given the old farm a fair chance. Perhaps I simply hadn't looked at rebuilding as an exercise open to that same thought process. With the creative juices once again flowing, we put our brand-new passive solar home on the market and began looking for an in-town candidate for our experiment. We were going to see if an existing house couldn't be *retrofitted* to approximate the passive solar performance of our new house.

In looking for the "right" house we had a lot of factors on our side. Brunswick is a popular town, and its real estate is scarce. While the competition was looking for the perfect specimens, we searched for cracked ceilings and walls, tacky wallpaper and paint, no insulation, an old clunker of a furnace, and—best of all—out-of-sight fuel bills. That was what we would not be paying for, things we were about to destroy. The real estate agent rolled her eyes in disbelief as we ran from room to room exclaiming over each new imperfection. We were lucky; no, not lucky. We recognized the value of the fourteen-room two-story house the moment we saw it because we had analyzed beforehand what we were about to do. The house was in perfect exterior condition; sound of frame and straight on a good lot. But the interior! The interior needed some tender loving care, some "redecoration," as the real estate lady so delicately put it.

Redecoration, our eyes! It needed *retrofit;* it needed thermal upgrading; it needed to be hauled to the dump!

Once again we promised to keep the neighbors entertained for the summer. They knew something was up as soon as they saw plaster lath and acoustic tile sailing out of the windows, but they really settled into their porch rockers when they saw the entire heating system emerging from the basement.

The first decision we faced was whether to gut the house. To *gut;* a better word could not be found. We agreed to gut a section of the house totaling 1,600 square feet. We hired two helpers with inclinations toward the act and outfitted ourselves with helmets, goggles, face masks, gloves, steel-toed shoes, crowbars, a chain saw, and Coca-Cola. Kids loved it, and some arrived from miles around. Down came the acoustic tile; down came the plaster; down came the lath; and down came Susan through the ceiling! The chain saw got its first exercise since the woods of Woolwich, and out came the walls. Not only was openness familiar and appealing to us, but necessary for our revolutionary heating system— a wood stove! After two weeks we were through. Two hundred and twenty barrels of plaster and lath had gone to the dump. We had more than two-thirds of a new house. The house looked exactly as it must have one hundred years ago before the carpenters finished off the interior. What a dramatic space! A thirteen-thousand-cubic-foot lump of clay had been handed to us to do with what we wished!

Now the fun could begin. First we put up a huge, hand-planed native spruce beam where once a supporting wall had been. *Voilà*—three small rooms and a hall became a 20′ × 26′ living and dining area with room left over for a wall-sized bookcase and a baby grand piano.

Next the kitchen. We built open shelves for the dishes and turned a former bathroom into a pantry for pots, pans, and foodstuffs. We made kitchen cabinets the easy way by recycling the old drawers and installing new preformed counter tops. Upon taking up the old linoleum we found a beautiful old maple floor as tight as a drum. A little sanding and several coats of tung oil yielded the most carefree kitchen floor we've ever experienced.

We worried about the lovely old pumpkin pine floors in the livingroom as we carelessly rolled four-hundred-pound barrels of plaster over them and dropped gobs of joint compound on them. Worry was unnecessary; we washed the floors with steel wool and water, gave them a fresh coat of polyurethane, and found that the abuse had only added to their beauty. Just as in a new house, insulating was a snap: 12″ of fiberglass between and over the attic joists, 4″ of urea-formaldehyde foam in the walls, and 6″ of fiberglass between the basement floor joists. Over all of it a 6-mil polyethylene vapor barrier, protecting not only the insulation from condensation, but us from infiltrating wind.

The single-glazed windows were in good repair but rattled in their frames. First we cut off the old sash weights and taped the pulley holes closed. After puttying and painting we caulked and nailed the top sash in place. That solved one-half of the leaky window problem! To the bottom sash we attached V-type aluminum door weather stripping on three sides, reducing the infiltration to the level of a brand-new window. We still weren't satisfied with the night heat loss through the glass, however. The Cornerstones students helped us evolve an interior insulating shutter that is a marriage of the old Indian shutter and modern space-age material. The shutters turn daytime windows into nighttime walls. We covered them with decorative fabric and eliminated the need for curtains or drapes. The shutters are attractive and easy for even the novice to make. We even made one to cover a sliding glass door.

Twelve weeks and $8,200 later we had a brand new sixteen-hundred-square-foot house—a house with new interior surfaces, new wiring, new plumbing, new bathroom, and new kitchen. A house that, without benefit of a solar orientation, gets through the Maine winter on four cords of wood.

From the Walls In is the culmination of a love/hate relationship begun upon that old fungus pile in Woolwich. It ends on a note of love. It is to old houses what *From the Ground Up* is to new—a compendium of insights, a pile of my lectures, and, I hope, a guide to clear thinking about retrofit.

What Have We Here?

1.

A Short Course in American Architecture

This chapter is intended to aid you in deciding whether your house should be extensively retrofitted or whether it is too valuable a part of the American architectural heritage to bear any change. To put retrofit into perspective, we should first compare it to other commonly used terms.

> *Preservation* means vigilant maintenance of a building in its original form.
> *Reconstruction* means duplication of an old building, using either new or used materials.
> *Restoration* means undoing all changes made after original construction.
> *Renovation* means changing in any way to make more useful.
> *Retrofit* means improving the energy efficiency of a building.

Some aspects of retrofit (such as caulking building joints) do not conflict with any of the other terms. Others, such as installation of solar collectors, are contradictory to preservation, reconstruction, and restoration. We are particularly concerned in this chapter about the conflict with preservation.

If you find yourself living in a house of historic value, you have a tough choice to make. The number of such houses is so small that their retrofit is insignificant to the overall energy budget of the world. Their energy consumption is not an insignificant part of your personal budget, however, and that is precisely why you are reading this book. The possibility of dry-rot damage in the wall framing and sheathing of buildings insulated without proper vapor barriers is widely acknowledged. This is probably the topic of greatest current interest to historic preservationists. The occupants of historic houses carry a large burden. Most of us are weighing the risks over the next thirty to forty years; they must consider the preservation of their houses for the coming centuries.

I personally believe that the value of the truly historic house lies not only in the preservation of its architectural embellishments but also in the demonstration of an earlier way of life. Seen this way, the question is no longer *whether* to insulate. The question is whether or not you are interested in living with and within the old house the way it was originally intended to function.

I was recently invited to serve on a panel discussing the pros and cons of insulating old houses. As an antidote to my strictly scientific handling of the subject, the sponsor wisely provided a lover

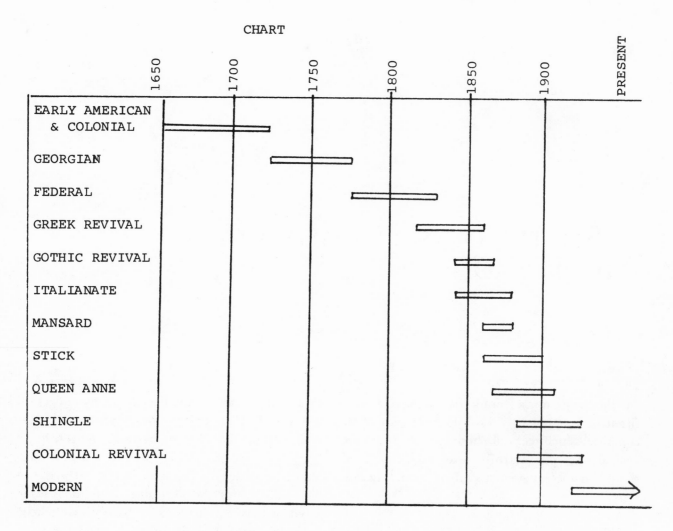

of old houses, architect Christopher Glass of Camden, Maine. I am forever indebted to Mr. Glass for his summary suggestion that, in the case of historic houses, perhaps what needs retrofitting is not the house, but the occupant.

The decision has to be yours. I can only provide you with a starting kit of tools with which to make your decision. Illustration 1 is a time chart showing the span of major activity for each of a dozen styles of American architecture. Illustrations 2 through 13 are representative examples of each. The characteristics listed for each of the recognized old house styles are meant only as clues to start you off on your detective work. There is no such thing as a pure example of any of the styles. Differences abound due to variation in regional taste and the influence of local builders. Moreover, very few houses have escaped major renovation by at least one of perhaps a dozen different owners. Most of the states have historic preservation commissions, established to handle federal historic preservation funds. They can refer you to historic preservation groups in your area or otherwise guide you in your detective work.

3

Georgian (1725-1775)

The Georgian style overlaps the various Colonial styles but differs from them in being more elegant. It suited the more gracious life-style now afforded by many of the colonists. Simplicity was still considered elegant, and so overhangs and decoration were modest. Some of the changes include:

a central hall
two chimneys instead of the one central chimney
 (not always)
a higher foundation exposure
fancy interior woodwork
some wallpaper above the chair rail height.

5

Greek Revival (1820-1860)

In the early 1800's the world fell out of love with the Romans (Georgian style) and into love with the Greeks. The result was perhaps the strongest style ever to assert itself in American architecture, embracing the spectrum from government buildings to rude farmhouses. In some cases the only thing Greek about the building was its facade. Imagine an otherwise undistinguished building with a facade like the Parthenon! In the finer houses, however, the Greek influence permeated the inside as well. Common, but as usual not universal, features include:

pediments (roof triangles) at the gables and
  sometimes over doors and even windows
deemphasis of chimneys
larger windows, often with shutters
wide corner trim, sometimes resembling columns
entrance often in the gable end, emphasizing the
  temple aspect
larger overhangs with wide cornices
wood walls that are sometimes smooth in order
  to resemble stone.

Gothic Revival (1840-1870)

The Gothic Revival style was the first of the general class of Victorian styles. It evolved in response to the new balloon style of framing, which utilized closer and smaller framing members than the previous large-member braced frames. The balloon frame allowed more flexibility and complexity in building. The Gothic Revival style took advantage of this fact, giving the designer more freedom to create interior spaces by adding wings, ells, and bays. No longer did the requirement for external symmetry dictate the interior space;

in fact, the interior now controlled the exterior. The ornate exterior decoration characteristic of this style probably evolved as an attempt to tie the exterior together in some semblance of order. Distinguishing features include:

    porches and verandas
    bay windows
    intersecting sections
    high-pitched roofs
    dormer windows
    thin, often fancy, chimneys
    fancy scrollwork trim on gables and porches.

8

Mansard (1860-1880)

The Mansard style is easily recognized by its one dominant feature—the mansard roof. Since the "roof" functions as a wall, the purpose of the builders is not entirely clear. A prevalent theory is that the Mansard style allowed construction of a three-story building that would be taxed on the basis of two stories. One shouldn't get the impression that one style excluded the others during the Victorian era, which roughly spanned the years 1840–1900. All of the styles coexisted with others, including many not cited here. The balloon frame revolution, the availability of fancy machine-cut trim, and the growing number of books on building encouraged builders to play architect. The result was that the majority of houses built during this period are rather disparagingly termed "Carpenter Gothic."

In addition to the obvious mansard roof, the Mansard style is characterized by:

> at least two dormers projecting from every side of the roof
> heavy, overhanging eaves, often with supporting brackets
> bay windows
> double entrance doors.

Stick (1860-1900)

The Stick style usually has strongly projecting gable eaves falsely supported by decorative braces. Other features include:

decorative effects on walls and in porch railings through the use of thin pieces of wood (sticks)

generous overhangs all around, supported at the corners and peaks by decorative braces

thin chimneys

steep roofs

dormers

porches with roofs supported by columns having diagonal braces at tops.

10

Queen Anne (1870-1910)

The last of the Victorian styles, the Queen Anne, is known for its turrets of round and octagonal sections, a variety of decorative shingle effects, and stained glass windows. Other signs are:

houses complex but massive-appearing

mixtures of turrets, dormers, and projecting
  gables in the roof

windows with a mixture of clear and stained glass

shingles cut and applied in geometric patterns

thin chimneys with decorative relief.

12

Colonial or Georgian Revival
(1880-1930)

The American centennial revived interest in the classic pre-Revolutionary styles. In a revolt against the amorphous shingle style and the un-disciplined Victorian styles, many architects returned to the strict symmetry of the Georgian style:

symmetry inside and outside
a widespread use of brick
dormers and end chimneys, giving the roof added
   symmetry
classic cornices
porticos with columns protecting the front and
   often side entrances.

13

Nondescript (1700-present)

I would say conservatively that the majority of houses built in the United States over its entire history do not fit into any one of the above categories. More affluent owners built in the style of their day, built better houses, and subsequently put more into their upkeep. A screening process has therefore eliminated most of the really old nondescript houses. But nondescript houses were built in every age simply because, as today, their owners were more interested in getting a roof over their heads than in architectural detail. I offer the following for the disappointed owners of the nondescript houses.

What of architectural beauty I now see, I know has gradually grown from within outward, out of the necessities and character of the indweller, who is the only builder,—out of some unconscious truthfulness, and nobleness, without ever a thought for the appearance; and whatever additional beauty of this kind is destined to be produced will be preceded by a like unconscious beauty of life. The most interesting dwellings in this country, as the painter knows, are the most unpretending, humble log huts and cottages of the poor commonly; it is the life of the inhabitants whose shells they are, and not any peculiarity in their surfaces merely, which makes them *picturesque;* and equally interesting will be the citizen's suburban box, when his life shall be as simple and as agreeable to the imagination, and there is as little straining after effect in the style of his dwelling.

—Thoreau, *Walden*

2.

A Shorter Course in Economics

When most of us think of economics, we picture clean-shaven men in dark suits and striped ties, consulting payback tables in mahogany-paneled rooms. They make decisions involving tens of thousands of dollars, tens of years, interest rates, inflation, depreciation, and on and on. Few of us realize that we make decisions of equal magnitude in our own lives. For whatever reason, Americans are accustomed to thinking in the short term. "Can I make the down payment now? How much can I borrow? What's the monthly payment?" We are a society of the moment, of instant gratification, of fleeting fashion and interest.

I had an illuminating conversation with a neighbor once, which will probably not at first glance strike you as extraordinary.

The neighbor said, "My fuel bills are killing me!"

"Is your house well insulated?" asked I.

"None at all," was the reply.

"You know," I said, "insulating your attic pays for itself in one year."

"I know that—but I can't afford to buy the insulation."(!)

The average homeowner will pay the bank in excess of $100,000 in mortgage payments over a thirty-year period. In addition, in the northern areas of the country, he may pay in excess of $30,000 in order to maintain his home at 70° F. It behooves us to sit down for a moment and consider the ways of the economist. As the saying goes, "The rich get richer and the poor get poorer," and there's probably a logical explanation.

LIMITS

Ever since the discovery of coal and oil in Pennsylvania, the United States has been on a production binge, fed by unrestrained consumption of fossil fuels. The United States has an "energy economy." Our high standard of living depends on 6 percent of the world's population consuming one-third of all the world's energy. This statistic is made less obscene only by the inclusion of the other industrialized nations, whose goals apparently are to emulate and perhaps even exceed the U.S. figures. In fact, U.S. per-capita energy consumption is one hundred times that of the least developed nations.

That this situation alarmed few people before 1973 is not surprising. Because of technological improvements in drilling and mining and price controls imposed on fuels, during the twenty years preceding the Arab oil boycott fuel prices actually rose at a rate slower than general inflation. In other words, relative to the other costs of purchasing and maintaining homes, fuel costs continually decreased in importance. A second factor was the sheer magnitude of the numbers used in describing fossil fuel reserves. I don't recall anytime during my formal education having to deal with numbers in excess of four digits—with the single exception of the speed of light, which everyone knows is practically infinite. Any number so large that we are not sure of its verbalization is stored away in memory as simply infinite, or something not to worry about. The problem is that annual consumption is also getting to be such a number.

To illustrate how annual consumption could have increased from a few barrels of oil per year to a figure presently beyond our comprehension, I'll borrow from *Limits to Growth,* by Meadows and Meadows, the publication of which in 1972 rudely awakened many slumbering minds.

Unrestrained growth in nature invariably follows what is known in mathematical circles as the exponential curve (Illustration 14).

The exponential, or natural growth curve, is characterized by a doubling of quantity each successive period of time, t. In other words, starting at an arbitrary quantity of 1 at time $t=0$, the quantity at successive times is

Elapsed Time	Quantity
0t	1
1t	2
2t	4
3t	8
4t	16

Energy consumption in the United States has been following such a curve for 100 years. You probably don't find this growth pattern particularly disturbing. If you don't find the pattern upsetting, you are in the vast majority. You also have no right to judge the king who lost his kingdom to a clever courtier.

In payment for a beautiful chessboard the courtier asked only for rice: one grain for the first square, two for the second, four for the third, and so on, doubling the number of grains for each successive square. The king lost his kingdom in paying for the chessboard, for, as your calculator will tell you, one doubled 64 times equals 184 followed by 17 zeroes!

A parable that even better illustrates our

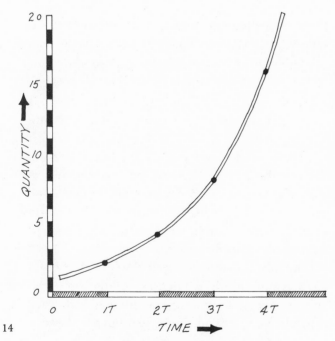

16

energy predicament is that of the lily pond (Illustration 16). It seems a man noticed the sudden appearance of a lily pad in his pond. Being an educated man, he knew that the lily pad choked out other forms of life and, furthermore, doubled its numbers every day. Being an extremely busy modern man, he took mental note of the potential problem and promised to rid the pond of lily pads as soon as they had covered one half of the pond. *Question:* If the lily pads were to cover the pond completely on day 30, on which day would the man have begun to remove the growth?

Everyone agrees that the total quantity of fossil fuels on earth is a fixed number. (They don't all agree on the precise number, but they do agree that it is fixed.) Everyone also agrees that our annual rate of consumption of fossil fuels is doubling every eighteen years. Let's plot the past rate of consumption of fossil fuels as a function of time in Illustration 17. The curve is an exponential curve. In other words, the growth of energy consumption has until now been a natural or unrestrained growth. The coordinates of the graph in Illustration 17 are *amount consumed per year* and *year*. If we multiply the two coordinates we get simply *amount consumed.* The area under the curve from the origin to the present year represents the total amount consumed until now. If the total amount of fossil fuels is fixed and the area under the consumption curve is the amount consumed, then obviously the consumption curve must at some point turn downward in order that the amount consumed not exceed the amount initially available, q.

The most famous and universally accepted dictum of economics is the rule of supply and demand, which states that when demand exceeds supply, prices rise in order to decrease demand. The more the demand exceeds the supply, the faster prices rise. I refer you to Illustration 18, showing the U.S. fuel price index measured against the general consumer price index for the past three decades.

Economists have wasted a lot of time in refuting fine points in *The Limits to Growth.* They do us a disservice; they distract us from the job at hand. The question today is when are we going to clean up our pond?

TOOLS OF THE ECONOMIST

The question addressed above is probably the most important ever faced by mankind. We're all going to have to do our best to resolve it. This book is part of my contribution. I hope here to make you aware that there is something you can do to turn the consumption pattern downward. I don't have to rely on your conscience entirely, however. There are powerful economic incentives already at work. If you don't already know them,

17

AMOUNT CONSUMED PER YEAR

EXPONENTIAL CURVE

PRICE PAID

ACTUAL USE

Q = AREA

YEARS ➡

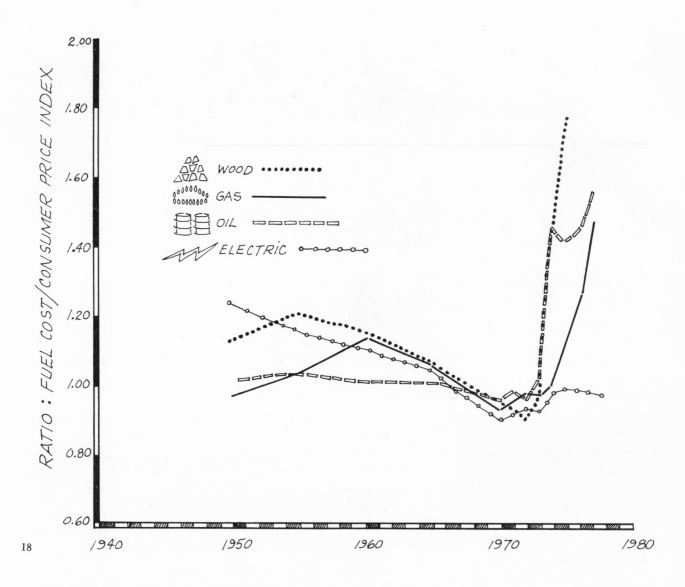

take time to study and understand the tools of the economists. These tools are as important as the hammer and saw in retrofitting your home.

LIFE-CYCLE COST

Our attitudes toward the costs of home ownership are largely derived from the attitudes of the institutions financing them. During the decades of cheap energy, the measure of credit-worthiness of a borrower was the so-called PITI ratio—a ratio of monthly income to the sum of monthly payments for *principal, interest, taxes,* and *insurance.* Recently, banks have been forced to calculate the PITIEM ratio, incorporating the additional monthly costs of *energy* and *maintenance.* For many homeowners the monthly energy bill is rapidly approaching the monthly mortgage payment. As energy costs spiral upward, a new awareness grows—an awareness that the true cost of owning a home is not simply next month's mortgage payment but the *life-cycle cost,* or the total cost of building, financing, maintaining, and fueling the house over its useful life.

This book is about saving money by saving energy. Fortunately, we can focus on two items: *principal* (cost of improvement) and *energy* (cost of fueling the house over the lifetime of the house). Most economists agree that interest, taxes, and insurance, in combination with income tax deductions and rebates, very nearly equal inflation. Since they approximately balance in the life-cycle cost equation, we will ignore them.

Certain energy conservation actions, such as insulating the attic, obviously pay for themselves in reduced fuel bills. The payback of others is not so certain, however. And far from obvious are the exact amounts and combinations of improvements that will result in the maximum possible lifetime savings. The purpose of life-cycle-benefit-cost analysis is the determination of that combination of energy actions which will result in the lowest total cost of improvement plus fuel over the life of the house.

PRESENT VALUE (PV)

First, in order to compare fairly the value of future fuel savings and costs of improvements made today, we need the concept of present value. As we all know, a dollar under the mattress today will buy less bread tomorrow. Similarly, a dollar saved on a future fuel bill will be less valuable than one saved today. Mathematically,

$$PV = \frac{FV}{(1+i)^t}$$

PV = present "real dollar" value of future savings
FV = "face value" of future savings t years from now
i = annual inflation rate
t = number of years from now

For example, if inflation were 7 percent per year (i=.07), then a "dollar" next year would be worth:

$$PV = \$1.00 \div 1.07 = 93¢$$

Similarly, a "dollar" two years from now will be worth only:

$$PV = \$1.00 \div (1.07 \times 1.07) = 86.5¢$$

On the other hand, fuel prices are increasing every year. Suppose fuel prices rise at 10 percent per year. Then an amount of fuel costing $1.00 today will cost $1.10 in one year and $1.21 two years from now. There are thus seen to be two monetary forces at work here, one pushing upward, the other pulling downward. Mathematically,

$$PV = \frac{(1+p)^t}{(1+i)^t}$$

PV = real dollar value of fuel savings to be made in t years from now
t = number of years from now
i = annual inflation rate
p = rate at which fuel prices increase

PRESENT WORTH FACTOR (PWF)

Of course we will be saving fuel dollars every year from the time of the improvement. Therefore, t takes on successive values. The present worth factor, PWF, is the sum of the present values for all the years considered (the lifetime of the improvement).

If you play with the numbers, you will soon find that the important factor is not p or i but (p–i), the rate at which fuel prices increase relative to inflation. If p=i, then energy savings in the future have the same real value as energy savings today and PWF equals simply the number of years considered. If p is greater than i, then future energy savings have greater value than energy savings today, and PWF is consequently greater. Table 1 lists PWF for several values of (p–i). Going from the future value of one dollar saved to the future value of total annual saving is easy:

Present Value of Life-Cycle Savings
= First-Year Saving × PWF

BENEFIT-COST RATIO (BCR)

We now have a method of figuring total real savings over the life of the house. However, we still don't know the relative priorities of various conservation improvements we might make. What we need to know is the relative number of dollars returned compared to the number of dollars spent on the various improvements. If Improvement A promises to save $10 for each dollar spent, and Improvement B only $2 for each dollar spent, we should implement A before B. *Benefit* is simply the present value of life-cycle savings as calculated above. *Cost* is the number of dollars actually spent today to effect the improvement. If we assume a home improvement or second mortgage interest rate balanced by inflation and tax breaks, then it makes no difference whether we use out-of-pocket dollars or borrowed dollars. In both cases, use today's dollars. The benefit-cost ratio is

$$BCR = \frac{benefit\ due\ to\ improvement}{cost\ of\ improvement}$$

The BCR is a direct measure of the relative priority of an improvement. After calculating the benefits and the costs of all the improvements contemplated, compile a priority list, starting with the project having the highest BCR. Spending money in order of priority will automatically achieve the greatest return on investment. Note: (1) If the BCR of a project is less than 1.0, then it's economically not worth doing. (2) If your budget doesn't allow completing one of the higher-priority jobs immediately, drop to the next lower item and return when you have the funds.

PAYBACK PERIOD

The number of years required for savings to surpass initial cost is often used as a measure of priority. If all improvements had equal life expectancies, the payback period would be a valid criterion. However, while insulation in the attic may last forty years, an aluminum storm door on a house containing six children may last only five years. The benefit-cost ratio reflects this

Table 1. Present Worth Factors for Values of (p-i)

life (years) t	(percentages)					
	1	2	3	4	5	6
1	1.00	1.00	1.00	1.00	1.00	1.00
2	2.01	2.02	2.03	2.04	2.05	2.06
3	3.03	3.06	3.09	3.12	3.15	3.18
4	4.06	4.12	4.18	4.25	4.31	4.37
5	5.10	5.20	5.31	5.42	5.53	5.64
6	6.15	6.31	6.47	6.63	6.80	6.98
7	7.21	7.43	7.66	7.90	7.14	7.39
8	8.29	8.58	8.89	9.24	9.55	9.90
9	9.37	9.75	10.16	10.58	11.03	11.49
10	10.46	10.95	11.46	12.01	12.58	13.18
11	11.57	12.17	12.81	13.49	14.21	14.97
12	12.68	13.41	14.19	15.03	15.92	16.87
13	13.81	14.68	15.62	16.63	17.71	18.88
14	14.95	15.97	17.09	18.29	19.60	21.02
15	16.10	17.29	18.60	20.02	21.58	23.28
16	17.26	18.64	20.16	21.82	23.66	25.67
17	18.43	20.01	21.76	23.70	25.84	28.21
18	19.61	21.41	23.41	25.65	28.13	30.91
19	20.81	22.84	25.12	27.67	30.54	33.76
20	22.02	24.30	26.87	29.78	33.07	36.79
25	28.24	32.03	36.46	41.65	47.73	54.86
30	34.78	40.57	47.58	56.08	66.44	79.06
35	41.66	49.99	60.46	73.65	90.32	111.43
40	48.89	60.40	75.40	95.03	120.80	154.76
45	56.48	71.89	92.72	121.03	159.70	212.74
50	64.46	84.58	112.80	152.67	209.35	290.34

important difference by either assigning a five-year life to the door or requiring that the cost include the installation of *eight* doors over the next forty years! Because of short life expectancies, some "improvements" that at first seem to have reasonable payback periods are, in fact, not worth doing. This is reflected either in a BCR of less than 1.0 or a payback period that exceeds the life expectancy. With this warning in mind, payback periods are still quite useful because they are in line with our usual way of thinking.

To Gut or Not to Gut

The first part of this chapter dealt with the economics of energy conservation. We considered cost of implementation, present worth factors, future fuel savings, and payback periods. Individual energy-related improvements are best dealt with in this way. But a house is larger overall than the sum of its parts. Particularly when considering an extensive retrofit involving non-energy-related improvements, we must address the larger question of the "value" of a house. The most drastic thing we can do to a house is gut it; whether gutting pays back is a serious question.

THE VALUE OF A HOUSE

What is the "value" of a house? A lot of elements come into play when we consider the value of our own house. Particularly if we've grown up in the house, part of our identity is involved; therein is our idea of "houseness." Like an old sweater or pair of shoes, no other house could ever be as comfortable—at least to our psyches. No matter how skilled the craftsmen, this house could never be reproduced: the memories, good and bad, the secret messages penciled in the attic or basement, the old tree-house tree, and the family dog buried under the lilac.

Soon after we purchased and retrofitted our house, we opened it to the neighbors. Nearly two hundred people came to see the foamed walls, the bright enameled wood stoves, insulating window shutters, and large open spaces where once had been cramped rooms. We graciously accepted the "ooh's" and "aah's" from the duly impressed neighbors. Some gushed; some wanted information on how-to; some merely strolled through as if afraid to commit themselves to personal opinion; but in the corner stood an old lady with tear-filled eyes. She had grown up in this house.

Beyond possible emotional ties are factors such as historic value (Chapter 1), value of the improved lot, proximity to schools, parks, and shopping, and the values of surrounding properties. As a single example, a run-down property in the middle of a generally well-kept neighborhood has a greater potential value than an identical one in a run-down area.

The purpose of this chapter is to help you make sound economic decisions regarding the "value" of your property and improvements thereto. When shopping for a house to retrofit or even when considering extensive renovations to your present house, fantasy is an ever-present danger. Retrofitting is a creative act, and fantasy is a necessary ingredient in architectural creativity. But fantasy knows no limits; unbridled fantasy magnifies results while reducing cost and labor estimates. My personal fantasy factor is 2x—everything costs twice as much, takes twice as long, is twice as hard—as I have learned from hard experience. As a younger man I started at between 3 and 4, but try as I may, I can't seem to get below 2. I'd be very surprised if you can do much better. So listen hard to what may be the best advice I have to offer. *THE KEY TO SUCCESS IS FANTASY BOUNDED BY REALITY.* You must supply the fantasy; here is some reality.

ESTIMATING RETROFITTING

One of your concerns should be that you don't begin a project that will prove to be beyond your resources. In such a case you would be better off never to start. The other concern is that the value

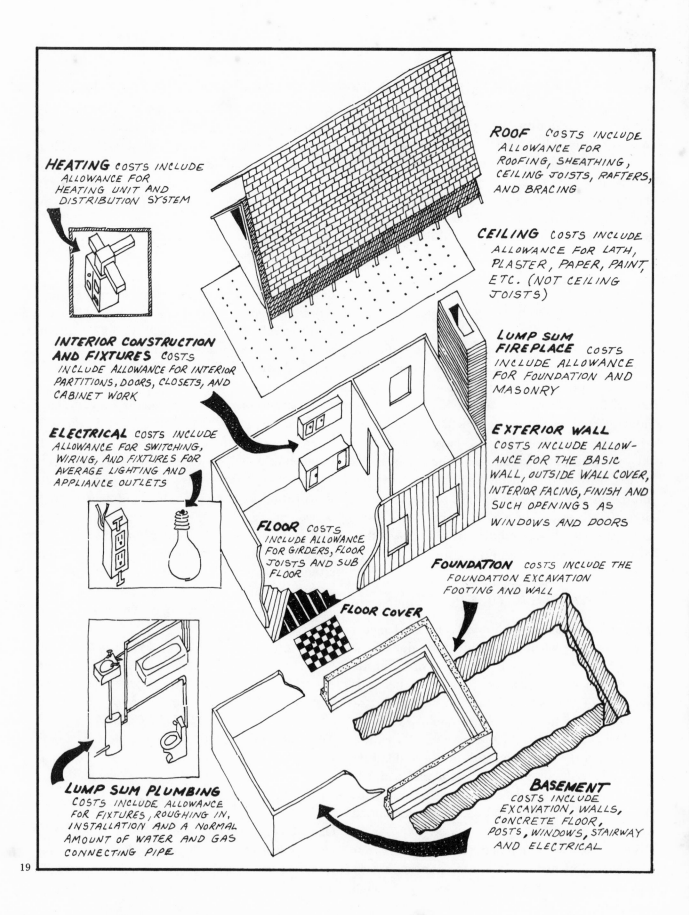

HEATING COSTS INCLUDE ALLOWANCE FOR HEATING UNIT AND DISTRIBUTION SYSTEM

ROOF COSTS INCLUDE ALLOWANCE FOR ROOFING, SHEATHING, CEILING JOISTS, RAFTERS, AND BRACING

CEILING COSTS INCLUDE ALLOWANCE FOR LATH, PLASTER, PAPER, PAINT, ETC. (NOT CEILING JOISTS)

INTERIOR CONSTRUCTION AND FIXTURES COSTS INCLUDE ALLOWANCE FOR INTERIOR PARTITIONS, DOORS, CLOSETS, AND CABINET WORK

LUMP SUM FIREPLACE COSTS INCLUDE ALLOWANCE FOR FOUNDATION AND MASONRY

ELECTRICAL COSTS INCLUDE ALLOWANCE FOR SWITCHING, WIRING, AND FIXTURES FOR AVERAGE LIGHTING AND APPLIANCE OUTLETS

EXTERIOR WALL COSTS INCLUDE ALLOWANCE FOR THE BASIC WALL, OUTSIDE WALL COVER, INTERIOR FACING, FINISH AND SUCH OPENINGS AS WINDOWS AND DOORS

FLOOR COSTS INCLUDE ALLOWANCE FOR GIRDERS, FLOOR JOISTS AND SUB FLOOR

FOUNDATION COSTS INCLUDE THE FOUNDATION EXCAVATION FOOTING AND WALL

FLOOR COVER

LUMP SUM PLUMBING COSTS INCLUDE ALLOWANCE FOR FIXTURES, ROUGHING IN, INSTALLATION AND A NORMAL AMOUNT OF WATER AND GAS CONNECTING PIPE

BASEMENT COSTS INCLUDE EXCAVATION, WALLS, CONCRETE FLOOR, POSTS, WINDOWS, STAIRWAY AND ELECTRICAL

19

Early American or Colonial (1640-1775)

If you have such a house, the chances are very small that you don't already know it. Included in this group are such diverse styles as the one-story Cape Cod, one-and-a-half- or two-story Colonial (farmhouse), brick Dutch Colonial, Colonial with Lean-to (the Saltbox), and the two-story Colonial with Overhang (Garrison). The common characteristics include:

 full or partial stone cellars
 small-paned 9/6, 12/8, 12/12 double-sashed windows
 center chimneys
 post and girt (braced) frame
 little if any roof overhang either at gable or eave
 no exterior shutters.

Federal (1775-1830)

The Georgian gradually changed into the Federal style through a growing freedom of interior design behind a strictly Roman classical exterior:

 extremely symmetrical exterior with an emphasis
  on horizontal lines
 evenly spaced windows
 doorways with sidelights and semicircular or
  elliptical fanlights
 chimneys in the end walls
 the use of brick in building, even in New England
 interior spaces with many curved walls
 elegant interior woodwork.

Italianate (1840-1880)

Many architectural historians feel that the Italianate style marks the beginning of a downward slide in American architecture. Some rigor was lost with the introduction of the Gothic Revival, but here the exterior begins to lose all coherence. To distinguish Italianate from Gothic Revival, some clues may be:

 round-top windows
 heavier, more massive appearance
 double entrance doors
 lower-pitched roofs
 cupolas on the roof.

Shingle (1880-1930)

There could be no other name for this style of architecture. It resembles nothing so much as a mound of shingles. Both the roof and the walls are shingled, and with typically no more roof overhang or trim than in the early Colonial styles, the effect is overwhelming. Some features are:

 either low-pitched or gambrel roof with little
  if any overhang
 absence of strong lines or shadows
 porches that form indentations in the main
  structure
 more shingles than you could shake a stick at.

2 *Early American or Colonial Style*

4 *Federal Style*

7 *Italianate Style*

11 *Shingle Style*

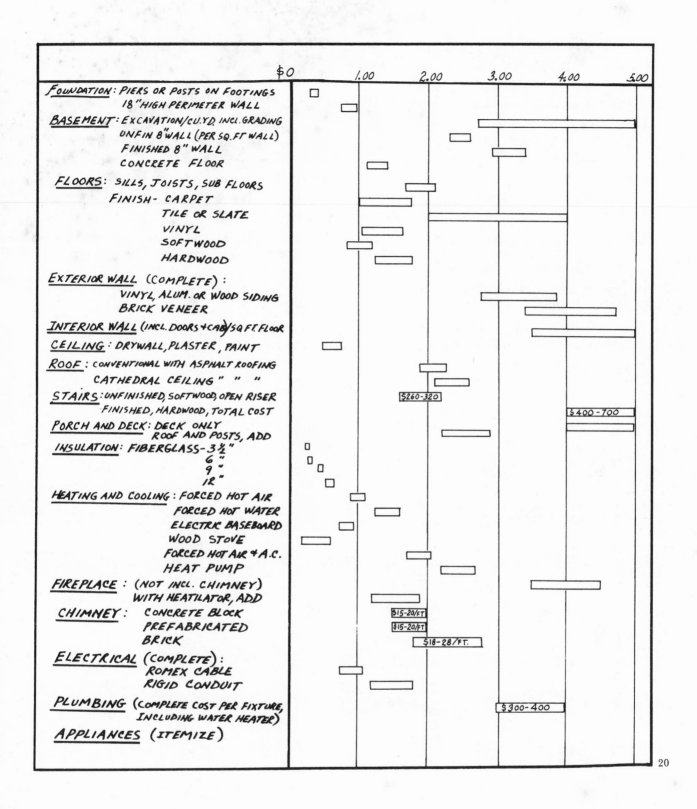

FOUNDATION: PIERS OR POSTS ON FOOTINGS
           18" HIGH PERIMETER WALL
BASEMENT: EXCAVATION/CU.YD. INCL. GRADING
          UNFIN. 8" WALL (PER SQ.FT WALL)
          FINISHED 8" WALL
          CONCRETE FLOOR

FLOORS: SILLS, JOISTS, SUB FLOORS
       FINISH- CARPET
            TILE OR SLATE
            VINYL
            SOFTWOOD
            HARDWOOD

EXTERIOR WALL (COMPLETE):
         VINYL, ALUM. OR WOOD SIDING
         BRICK VENEER

INTERIOR WALL (INCL. DOORS + CAB)/SQ.FT. FLOOR

CEILING: DRYWALL, PLASTER, PAINT

ROOF: CONVENTIONAL WITH ASPHALT ROOFING
       CATHEDRAL CEILING " " "

STAIRS: UNFINISHED, SOFTWOOD, OPEN RISER $260-320
       FINISHED, HARDWOOD, TOTAL COST $400-700

PORCH AND DECK: DECK ONLY
            ROOF AND POSTS, ADD

INSULATION: FIBERGLASS- 3½"
              6"
              9"
              12"

HEATING AND COOLING: FORCED HOT AIR
              FORCED HOT WATER
              ELECTRIC BASEBOARD
              WOOD STOVE
              FORCED HOT AIR & A.C.
              HEAT PUMP

FIREPLACE: (NOT INCL. CHIMNEY)
           WITH HEATILATOR, ADD

CHIMNEY: CONCRETE BLOCK $15-20/FT
         PREFABRICATED $15-20/FT
         BRICK $18-28/FT.

ELECTRICAL (COMPLETE):
         ROMEX CABLE
         RIGID CONDUIT

PLUMBING (COMPLETE COST PER FIXTURE, $300-400
          INCLUDING WATER HEATER)

APPLIANCES (ITEMIZE)

Scale: $0   1.00   2.00   3.00   4.00   5.00

20

of the improvement be at least as great as the investment. All too often the percentage of a house replaced is so great that demolition and new construction would have been cheaper.

Emotional considerations aside, the value of a property is the price it will bring on the open market. This is the famous "bottom line." Don't attempt to set that figure yourself: too much fantasy here! Get the opinions of several real estate brokers familiar with the local market. Show them the property and give them a realistic picture of the improvements you plan to undertake. By comparing the features of the to-be-retrofitted house to other similar properties in the area, they should be able to place the value within ±10 percent. Call this figure item A.

Item B will be the estimated total cost of the planned improvements. Illustrations 19 and 20 show the costs of new house construction broken into major components. The costs shown are for "fair" to "good" construction. Low-quality mass-produced houses cost a little less than the lowest figures and one-of-a-kind architect-designed houses much more. The figures listed represent national averages as of June 1977. To project future costs, use Illustration 21, which traces per-square-foot costs of construction from 1946 to 1977. The graph shows that construction costs have risen at a constant 8 percent per year from 1970 to 1977. To arrive at item B, list all of the work to be done, the number of square feet involved, the per-square-foot cost, and finally the cost of each task.

You must make some interpretive adjustments

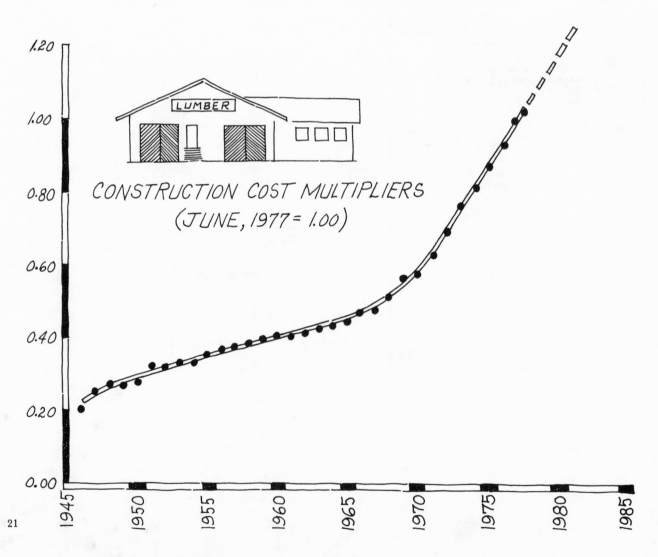

21

in arriving at the costs. (1) Older houses were not built with standard or modular dimensions. Therefore, new work in old houses tends to be more wasteful of materials. Increase costs from 0 to 20 percent, depending on the age of the house. (2) If the house has settled so that the corners are no longer square and the floors slope, again increase costs slightly to reflect more labor. (3) Often only part of the section has to be replaced. For example, if only the drywall has to be replaced on an exterior wall, don't use the exterior wall figure; use the drywall ceiling figure. (4) If an item doesn't seem to fit in the table or if there is a serious question about a particular job, get estimates from local contractors. They're far better than the table in estimating particular jobs. (5) The costs listed are for material plus labor. As a general rule of thumb, labor cost=material cost. Think hard before you divide all of the costs in half because you plan on doing the work. If you're doing the work during time customarily spent snoozing in front of the TV,

Table 2. Example Retrofit Analysis

Item A   Estimated Fair Market Value after Retrofit $50,000

Item B   Cost of Work

task	sq. ft.	dollars per sq. ft.	cost (dollars)
1. Carpet 50% of floor area, average quality	775	1.40	1,085
2. Insulate attic with 12″ fiberglass	775	0.60	465
3. Insulate under first floor with 6″ fiberglass	775	0.30	233
4. Insulate exterior walls with urea formaldehyde (estimate from contractor)	1,550	0.60	930
5. Drywall and paint exterior walls	1,550	0.50	775
6. Drywall and paint ceilings	1,550	0.50	775
7. Remove all interior walls and cabinets; drywall and paint 50% of interior walls	500	0.50	250
8. Kitchen and bathroom cabinets (bid job)			1,800
9. Install two wood stoves in present chimneys	2×350		700
10. Replace electrical wiring	1,550	0.80	1,240
11. Replace plumbing (kitchen sink, hot water heater, 3 bath fixtures)	5×300		1,500
12. New kitchen range			400
13. Make and install insulating shutters on all house windows	420	1.50	630
Total Item B		$10,783	$10.783

Item C   Demolition and Cleanup (10% of B) $ 1,078

Item D   Value of Existing Property (A – B – C) $38,139

Price Paid $31,500

Estimated Profit $ 6,639

O.K., but don't discount the value of your labor or your "free" time.

Item C is the cost of demolition. I don't mean that you should at this point give up and call the bulldozer. You should, however, recognize that in rebuilding a house, some of the original material must be removed and properly disposed of. My own experience is that the labor cost of rubbish generation, removal, and final cleanup is about 10 percent of item B.

Item D is computed as item A less items B and C. In searching for a retrofit house, this is the very most you should pay. When retrofitting your existing house, if item D is not greater than or equal to the present market value of your house, the investment is economically questionable.

Example: I'll use my own house as an example. We bought a 2,800-square-foot house for $31,500. Of the 2,800 square feet, 1,250 was a new addition needing no improvements. The remaining 1,550 square feet had no insulation, a nonfunctioning heating system, inadequate wiring, an out-of-date kitchen, cracked plaster walls and ceilings, and one totally worthless bathroom. We wished to convert to wood heat and doing that additionally pointed toward opening up the spaces. Table 2 shows the analysis.

The analysis predicted the cost of work to be done to be $11,861. The actual cost of material totaled $6,200, contracted labor $2,000, and my own labor, figured at $5 per hour, $3,200.

Several factors contributed to the economic success of this retrofit. (1) The purchase was made immediately after a hard winter, which saw heating costs rise dramatically. With no insulation, the house had been a financial burden to the previous owner. (2) Equally significant is the fact that all of the items replaced in the house had no present value. The walls and ceilings were cracked, the kitchen and bath were outdated, the furnace was broken, the wiring was inadequate and dangerous. (3) The roof, windows, doors, exterior walls, and foundation of the house needed no attention at all.

What Holds It Up

3.

Forces and Loads

Introduction

We will investigate over the next four chapters the nature of the forces in and on buildings and how the frame of the building deals with them. Understanding this, we can repair a damaged frame or even alter the structure at will to fit our future needs and life-style. Understanding the forces on the frame is critical to such a venture; indeed, it is dangerous (as your intuition will tell you) to deal with such large forces without understanding.

This series of four chapters also will stand alone to serve as a short course in building structural analysis. I hope that carpenters will find a new design freedom here. It should not be used, however, as the basis for design of larger than residential structures.

FORCE UNITS

I assume that you, the reader, presently know nothing of the subject. Therefore we will begin at the beginning by defining the words we will use to describe forces. These words are technically called *units*. Units are very important in calculations because they keep our thinking straight.

Whenever we perform a calculation such as multiplying two numbers, we keep the units as a check on our logic. For example, suppose we were calculating the volume of a box and were supposedly using the units of feet. If, after our cranking the calculator and combining the units, the answer came out with the combined units *pounds per week*, we might well wonder whether the numbers had any meaning as well. In this age of calculators, units are more important than ever. Calculators never make mistakes; their operators do. In many a computer room hangs a sign "Garbage in—garbage out." Enough said; the units we will use are listed in Table 3.

Table 3. Units of Measurement

distance	area	volume	force	pressure
inches (in.)	square inches (sq. in.)	cubic inches (cu. in.)	pounds (lb.)	pounds per square inch (lb./sq. in. or psi)
feet (ft.)	square feet (sq. ft.)	cubic feet (cu. ft.)	pounds (lb.)	pounds per square foot (lb./sq. ft. or psf)

FORCES="LOADS" AND "REACTIONS"

In building we never use the word *force*, for it is so general as to be useless. Forces are either *loads* or *reactions*. The most basic of all the laws of physics (here structural analysis) may be stated:

> *Whenever there is no motion, you can be sure that the forces on a body are balanced.*

Illustrations 22 and 23 show the balanced forces on several bodies. In 22 we see that the weight W does not move downward under the influence of gravity because the post is pushing back with an equal and opposite force. (We say that the forces are balanced when they are equal and opposite.) Similarly, the bottom of the post doesn't sink into the ground because the soil beneath is pushing back. Actually, the bottom of the post does sink slightly until the soil, by compaction, achieves a sufficient "soil-bearing capacity."

Illustration 23 shows that a man standing on the ground is no different from the post. The soles of his feet push down on the ground with a force we call his weight; and the ground pushes back with an equal and opposite force. If the ground did not push back, the population problem would be solved very quickly. If he had no weight at all, the same would be true, I suppose.

Illustrations 22 and 23 both dealt with vertical forces. Other forces exist. Illustration 24 shows the lateral force of the wind against the side of a building. Why does the building not skitter across the ground like an empty cardboard box across a frozen pond? Because the ground beneath the building pushes back with an equal and opposite force due to the weight of the building, friction, and a few anchor bolts tying the building to its foundation.

It's important to note that these secondary forces do not exist by themselves; the ground is not full of upward forces waiting to be stepped on! These forces come into play only in reaction

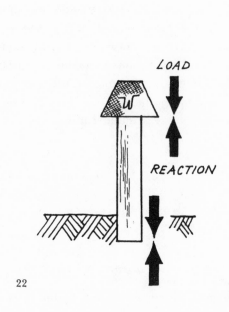

22

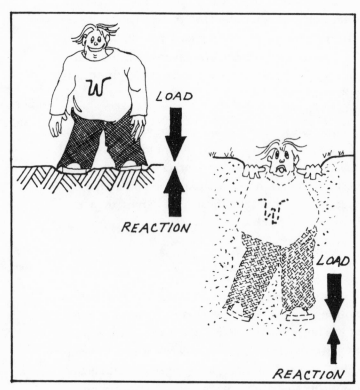

23

WIND
LOAD

REACTION

24

to loads placed upon them. For this reason the two different types of force are called *loads* and *reactions: loads,* the primary causative forces, and *reactions,* the forces that arise in reaction. A building is not in trouble until either its frame or foundation is unable, through poor design or the wear of time, to rise to the occasion and provide a reaction equal to the load.

BUILDING LOADS

Building codes recognize several types of laod imposed on a building by nature and man:

> dead load: the weight of the building materials
>   themselves
> live load: the additional load on floors due to
>   occupancy
> snow load: the weight of the maximum depth
>   of snow expected on a roof in that geographic
>   area
> wind load: the pressure normal to exterior
>   building surfaces exerted by the maximum
>   expected wind.

The *dead load* may be calculated from the type and thicknesses of the building materials. On the other hand, the dead load is so small compared to the other loads that it is usually taken to be a fixed figure roughly determined by the style of construction. For any normal construction not involving masonry (for example, a slate roof or a tile floor), 10 psf is an ample figure.

The *live load* is not subject to calculation in

residential construction; it is dictated by the building codes:

> first floor (interpret as social areas), 40 psf
> second floor (interpret as sleeping areas), 30 psf
> attic (interpret as unoccupied areas), 20 psf
> stairs and landings, 100 psf

A word on interpretation: if you plan to reverse the order of things by making the second floor your living room, the obvious interpretation calls for 40 psf. If the attic might someday be finished off to accommodate a mother-in-law, it should be built for 30 or 40 psf, rather than 20.

The *snow load* commonly used is that which is expected to occur once in fifty years. Snowfall sometimes varies dramatically within small distances, particularly with elevation. If there is any question as to the snow load in your area, ask a local architect or contractor. They're not likely to put up a building a second time using the wrong snow load!

Because a roof is generally pitched, forming the hypotenuse of a triangle, it has a greater square foot area than the floor below it, even after discounting the overhang. In computing snow loads, which area should we use: the roof or the floor beneath? Counter to your intuition, you should use the floor area or horizontal projection of the roof. The reason for this is simply that no more snow falls out of the sky onto a roof than would onto a level piece of ground of the same area as the horizontal projection. Remember this when we begin to deal with roof rafter sizes.

Wind load depends on exposure and geographical location. Use 15 psf for interior and sheltered areas, 25 psf for coastal and exposed areas, and 35 psf for mountaintop and Florida coastal areas. These pressures correspond to the highest wind velocities ever recorded, including hurricanes, but excluding tornadoes. Forget tornadoes; unless your house is of masonry construction (like the third little pig's), wind pressure will be of only academic interest after the big blow. You are at an advantage in retrofitting, however. If your house is still standing after fifty or more years, it obviously can handle the wind pressures in your area. Calculate wind load only if you are doing major modification of the walls or a new addition.

HOW UNIFORM LOADS ARE DISTRIBUTED

Uniform loads are loads distributed over a surface like so much peanut butter. To get from the load in pounds per square foot of area (psf) to the total load on a given area (lb.) we use the pressure formula:

$$Total\ Load\ (lb.) = Pressure\ (psf) \times Area\ (sq.ft.)$$

In other words, the total load on an area is simply the load on one square foot multiplied by the number of square feet subject to the uniform loading.

To go one step farther, we most often need to know the total load carried by a single framing member. The key is obviously in finding the area supported by that member. We will use a concept I borrow from the United Fund: the *fair share*.

Illustration 25 shows two people carrying a ladder. If one were stupid enough to pick the ladder up at the midpoint, he would be carrying the entire weight, the other fellow being superfluous. However, if the two carried the ladder by its opposite ends, each would be lifting an equal

weight—one-half of the total weight. This illustrates perfectly the concept of *fair shares*. In general, any framing member carries its fair share, or exactly one-half of the total load between it and the adjacent members to each side. The member spacing makes no difference; remember only the fair share, one-half.

Suppose, for example, we wished to find the total load carried by the floor joist in Illustration 26. The joists recur in a regular pattern at an interval called the "on-center spacing" (o.c.). We are generally interested in the load that will bend the joist, and so we are interested only in the load over the length of the joist that is unsupported from below. We call this length the "clear span," L. (Any load occurring over the support will serve simply to compress the joist, but not bend it.) Using the fair share concept, we see that the joist is carrying the load of a rectangle having sides o.c. and L. The general rule for the load carried by repetitive members is therefore

$$\underset{Total\ Load\ (lb.)}{W} = \underset{(psf)}{w} \times \underset{(ft.)}{o.c.} \times \underset{(ft.)}{L}$$

Not all loads are uniformly distributed, however. A post supported by a beam at some intermediate point constitutes a *concentrated load*. But this is as far as it goes. Beams are loaded by

25

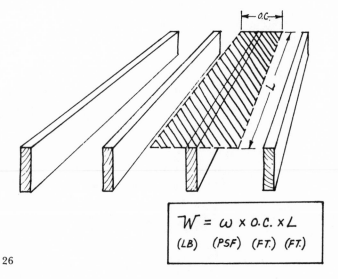

$$W = w \times o.c. \times L$$
$$\text{(LB)} \quad \text{(PSF)} \quad \text{(FT.)} \quad \text{(FT.)}$$

26

Example: Suppose your first floor is supported by joists spaced at an average of 27″ from center to center. The distance from the last point of support at the sill to the last point of support by a heavy beam running down the middle of the house measures 11′ 4″. Assuming a dead load of the floor itself of 10 psf and the live load specified by the building code, what is the total load, W, carried by a single joist?

Answer: First we must convert o.c. and L to the proper units, ft. Twenty-seven inches is 2.25 ft. and 11′ 4″ is 11.33 ft. Then,

$$
\begin{aligned}
W &= w \times o.c. \times L \\
&= (10\ psf + 40\ psf) \times 2.25\ ft. \times 11.33\ ft. \\
&= 1,275\ lb.
\end{aligned}
$$

uniform loads, concentrated loads, or a combination of both. What to do with the calculated loads will be seen in the following chapters.

In the next chapter we will discover how a building deals with its imposed loads.

4.

How a Building Supports Its Loads

In discussing forces in the previous chapter we considered only "pushing" types of force. Other sorts of force exist in nature and in buildings. Some push; others pull, bend, and shear. Wood is an amazing substance, surpassed in strength per weight by only a few man-made materials. We will consider the strength of wood in resisting the various forces.

Stress Types

Forces that exist inside wood, as opposed to those imposed on the outside, are called *stresses*. Distortions of the wood that result from stresses are called *strains*. Illustration 27 shows the stresses we will be concerned with.

If a load and its accompanying reaction act on a member so as to shorten or compress it, the stress is called *compression*. Wood is extremely strong in compression.

If, on the other hand, a member is used to tie two points together (the load and the reaction here pulling apart), the combination of forces tends to extend the member, and the stress is

called *tension*. Short pieces of wood are nearly equally strong in tension and compression.

When loads and reactions are equal and opposite but not along the same line, the combination of forces tends to bend the member. We call this phenomenon *bending*. Notice that I did not call bending a stress but a phenomenon. As Illustration 28 shows, the upper and lower edges of a bending member form arcs of a circle. Since the circumference of a larger circle is greater than that of a smaller circle, it is obvious that the upper edge is getting shorter, the midpoint staying the same length, and the bottom edge getting longer. In other words, the wood above the midplane is in compression while the bottom wood is in tension. Since the bottommost wood fiber is subject to the greatest tension of all, the measure of strength of a beam in bending is called the *extreme fiber stress in bending,* which we designate as f. We will return to this point.

Above I said it was obvious that the bending beam conformed to the arc of a circle with the upper edge shortening and the lower edge lengthening. If the beam consisted of two beams on top of one another, the same amount of bending would produce only half the extension and com-

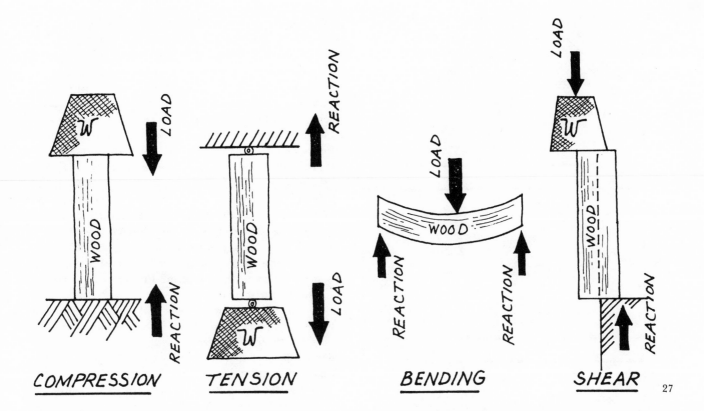

COMPRESSION   TENSION   BENDING   SHEAR

27

pression of the edge fibers. The adjacent faces (bottom of the top beam and top of the bottom beam) would slide past each other. The sliding would be greatest at the ends and nil at the midpoint of the beams. In a simpleminded way, the single beam would be happier (its stress would be relieved) if it were to split into the two beams. It sometimes happens. The phenomenon is called *horizontal shear*. We will treat it, like bending, as if it were one of the fundamental stresses rather than a combination of compression and tension.

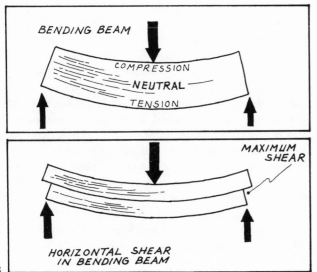

28

Stresses in the House Frame

A section of conventional house frame is shown in Illustration 29. I will use this type of frame because it is both the most common and the most complicated you will be able to understand with the information presented here.

(1) *Compression due to a vertical load.* The roof dead load, the snow load, and the dead and live loads of the attic floor are all supported by the studs and posts of the walls. In general, vertical framing members are primarily in compression.

(2) *Tension due to a vertical load.* Without the attic floor joists, the building would probably collapse under the

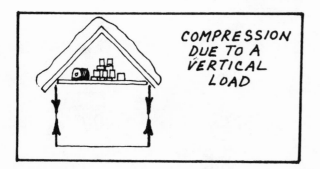

COMPRESSION DUE TO A VERTICAL LOAD

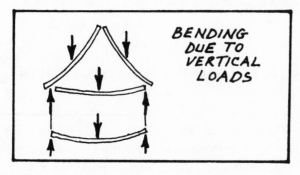

TENSION DUE TO A VERTICAL LOAD

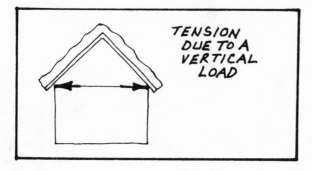

RACKING (SHEAR) DUE TO A HORIZONTAL LOAD

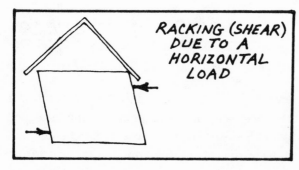

BENDING DUE TO VERTICAL LOADS

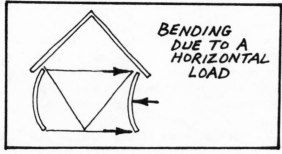

BENDING DUE TO A HORIZONTAL LOAD

29

snow load, as shown in the illustration. Two sets of forces are required to hold the roof rafters in position: (a) the upward force from the walls as in 1 above, and (b) a set of inward forces at the rafter bottom ends. These horizontal forces could be supplied from the outside by buttresses, as in many of the cathedrals of the fifteenth and sixteenth centuries, allowing a dramatic, clear inside space (the cathedral ceiling). Almost universally, however, these forces are supplied by attic joists or collar ties in tension.

(3) *Racking (shear) due to a horizontal load.* Even after we have solved the problem of the spreading rafters, our building is not rigid. If the wind were to blow against the billboard-like exterior wall, the horizontal force on the wall is resisted only by the horizontal reaction at ground level. This constitutes a shear, and the building's response is to distort into a parallelogram. What is the solution to this problem? I'm sure you've already guessed: the triangular brace.

We've seen two examples now of the use of a triangle to brace a structure, 2 and 3. Of all the geometric figures, only the triangle is perfectly rigid. This unique quality is due to the fact that the only way to change one of the angles of a triangle (not limited to the right triangle) is to change the length of one or more of its sides. Wood is phenomenally strong in both tension and compression. We have witnessed a marriage of material and form in the wood-braced frame. (Fuller's geodesic domes are the ultimate expression of this combination.)

(4) *Bending due to a vertical load.* We have seen how to deal with the stability of the framing member end points, but what about the members themselves? Vertical loads—dead, live, and snow—cause bending of any member that is either horizontal or has a horizontal projection. Since there is no support for this load between the end points, the reaction must come from the interior strength of the member itself.

It is common to use trusses in roof framing. The truss differs from the common rafter system shown in the figure by the addition of various members connecting rafter and attic joist into a combination of triangles. Rigidity is thus achieved by geometry rather than mere size of the rafter. Large spans can be achieved by relatively small pieces of wood when the latter are formed into trusses. It is beyond the scope of this book to discuss trusses; they are best left to structural engineers.

(5) *Bending due to a horizontal load.* We don't often consider this phenomenon, but if you were to turn Illustration 27E counterclockwise by 90°, would not the pressure of the wind on the side wall act exactly like the dead and live loads on the floor and the snow load on the roof? Particularly in tall structures, we must consider the horizontal bending forces on the wall framing as well as the vertical compressive forces.

The Strength of Wood

Before considering exactly how to deal with each of these forces, we will need a set of numbers describing the mechanical properties of common species of wood. Dozens of properties of wood are tested but we are here interested in only four:

f, extreme fiber stress in bending—a measure of the tension that may be exerted in the bottom fibers of a beam in bending.

$c_\parallel$, *compression parallel to grain*—the vertical load that a short column or post will carry in the direction of the grain (its normal orientation).

h, horizontal shear—a measure of ability to withstand displaced opposing forces along the direction of grain without splitting into two pieces.

E, modulus of elasticity—a measure of stiffness or ability to carry a load without bending.

All of the above properties are measured in the laboratory on both clear and imperfect specimens. Lumber grading consists of assigning lumber, on the basis of either visual or mechanical tests, to categories or grades described by the above qualities. In order to deal with the almost infinite variety of lumber sizes the strength variables are given in pounds per square inch, psi.

Table 4 lists ten species of wood that one might consider for framing purposes. I have listed the values for the 2″ to 4″ thick, 6″ and wider grade from *The National Design Specification for Stress-Grade Lumber and Its Fastenings,* National Forest Products Association, 1973. Be aware, however, that there are both higher and lower grades. The more select grades are generally 20 to 30 percent stronger, while the more utilitarian grades may be weaker by the same percentage.

After you either do a few beam calculations or consult the tables at the end of this chapter you may suddenly panic, realizing that the carport you built last summer is in imminent danger of collapse. Relax. Although you have probably violated the local building code by ignoring in your design the officially recognized stress values,

Table 4. Allowable Stresses for Wood (psi), for 2″–4″ thick, 6″ and wider, #2 grade

species	extreme fiber stress in bending (f)	compression parallel to grain (c∥)	tension parallel to grain (t∥)	horizontal shear (h)	modulus of elasticity
Western hemlock	1,250	975	725	90	1,400,000
Lodgepole pine	1,050	750	600	70	1,200,000
Douglas fir/ larch	1,450	1,050	825	95	1,700,000
California redwood	1,400	1,200	800	80	1,200,000
Hem-fir	1,150	850	650	75	1,400,000
Eastern spruce	1,000	750	600	65	1,200,000
Eastern hemlock	1,200	900	700	85	1,100,000
Eastern white pine	950	700	550	70	1,100,000
Northern white cedar	825	575	450	65	700,000
Southern pine	1,200	900	700	75	1,400,000

Source: *The National Design Specification for Stress-Grade Lumber and Its Fastenings,* National Forest Products Association, 1973.

Note: Increase f by: 15 percent for snow load
33-1/3 percent for wind load

your carport will probably not collapse. In the interest of public safety, allowable stress values incorporate a safety factor of approximately eight. That is, you are officially allowed to load a graded piece of lumber by only one-eighth of the ultimate capacity of a perfect piece of wood. Do not take this as permission to use higher figures, however, as lumber is notoriously unpredictable in strength.

Simple Procedures for Calculating What You Need for Every Situation

We have identified the stresses existing in a house frame and the average strength qualities of the common framing woods. What we need now is a procedure to determine how big a piece of wood is called for in any situation. If you're the sort of person who already owns a calculator, you'll enjoy the application of your toy to these problems. If not, the span tables for rafters and joists at the end of the chapter will probably suffice for all but the most daring structural modifications you're considering.

COMPRESSION DUE TO A VERTICAL LOAD

Posts, studs, and columns carry loads in compression parallel to their grain. Illustration 30 shows such a vertical member; it can fail in either of two modes: (1) crushing of the fibers in the direction of the grain, or (2) sideways buckling due to the combination of load and an initial bow or defect. A measure of the resistance to crushing is the compressive strength parallel to grain, $c_{||}$. A measure of the tendency to buckle is the "slenderness ratio"—the unsupported length divided by the width—combined with the stiffness or modulus of elasticity, E.

When a number of vertical members are joined to each other laterally, they support each other against buckling. The studs in a wall are a perfect example, being connected by the interior and exterior wall sheathing. The unsupported length in the slenderness ratio is the distance between such lateral supports.

Example: Suppose a post holds up (by fair shares) 1/4 of the total load of a $20' \times 20'$ second story. The Eastern spruce post measures $4'' \times 6'' \times 8'$ and is unsupported laterally. Is the post adequate?

procedure	example
1. Look up the allowable compressive stress, $c_{||}$, and the modulus of elasticity, E, for the wood.	1. Eastern spruce: $c_{||} = 750$ psi $E = 1,200,000$ psi
2. Calculate both slenderness ratios.	2. $L/d = \dfrac{8' \times 12''}{4''} = 24$ $L/d = \dfrac{8' \times 12''}{6''} = 16$
3. Calculate the total load carried by the post.	3. $W = w \times A$ $= (10 \text{ psf} + 30 \text{ psf}) \times 1/4 \times 20' \times 20'$ $= 4,000$ lb.
4. Calculate the compressive stress, c, at the maximum total load.	4. $c = \dfrac{W}{b \times d} = \dfrac{4000 \text{ lb.}}{4'' \times 6''} = 167$ psi
5. Check: crushing, $c < c_{||}$? buckling, $L/d < 50$? buckling, $c < \dfrac{0.3E}{(L/d)^2}$?	5. 167 psi $<$ 750 psi, O.K. $24 < 50$; $16 < 50$, O.K. $167 < \dfrac{0.3 \times 1,200,000}{(24)^2}$ $167 < 625$, O.K.

The post in question passes all tests with flying colors!

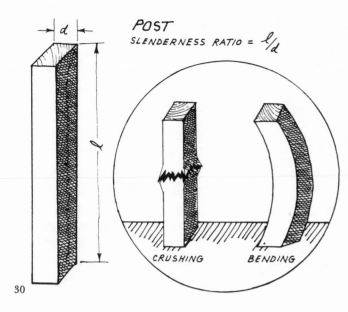

POST

SLENDERNESS RATIO = ℓ/d

CRUSHING   BENDING

30

joist and rafter sufficient? The first question relates to the tension parallel to grain, $t_\parallel$, and the cross-sectional area of the joist. The second relates to the number and size of nails making the connection.

First find the tension existing in the ceiling joist. This can be accomplished simply by drawing a picture. First calculate the total load carried by a single rafter as discussed before.

$$W = w \times o.c. \times L$$
where W = total load on the rafter in lb.
w = combined dead and snow load in psf
o.c. = on-center spacing in ft.
L = span of a single rafter in ft.

Next, draw to scale a triangle with sides representing the rafter, its horizontal projection (span or run), and its vertical projection (rise) as in Illustration 31. Letting the length of the vertical leg represent one-half of W, the tension in the ceiling joist can be read as the length of the horizontal leg. One more piece of information is required: the load sustained by each nail. Without getting into a table of values, we'll use the figure of 150 lb. per sixteenpenny spike.

TENSION DUE TO A VERTICAL LOAD

Tension is produced in ceiling joists when they form the base of a triangle with the roof rafters. We are concerned with two questions: (1) Is the ceiling joist itself capable of sustaining the tension? and (2) Is the fastening between the ceiling

Example: How many nails are required to fasten the rafter/ceiling joist connection in a roof where the rafter and its vertical and horizontal projections form a triangle with sides 15, 9, and 12 feet. The dead load is 10 psf and the snow load 40 psf. The ceiling joist is Hem-fir of dimensions 1-1/2″ × 5-1/2″ and spaced at 24″ on-center.

procedure	*example*
1. Look up the rafter allowable tension parallel to grain.	1. Hem-fir, $t_\parallel$ = 650 psi
2. Calculate the total load carried by a single rafter.	2. W = w × o.c. × L = (10 psf + 40 psf) × 2′ × 12′ = 1,200 lb.
3. Calculate the tension in the ceiling joist.	3. [triangle: 15′ hypotenuse, 9′ vertical, 12′ horizontal] = 800 lb. tension = 800 lb.
4. Check psf of tension stress in joist: tension/b × d < $t_\parallel$?	4. $\dfrac{800\ lb.}{1\text{-}1/2'' \times 5\text{-}1/2''}$ < 650 psi? 97 psi < 650 psi, O.K.
5. Check nailing How many 12d or 16d nails?	5. Nails = $\dfrac{tension}{150\ lb.}$ = 6 nails

The number of nails required to fasten the ceiling joist to rafter under the maximum snow load condition is surprisingly large, 6, illustrating the importance of this connection!

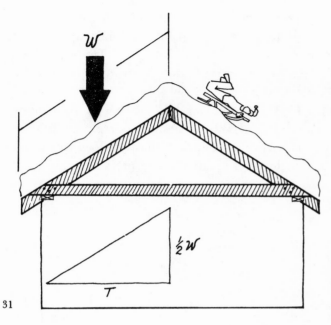

31

RACKING DUE TO A HORIZONTAL LOAD

No procedure is required in determining racking resistance provided one follows standard carpentry practice: *For a single story or top story of a multistory dwelling,* adequate racking resistance is supplied by:

> diagonal sheathing, or
> one full 4′ X 8′ plywood panel near each corner of
>   each wall, or
> one 8′ or three 4′ let-in braces for each wall.

For the bottom story of a multistory dwelling:

> diagonal sheathing, or
> one full 4′ X 8′ plywood panel near each corner of
>   each wall, or
> two 8′ or five 4′ let-in braces for each wall.

BENDING DUE TO A VERTICAL LOAD

Any framing member with the primary function of resisting bending forces is called a "beam." Rafters and joists are beams; when subject to wind, wall studs are beams. The resistance of a beam to bending is provided entirely by the inherent strength of the wood fibers (the *extreme fiber stress in bending, f*) and the size of the beam

(the *section modulus, S*). The section modulus of a rectangular beam of breadth b and depth d is given by the relation

$$S = \frac{b \times d^2}{6}$$

where b = breadth in inches
d = depth in inches

On the other side, both the load and its relative position on the beam influence bending. In the case of a diving board, for example, it is obvious that a load placed at the end of the board has a greater chance of breaking the board than one placed near the supports. The measure of the tendency to break is called the *bending moment,* M, and it involves both the load and its distance from the supports.

I like to think of the question as to whether a beam will break under bending forces as a moral tug-of-war. The bending beam equation is:

bending moment		section modulus		extreme fiber stress in bending
M	=	S	X	f

32

On the left we have the force of evil trying to break the beam. On the right are the forces of good working together to preserve the integrity of the beam. Beams are designed using this equation as if the beam were just on the point of breaking: on the one side the maximum or design loads and on the other side the section of the beam and the maximum allowable stress values. Of course equality does not actually represent the point of failure because there is a safety factor in the allowable fiber stress in bending, f.

Ordinarily, designing a beam for bending alone is sufficient. However, as shown in Illustration 32, there are two further considerations of which we should be aware: failure by shear in short beams and excessive deflection in long beams. Procedures for each of these calculations follow the procedure for bending.

Example: Calculate the size of joist needed to support a second floor. The joist is to be rough sawn Eastern hemlock spaced at 16″ on-center, with a clearspan of 10′.

Procedure for Calculating a Beam Supported at Its Ends and Subject to a Uniformly Distributed Load

procedure	*example*
1. Pick a wood species and find in Table 4 value for f.	1. Eastern hemlock f = 1,200 psi
2. Define dead load, live load, on-center spacing, and clearspan.	2. w = (10 psf + 30 psf) o.c. = 4/3 ft., L = 10 ft.
3. Calculate the total uniformly distributed load on the beam, W.	3. W = w × o.c. × L = 40 psf × 4/3 ft. × 10 ft. = 533 lb.
4. Calculate bending moment $$M = \frac{W \times L}{8}$$ Note: L is in inches.	4. $M = \dfrac{W \times L}{8}$ $\quad = \dfrac{533 \text{ lb.} \times 10 \text{ ft.} \times 12 \text{ in.}}{8}$ $\quad = 8,000 \text{ in. lb.}$
5. Calculate the required beam section modulus from the bending beam equation $$S = M/f$$	5. S = M/f $\quad = \dfrac{8,000 \text{ in. lb.}}{1,200 \text{ psi}}$ $\quad = 6.67 \text{ in.}^3$
6. Locate a beam with sufficient section modulus from Column 2 of the span tables (Tables 5–12), or pick beam breadth, b, and calculate depth, d, from the relation $$S = \frac{bd^2}{6}$$ or $$d = \sqrt{\frac{6S}{b}}$$	6. From the span tables (Tables 5–12), find the following joists having S greater than 6.67. $\quad$ S4S (surfaced four sides) — RGH (rough-sawed) $\quad$ 2 × 6 — 2 × 6 $\quad$ 2 × 8 — 2 × 8 $\quad$ etc. — etc. or from the equation, using b = 2″: $\quad d = \sqrt{\dfrac{6 \times 6.67 \text{ in.}^3}{2 \text{ in.}}}$ $\quad$ d = 4.5 in.

We have just found a floor joist of sufficient dimension to resist breaking by bending. However, as discussed above, another mode of failure for beams is horizontal shear, primarily in very short beams carrying very heavy loads.

Procedure to Check Horizontal Shear

procedure	example
1. Find the allowable horizontal shear stress, h, for the beam in Table 4.	1. Eastern hemlock, h = 85 psi
2. Calculate the existing shear stress in the beam at maximum design load. $$\text{Existing shear} = \frac{3W}{4\,b \times d}$$	2. Existing shear $= \dfrac{3W}{4\,b \times d}$ $$= \frac{3 \times 533 \text{ lb.}}{4 \times 2 \text{ in.} \times 6 \text{ in.}}$$ $$= 33.3 \text{ psi}$$
3. Check: Existing shear < Allowable shear, h?	3. 33.3 psi < 85 psi, O.K.

After checking the bending strength and shear, we are assured that the joist will not fail. Whether the floor will be acceptable to the occupant, however, is subject to one further consideration—deflection. A joist can be perfectly safe and yet be bouncy enough to prove objectionable. If, when you walk across the floor, a hi-fi record needle jumps and the dishes rattle, your floor has excessive deflection.

Example: Let's use the same joist as in the previous examples. Note, however, that the total load W in the deflection formula refers to the live load only. Since the joist supports a second floor, the deflection ratio we are looking for is 1/240.

Procedure for Checking Deflection

procedure	example
1. Find the modulus of elasticity (E) in Table 4.	1. Eastern hemlock E = 1,100,000 psi
2. Find the moment of inertia, I, for the proposed beam from the span tables (Tables 5–12) or the equation $$I = \frac{bd^3}{12}$$	2. $I = \dfrac{bd^3}{12}$ $$= \frac{2 \text{ in.} \times 6 \text{ in.} \times 6 \text{ in.} \times 6 \text{ in.}}{12}$$ $$= 36 \text{ in.}^4$$
3. Calculate the total live load, W.	3. W = w × o.c. × L = 30 psf × 1-1/3 ft. × 10 ft. = 400 lb.
4. Calculate the deflection in inches from $$D = \frac{5WL^3}{384EI}$$ where L is inches.	4. $D = \dfrac{5WL^3}{384EI}$ $$= \frac{5 \times 400 \text{ lb.} \times (10 \text{ ft.} \times 12 \text{ in.})^3}{384 \times 1,100,000 \text{ psi} \times 36 \text{ in.}^4}$$ $$= 0.23 \text{ in.}$$
5. Calculate the deflection ratio D/L.	5. $D/L = \dfrac{0.23 \text{ in.}}{10 \text{ ft.} \times 12 \text{ in.}} = 1/530$
6. Check D/L against standard.	6. 1/530 < 1/240, O.K.
7. If D/L is excessive, increase depth d by 2 in. and repeat from step 2.	

Deflection is the distance the center of the beam drops from its normal position to its fully loaded position.

The criterion used to judge whether the deflection is excessive is the deflection ratio—the deflection divided by the clearspan. Since deflection is not a safety consideration, it is not specified by building codes. However, the following acceptable deflection ratios are commonly used by architects and builders:

> first floor   1/360
> second floor   1/240
> attic and roof 1/180.

The formula for the maximum deflection of a uniformly loaded beam supported at both ends involves the clearspan, live load, modulus of elasticity (stiffness), and a quantity similar to the section modulus but called the moment of inertia (I), $I = bd^3/12$. We do not include the dead load because we are concerned only with the change between the unloaded and loaded condition.

BENDING DUE TO A HORIZONTAL WIND LOAD

Bending of the wall studs and posts under a horizontally acting uniform wind load is exactly the same as the bending of floor joists or rafters under vertical loads, except there is no need to check shear or deflection. Since the maximum wind load occurs for such a short time, we are allowed to increase the fiber stress in bending, f, by 33-1/3 percent. All that remains is determination of the maximum wind load for your location in psf. Unless you live on top of a high bald hill, I suggest you use the figures:

> Interior: 15 psf
> Coast: 25 psf
> South Florida and Cape Hatteras: 35 psf

Span Tables for Floor Joists and Roof Rafters

Almost all of your structural calculations will involve either floor joists or roof rafters under uniform loads. Tables 5 through 8 assume rough-sawn lumber (RGH) of full dimension and total uniformly distributed loads of 30, 40, 50, and 60 psf. Tables 9 through 12 assume that the lumber is surfaced on four sides (S4S) or commercial lumber and the same loads. Table 13 lists spans limited by the deflection ratio of 1/360.

With a little ingenuity the span tables can be used for other than joists and rafters, as shown in one of the following examples.

Example: Disregarding deflection, what is the maximum allowed first floor span for S4S Eastern spruce 2×8 joists at 16″ on-center?

Answer: Assuming the lumber to be of the same grade as in Table 4, we find a value of extreme fiber stress in bending of 1,000 psi. The span table we are looking for is Table 11 (S4S lumber and a total uniform load of 50 psf: 10 psf dead load plus 40 psf live load). Entering Table 11, we find the section labeled "on-center spacing 16″" and run down the first column until we find 2×8. We then run across the 2×8 line to the f=1,000 psi column and find our answer, 11′=5″.

Example: What size rough-sawn Eastern hemlock rafter is required for a clearspan of 19′, on-center spacing of 48″, dead load 10 psf, and snow load 50 psf?

Answer: Table 4 assigns Eastern hemlock an f value of 1,200 psi. Note, however, that in the case of a snow load we are allowed to increase the listed f by 15 percent. We will therefore use f = 1.15 × 1,200 psi, or 1,380 psi. The table we are looking for is Rough-Sawn Lumber, Uniform Load 60 psf, Table 8. Enter the section of the table headed "on-center spacing 48″" and run down the column headed "f = 1,400 psi" until you find a span greater than 19′. A 4″×12″ is the smallest listed satisfactory rafter.

Table 5. Rough-sawn Lumber Spans
(Total uniformly distributed load 30 psf)

b × d	S	I	f = 1,000 psi	1,100	1,200	1,300	1,400	1,500
			On-center spacing 16″					
2 × 4	5.3	10.7	9–5	9–11	10–4	10–9	11–2	11–7
2 × 6	12.0	36.0	14–2	14–10	15–6	16–1	16–9	17–4
2 × 8	21.3	85.3	18–10	19–9	20–8	21–6	22–4	23–1
2 × 10	33.3	167	23–7	24–8	25–10	26–10	27–10	28–10
2 × 12	48.0	288	28–3	29–8	31–0	32–3	33–6	34–8
3 × 4	8.0	16.0	11–7	12–1	12–8	13–2	13–8	14–2
3 × 6	18.0	54.0	17–4	18–2	19–0	19–9	20–6	21–3
3 × 8	32.0	128	23–1	24–3	25–4	26–4	27–4	28–3
3 × 10	50.0	250	28–10	30–3	31–7	32–11	34–2	35–4
3 × 12	72.0	432	34–8	36–4	37–11	39–6	41–0	42–5
			On-center spacing 24″					
2 × 4	5.3	10.7	7–8	8–1	8–5	8–9	9–1	9–5
2 × 6	12.0	36.0	11–7	12–1	12–8	13–2	13–8	14–2
2 × 8	21.3	85.3	15–5	16–2	16–10	17–6	18–2	18–10
2 × 10	33.3	167	19–3	20–2	21–1	21–11	22–9	23–7
2 × 12	48.0	289	23–1	24–3	25–4	26–4	27–4	28–3
3 × 4	8.0	16.0	9–5	9–11	10–4	10–9	11–2	11–7
3 × 6	18.0	54.0	14–2	14–10	15–6	16–1	16–9	17–4
3 × 8	32.0	128	18–10	19–9	20–8	21–6	22–4	23–1
3 × 10	50.0	250	23–7	24–9	25–10	26–10	27–11	28–10
3 × 12	72.0	432	28–3	29–8	31–0	32–3	33–6	34–8
4 × 4	10.7	21.3	10–11	11–5	11–11	12–5	12–11	13–4
4 × 6	24.0	72.0	16–4	17–2	17–11	18–7	19–4	20–0
4 × 8	42.7	171	21–9	22–10	23–10	24–10	25–9	26–8
4 × 10	66.7	333	27–3	28–7	29–10	31–0	32–3	33–4
4 × 12	96.0	576	32–8	34–3	35–9	37–3	38–8	40–0
			On-center spacing 48″					
3 × 4	8.0	16.0	6–8	7–0	7–4	7–7	7–11	8–2
3 × 6	18.0	54.0	10–0	10–6	10–11	11–5	11–10	12–3
3 × 8	32.0	128	13–4	14–0	14–7	15–2	15–9	16–4
3 × 10	50.0	250	16–8	17–6	18–3	19–0	19–9	20–5
3 × 12	72.0	432	20–0	21–0	21–11	22–10	23–8	24–6
4 × 4	10.7	21.3	7–8	8–1	8–5	8–9	9–1	9–5
4 × 6	24.0	72.0	11–7	12–1	12–8	13–2	13–8	14–2
4 × 8	42.7	171	15–5	16–2	16–10	17–7	18–3	18–10
4 × 10	66.7	333	19–3	20–2	21–1	21–11	22–9	23–7
4 × 12	96.0	576	23–1	24–3	25–4	26–4	27–4	28–3
6 × 6	36.0	108	14–2	14–10	15–6	16–1	16–9	17–4
6 × 8	64.0	256	18–10	19–9	20–8	21–6	22–4	23–1
6 × 10	100.0	500	23–7	24–9	25–10	26–10	27–11	28–10
6 × 12	144.0	864	28–3	29–8	30–11	32–3	33–6	34–8
			On-center spacing 96″					
6 × 6	36.0	108	10–0	10–6	10–11	11–5	11–10	12–3
6 × 8	64.0	256	13–4	14–0	14–7	15–2	15–9	16–4
6 × 10	100.0	500	16–8	17–6	18–3	19–0	19–9	20–5
6 × 12	144.0	864	20–0	21–0	21–11	22–10	23–8	24–6
8 × 8	85.3	341	15–5	16–2	16–10	17–7	18–3	18–10
8 × 10	133.3	667	19–3	20–2	21–1	21–11	22–9	23–7
8 × 12	192.0	1,152	23–1	24–3	25–4	26–4	27–4	28–3
10 × 10	166.7	833	21–6	22–7	23–7	24–6	25–6	26–4
10 × 12	240.0	1,440	25–10	27–1	28–3	29–5	30–7	31–7
12 × 12	288.0	1,728	28–3	29–8	31–0	32–3	33–6	34–8

Table 6. Rough-sawn Lumber Spans
(Total uniformly distributed load 40 psf)

b × d	S	I	f = 1,000 psi	1,100	1,200	1,300	1,400	1,500
			On-center spacing 16″					
2 × 4	5.3	10.7	8–2	8–7	8–11	9–4	9–8	10–0
2 × 6	12.0	36.0	12–3	12–10	13–5	14–0	14–6	15–0
2 × 8	21.3	85.3	16–4	17–1	17–10	18–7	19–4	20–0
2 × 10	33.3	167	20–5	21–5	22–4	23–3	24–2	25–0
2 × 12	48.0	288	24–6	25–8	26–10	27–11	29–0	30–0
3 × 4	8.0	16.0	10–0	10–6	10–11	11–5	11–10	12–3
3 × 6	18.0	54.0	15–0	15–9	16–5	17–1	17–9	18–4
3 × 8	32.0	128	20–0	21–0	21–11	22–10	23–8	24–6
3 × 10	50.0	250	25–0	26–3	27–5	28–6	29–7	30–7
3 × 12	72.0	432	30–0	31–6	32–10	34–2	35–6	36–9
			On-center spacing 24″					
2 × 4	5.3	10.7	6–8	7–0	7–4	7–7	7–11	8–2
2 × 6	12.0	36.0	10–0	10–6	10–11	11–5	11–10	12–3
2 × 8	21.3	85.3	13–4	14–0	14–7	15–2	15–9	16–4
2 × 10	33.3	167	16–8	17–6	18–3	19–0	19–9	20–5
2 × 12	48.0	288	20–0	21–0	21–11	22–10	23–8	24–6
3 × 4	8.0	16.0	8–2	8–7	8–11	9–4	9–8	10–0
3 × 6	18.0	54.0	12–3	12–10	13–5	14–0	14–6	15–0
3 × 8	32.0	128	16–4	17–2	17–11	18–7	19–4	20–0
3 × 10	50.0	250	20–5	21–5	22–4	23–3	24–2	25–0
3 × 12	72.0	432	24–6	25–8	26–10	27–11	29–0	30–0
4 × 4	10.7	21.3	9–5	9–11	10–4	10–9	11–2	11–7
4 × 6	24.0	72.0	14–2	14–10	15–6	16–1	16–9	17–4
4 × 8	42.7	171	18–10	19–9	20–8	21–6	22–4	23–1
4 × 10	66.7	333	23–7	24–9	25–10	26–11	27–11	28–10
4 × 12	96.0	576	28–3	29–8	31–0	32–3	33–6	34–8
			On-center spacing 48″					
3 × 4	8.0	16.0	5–9	6–1	6–4	6–7	6–10	7–1
3 × 6	18.0	54.0	8–8	9–1	9–6	9–10	10–3	10–7
3 × 8	32.0	128	11–7	12–1	12–8	13–2	13–8	14–2
3 × 10	50.0	250	14–5	15–2	15–10	16–5	17–1	17–8
3 × 12	72.0	432	17–4	18–2	19–0	19–9	20–6	21–3
4 × 4	10.7	21.3	6–8	7–0	7–4	7–7	7–11	8–2
4 × 6	24.0	72.0	10–0	10–6	10–11	11–5	11–10	12–3
4 × 8	42.7	171	13–4	14–0	14–7	15–2	15–9	16–4
4 × 10	66.7	333	16–8	17–6	18–3	19–0	19–9	20–5
4 × 12	96.0	576	20–0	21–0	21–11	22–10	23–8	24–6
6 × 6	36.0	108	12–3	12–10	13–5	14–0	14–6	15–0
6 × 8	64.0	256	16–4	17–2	17–11	18–7	19–4	20–0
6 × 10	100.0	500	20–5	21–5	22–4	23–3	24–2	25–0
6 × 12	144.0	864	24–6	25–8	26–10	27–11	29–0	30–0
			On-center spacing 96″					
6 × 6	36.0	108	8–8	9–1	9–6	9–10	10–3	10–7
6 × 8	64.0	256	11–7	12–1	12–8	13–2	13–8	14–2
6 × 10	100.0	500	14–5	15–2	15–10	16–5	17–1	17–8
6 × 12	144.0	864	17–4	18–2	19–0	19–9	20–6	21–3
8 × 8	85.3	341	13–4	14–0	14–7	15–2	15–9	16–4
8 × 10	133.3	667	16–8	17–6	18–3	19–0	19–9	20–5
8 × 12	192.0	1,152	20–0	21–0	21–11	22–10	23–8	24–6
10 × 10	166.7	833	18–8	19–7	20–5	21–3	22–1	22–10
10 × 12	240.0	1,440	22–4	23–5	24–6	25–6	26–5	27–5
12 × 12	288.0	1,728	24–6	25–8	26–10	27–11	29–0	30–0

Table 7. Rough-sawn Lumber Spans
(Total uniformly distributed load 50 psf)

b × d	S	I	f = 1,000 psi	1,100	1,200	1,300	1,400	1,500
			On-center spacing 16″					
2 × 4	5.3	10.7	7-4	7-8	8-0	8-4	8-8	8-11
2 × 6	12.0	36.0	10-11	11-6	12-0	12-6	13-0	13-5
2 × 8	21.3	85.3	14-7	15-4	16-0	16-8	17-3	17-10
2 × 10	33.3	167	18-3	19-2	20-0	20-10	21-7	22-4
2 × 12	48.0	288	21-11	23-0	24-0	25-0	25-11	26-10
3 × 4	8.0	16.0	8-11	9-5	9-10	10-2	10-7	10-11
3 × 6	18.0	54.0	13-5	14-1	14-8	15-4	15-10	16-5
3 × 8	32.0	128	17-11	18-9	19-7	20-5	21-2	21-11
3 × 10	50.0	250	22-4	23-5	24-6	25-6	26-5	27-5
3 × 12	72.0	432	26-10	28-2	29-5	30-7	31-9	32-10
			On-center spacing 24″					
2 × 4	5.3	10.7	6-0	6-3	6-6	6-10	7-1	7-4
2 × 6	12.0	36.0	8-11	9-5	9-10	10-2	10-7	10-11
2 × 8	21.3	85.3	11-11	12-6	13-1	13-7	14-1	14-7
2 × 10	33.3	167	14-11	15-8	16-4	17-0	17-8	18-3
2 × 12	48.0	288	17-11	18-9	19-7	20-5	21-2	21-11
3 × 4	8.0	16.0	7-4	7-8	8-0	8-4	8-8	8-11
3 × 6	18.0	54.0	10-11	11-6	12-0	12-6	13-0	13-5
3 × 8	32.0	128	14-7	15-4	16-0	16-8	17-3	17-11
3 × 10	50.0	250	18-3	19-2	20-0	20-10	21-7	22-4
3 × 12	72.0	432	21-11	23-0	24-0	25-0	25-11	26-10
4 × 4	10.7	21.3	8-5	8-10	9-3	9-7	10-0	10-4
4 × 6	24.0	72.0	12-8	13-3	13-10	14-5	15-0	15-6
4 × 8	42.7	171	16-10	17-8	18-6	19-3	20-0	20-8
4 × 10	66.7	333	21-1	22-1	23-1	24-1	24-11	25-10
4 × 12	96.0	576	25-4	26-6	27-9	28-10	29-11	31-0
			On-center spacing 48″					
3 × 4	8.0	16.0	5-2	5-5	5-8	5-11	6-1	6-4
3 × 6	18.0	54.0	7-9	8-1	8-6	8-10	9-2	9-6
3 × 8	32.0	128	10-4	10-10	11-4	11-9	12-3	12-8
3 × 10	50.0	250	12-11	13-6	14-2	14-9	15-3	15-10
3 × 12	72.0	432	15-6	16-3	17-0	17-8	18-4	19-0
4 × 4	10.7	21.3	6-0	6-3	6-6	6-10	7-1	7-4
4 × 6	24.0	72.0	8-11	9-5	9-10	10-2	10-7	10-11
4 × 8	42.7	171	11-11	12-6	13-1	13-7	14-1	14-7
4 × 10	66.7	333	14-11	15-8	16-4	17-0	17-8	18-3
4 × 12	96.0	576	17-11	18-9	19-7	20-5	21-2	21-11
6 × 6	36.0	108	10-11	11-6	12-0	12-6	13-0	13-5
6 × 8	64.0	256	14-7	15-4	16-0	16-8	17-3	17-11
6 × 10	100.0	500	18-3	19-2	20-0	20-10	21-7	22-4
6 × 12	144.0	864	21-11	23-0	24-0	25-0	25-11	26-10
			On-center spacing 96″					
6 × 6	36.0	108	7-9	8-1	8-6	8-10	9-2	9-6
6 × 8	64.0	256	10-4	10-10	11-4	11-9	12-3	12-8
6 × 10	100.0	500	12-11	13-6	14-2	14-9	15-3	15-10
6 × 12	144.0	864	15-6	16-3	17-0	17-8	18-4	19-0
8 × 8	85.3	341	11-11	12-6	13-1	13-7	14-1	14-7
8 × 10	133.3	667	14-11	15-8	16-4	17-0	17-8	18-3
8 × 12	192.0	1,152	17-11	18-9	19-7	20-5	21-2	21-11
10 × 10	166.7	833	16-8	17-6	18-3	19-0	19-9	20-5
10 × 12	240.0	1,440	20-0	21-0	21-11	22-10	23-8	24-6
12 × 12	288.0	1,728	21-11	23-0	24-0	25-0	25-11	26-10

Table 8. Rough-sawn Lumber Spans
(Total uniformly distributed load 60 psf)

b × d	S	I	f = 1,000 psi	1,100	1,200	1,300	1,400	1,500
			On-center spacing 16″					
2 × 4	5.3	10.7	6-8	7-0	7-4	7-7	7-11	8-2
2 × 6	12.0	36.0	10-0	10-6	10-11	11-5	11-10	12-3
2 × 8	21.3	85.3	13-4	14-0	14-7	15-2	15-9	16-4
2 × 10	33.3	167	16-8	17-6	18-3	19-0	19-9	20-5
2 × 12	48.0	288	20-0	21-0	21-11	22-10	23-8	24-6
3 × 4	8.0	16.0	8-2	8-7	8-11	9-4	9-8	10-0
3 × 6	18.0	54.0	12-3	12-10	13-5	14-0	14-6	15-0
3 × 8	32.0	128	16-4	17-2	17-11	18-7	19-4	20-0
3 × 10	50.0	250	20-5	21-5	22-4	23-3	24-2	25-0
3 × 12	72.0	432	24-6	25-8	26-10	27-11	29-0	30-0
			On-center spacing 24″					
2 × 4	5.3	10.7	5-5	5-8	6-0	6-2	6-5	6-8
2 × 6	12.0	36.0	8-2	8-7	8-11	9-4	9-8	10-0
2 × 8	21.3	85.3	10-11	11-5	11-11	12-5	12-10	13-4
2 × 10	33.3	167	13-7	14-3	14-11	15-6	16-1	16-8
2 × 12	48.0	288	16-4	17-2	17-11	18-7	19-4	20-0
3 × 4	8.0	16.0	6-8	7-0	7-4	7-7	7-11	8-2
3 × 6	18.0	54.0	10-0	10-6	10-11	11-5	11-10	12-3
3 × 8	32.0	128	13-4	14-0	14-7	15-2	15-9	16-4
3 × 10	50.0	250	16-8	17-6	18-3	19-0	19-9	20-5
3 × 12	72.0	432	20-0	21-0	21-11	22-10	23-8	24-6
4 × 4	10.7	21.3	7-8	8-1	8-5	8-9	9-1	9-5
4 × 6	24.0	72.0	11-7	12-1	12-8	13-2	13-8	14-2
4 × 8	42.7	171	15-5	16-2	16-10	17-7	18-3	18-10
4 × 10	66.7	333	19-3	20-2	21-1	21-11	22-9	23-7
4 × 12	96.0	576	23-1	24-3	25-4	26-4	27-4	28-3
			On-center spacing 48″					
3 × 4	8.0	16.0	4-9	4-11	5-2	5-4	5-7	5-9
3 × 6	18.0	54.0	7-1	7-5	7-9	8-1	8-4	8-8
3 × 8	32.0	128	9-5	9-11	10-4	10-9	11-2	11-7
3 × 10	50.0	250	11-9	12-4	12-11	13-5	13-11	14-5
3 × 12	72.0	432	14-2	14-10	15-6	16-1	16-9	17-4
4 × 4	10.7	21.3	5-5	5-9	6-0	6-2	6-5	6-8
4 × 6	24.0	72.0	8-2	8-7	8-11	9-4	9-8	10-0
4 × 8	42.7	171	10-11	11-5	11-11	12-5	12-11	13-4
4 × 10	66.7	333	13-7	14-3	14-11	15-6	16-1	16-8
4 × 12	96.0	576	16-4	17-2	17-11	18-7	19-4	20-0
6 × 6	36.0	108	10-0	10-6	10-11	11-5	11-10	12-3
6 × 8	64.0	256	13-4	14-0	14-7	15-2	15-9	16-4
6 × 10	100.0	500	16-8	17-6	18-3	19-0	19-9	20-5
6 × 12	144.0	864	20-0	21-0	21-11	22-10	23-8	24-6
			On-center spacing 96″					
6 × 6	36.0	108	7-1	7-5	7-9	8-1	8-4	8-8
6 × 8	64.0	256	9-5	9-11	10-4	10-9	11-2	11-7
6 × 10	100.0	500	11-9	12-4	12-11	13-5	13-11	14-5
6 × 12	144.0	864	14-2	14-10	15-6	16-1	16-9	17-4
8 × 8	85.3	341	10-11	11-5	11-11	12-5	12-11	13-4
8 × 10	133.3	667	13-7	14-3	14-11	15-6	16-1	16-8
8 × 12	192.0	1,152	16-4	17-2	17-11	18-7	19-4	20-0
10 × 10	166.7	833	15-3	16-0	16-8	17-4	18-0	18-8
10 × 12	240.0	1,440	18-3	19-2	20-0	20-10	21-7	22-4
12 × 12	288.0	1,728	20-0	21-0	21-11	22-10	23-8	24-6

Table 9. S4S Dimension Lumber Spans
(Total uniformly distributed load 30 psf)

b × d	S	I	f = 1,000 psi	1,100	1,200	1,300	1,400	1,500
			On-center spacing 16″					
2 × 4	3.1	5.4	7–2	7–6	7–10	8–2	8–5	8–9
2 × 6	7.6	20.8	11–3	11–9	12–4	12–10	13–3	13–9
2 × 8	13.1	47.6	14–9	15–6	16–2	16–10	17–6	18–1
2 × 10	21.4	98.9	18–11	19–10	20–8	21–6	22–4	23–2
2 × 12	31.6	178	22–11	24–1	25–2	26–2	27–2	28–1
3 × 4	5.1	8.9	9–3	9–8	10–1	10–6	10–11	11–3
3 × 6	12.6	34.7	14–6	15–2	15–10	16–6	17–2	17–9
3 × 8	22.7	82.1	19–5	20–5	21–4	22–2	23–0	23–10
3 × 10	35.7	165	24–5	25–7	26–9	27–10	28–10	29–10
3 × 12	52.7	297	29–8	31–1	32–6	33–9	35–1	36–4
			On-center spacing 24″					
2 × 4	3.1	5.36	5–10	6–1	6–5	6–8	6–11	7–2
2 × 6	7.6	20.8	9–2	9–7	10–0	10–5	10–10	11–3
2 × 8	13.1	47.6	12–1	12–8	13–3	13–9	14–3	14–9
2 × 10	21.4	98.9	15–5	16–2	16–11	17–7	18–3	18–11
2 × 12	31.6	178	18–9	19–8	20–6	21–4	22–2	22–11
3 × 4	5.1	8.9	7–6	7–11	8–3	8–7	8–11	9–3
3 × 6	12.6	34.7	11–10	12–5	13–0	13–6	14–0	14–6
3 × 8	22.7	82.1	15–11	16–8	17–5	18–1	18–9	19–5
3 × 10	35.7	165	19–11	20–11	21–10	22–8	23–7	24–5
3 × 12	52.7	297	24–2	25–5	26–6	27–7	28–8	29–8
4 × 4	7.1	12.5	8–11	9–4	9–9	10–2	10–7	10–11
4 × 6	17.6	48.5	14–0	14–8	15–4	15–11	16–7	17–2
4 × 8	30.7	111	18–6	19–4	20–3	21–1	21–10	22–7
4 × 10	49.9	231	23–7	24–8	25–10	26–10	27–10	28–10
4 × 12	73.8	415	28–8	30–0	31–4	32–8	33–11	35–1
			On-center spacing 48″					
3 × 4	5.1	8.9	5–4	5–7	5–10	6–1	6–4	6–6
3 × 6	12.6	34.7	8–4	8–9	9–2	9–6	9–11	10–3
3 × 8	22.7	82.1	11–3	11–9	12–4	12–10	13–3	13–9
3 × 10	35.7	165	14–1	14–9	15–5	16–1	16–8	17–3
3 × 12	52.7	297	17–1	17–11	18–9	19–6	20–3	20–11
4 × 4	7.0	12.5	6–4	6–7	6–11	7–2	7–5	7–9
4 × 6	17.6	48.5	9–11	10–4	10–10	11–3	11–8	12–1
4 × 8	30.7	111	13–1	13–8	14–4	14–11	15–5	16–0
4 × 10	49.9	231	16–8	17–6	10–3	19–0	19–8	20–5
4 × 12	73.8	415	20–3	21–3	22–2	23–1	23–11	24–10
6 × 6	27.7	76.3	12–5	13–0	13–7	14–2	14–8	15–2
6 × 8	48.2	175	16–4	17–2	17–11	18–8	19–4	20–0
6 × 10	78.4	363	20–10	21–11	22–10	23–10	24–8	25–7
6 × 12	116.0	653	25–5	26–7	27–10	28–11	30–0	31–1
			On-center spacing 96″					
6 × 6	27.7	76.3	8–9	9–2	9–7	10–0	10–5	10–9
6 × 8	48.2	175	11–7	12–2	12–8	13–2	13–8	14–2
6 × 10	78.4	363	14–9	15–6	16–2	16–10	17–6	18–1
6 × 12	116	653	17–11	18–10	19–8	20–6	21–3	21–12
8 × 8	63.5	230	13–3	13–11	14–7	15–2	15–9	16–3
8 × 10	103	478	16–11	17–9	18–6	19–3	20–0	20–9
8 × 12	153	860	20–7	21–7	22–7	23–6	24–5	25–3
10 × 10	132	610	19–2	20–1	21–0	21–10	22–8	23–5
10 × 12	195	1,098	23–3	24–5	25–6	26–6	27–6	28–6
12 × 12	237	1,335	25–8	26–11	28–1	29–3	30–4	31–5

Table 10. S4S Dimension Lumber Spans
(Total uniformly distributed load 40 psf)

b × d	S	I	f = 1,000 psi	1,100	1,200	1,300	1,400	1,500
			On-center spacing 16″					
2 × 4	3.1	5.4	6-2	6-6	6-9	7-1	7-4	7-7
2 × 6	7.6	20.8	9-9	10-2	10-8	11-1	11-6	11-11
2 × 8	13.1	47.6	12-10	13-5	14-0	14-7	15-2	15-8
2 × 10	21.4	98.9	16-4	17-2	17-11	18-8	19-4	20-0
2 × 12	31.6	178	19-10	20-10	21-9	22-8	23-6	24-4
3 × 4	5.1	8.9	7-12	8-4	8-9	9-1	9-5	9-9
3 × 6	12.6	34.7	12-7	13-2	13-9	14-4	14-10	15-4
3 × 8	22.7	82.1	16-10	17-8	18-5	19-2	19-11	20-8
3 × 10	35.7	165	21-1	22-2	23-2	24-1	25-0	25-10
3 × 12	52.7	297	25-8	26-11	28-1	29-3	30-4	31-5
			On-center spacing 24″					
2 × 4	3.1	5.4	5-1	5-4	5-6	5-9	6-0	6-2
2 × 6	7.6	20.8	7-11	8-4	8-8	9-1	9-5	9-9
2 × 8	13.1	47.6	10-5	10-11	11-5	11-11	12-4	12-10
2 × 10	21.4	98.9	13-4	14-0	14-8	15-3	15-10	16-4
2 × 12	31.6	178	16-3	17-0	17-9	18-6	19-2	19-10
3 × 4	5.1	8.9	6-6	6-10	7-2	7-5	7-9	8-0
3 × 6	12.6	34.7	10-3	10-9	11-3	11-8	12-1	12-7
3 × 8	22.7	82.1	13-9	14-5	15-1	15-8	16-3	16-10
3 × 10	35.7	165	17-3	18-1	18-11	19-8	20-5	21-1
3 × 12	52.7	297	20-11	22-0	22-11	23-11	24-10	25-8
4 × 4	7.1	12.5	7-9	8-1	8-5	8-10	9-2	9-5
4 × 6	17.6	48.5	12-1	12-8	13-3	13-10	14-4	14-10
4 × 8	30.7	111	16-0	16-9	17-6	18-3	18-11	19-7
4 × 10	49.9	231	20-5	21-5	22-4	23-3	24-2	25-0
4 × 12	73.8	415	24-10	26-0	27-2	28-3	29-4	30-4
			On-center spacing 48″					
3 × 4	5.1	8.9	4-7	4-10	5-1	5-3	5-5	5-8
3 × 6	12.6	34.7	7-3	7-7	7-11	8-3	8-7	8-10
3 × 8	22.7	82.1	9-9	10-2	10-8	11-1	11-6	11-11
3 × 10	35.7	165	12-2	12-9	13-4	13-11	14-5	14-11
3 × 12	52.7	297	14-10	15-6	16-3	16-11	17-6	18-2
4 × 4	7.1	12.5	5-5	5-9	6-0	6-3	6-5	6-8
4 × 6	17.6	48.5	8-7	9-0	9-5	9-9	10-2	10-6
4 × 8	30.7	111	11-4	11-10	12-5	12-11	13-5	13-10
4 × 10	49.9	231	14-5	15-1	15-10	16-5	17-1	17-8
4 × 12	73.8	415	17-6	18-5	19-3	20-0	20-9	21-6
6 × 6	27.7	76.3	10-9	11-3	11-9	12-3	12-9	13-2
6 × 8	48.2	175	14-2	14-10	15-6	16-2	16-9	17-4
6 × 10	78.4	363	18-1	18-11	19-10	20-7	21-5	22-2
6 × 12	116.0	653	22-0	23-1	24-1	25-1	26-0	26-11
			On-center spacing 96″					
6 × 6	27.7	76.3	7-7	8-0	8-4	8-8	9-0	9-4
6 × 8	48.2	175	10-0	10-6	11-0	11-5	11-10	12-3
6 × 10	78.4	363	12-9	13-5	14-0	14-7	15-1	15-8
6 × 12	116	653	15-7	16-4	17-0	17-9	18-5	19-0
8 × 8	63.5	230	11-6	12-1	12-7	13-1	13-7	14-1
8 × 10	103	478	14-8	15-4	16-1	16-8	17-4	17-11
8 × 12	153	860	17-10	18-9	19-7	20-4	21-1	21-10
10 × 10	132	610	16-7	17-5	18-2	18-11	19-7	20-4
10 × 12	195	1,098	20-2	21-2	22-1	23-0	23-10	24-8
12 × 12	237	1,335	22-3	23-4	24-4	25-4	26-3	27-3

Table 11. S4S Dimension Lumber Spans
(Total uniformly determined load 50 psf)

b × d	S	I	f = 1,000 psi	1,100	1,200	1,300	1,400	1,500
			On-center spacing 16″					
2 × 4	3.1	5.4	5–6	5–10	6–1	6–4	6–7	6–9
2 × 6	7.6	20.8	8–8	9–1	9–6	9–11	10–3	10–8
2 × 8	13.1	47.6	11–5	12–0	12–6	13–1	13–7	14–0
2 × 10	21.4	98.9	14–8	15–4	16–0	16–8	17–4	17–11
2 × 12	31.6	178	17–9	18–8	19–6	20–3	21–0	21–9
3 × 4	5.1	8.9	7–2	7–6	7–10	8–2	8–5	8–9
3 × 6	12.6	34.7	11–3	11–9	12–4	12–10	13–3	13–9
3 × 8	22.7	82.1	15–1	15–10	16–6	17–2	17–10	18–5
3 × 10	35.7	165	18–11	19–10	20–8	21–7	22–4	23–2
3 × 12	52.7	297	22–11	24–1	25–2	26–2	27–2	28–1
			On-center spacing 24″					
2 × 4	3.1	5.4	4–6	4–9	4–11	5–2	5–4	5–6
2 × 6	7.6	20.8	4–1	7–5	7–9	8–1	8–5	8–8
2 × 8	13.1	47.6	9–4	9–10	10–3	10–8	11–1	11–5
2 × 10	21.4	98.9	11–11	12–6	13–1	13–7	14–2	14–8
2 × 12	31.6	178	14–6	15–3	15–11	16–7	17–2	17–9
3 × 4	5.1	8.9	5–10	6–1	6–5	6–8	6–11	7–2
3 × 6	12.6	34.7	9–2	9–7	10–0	10–5	10–10	11–3
3 × 8	22.7	82.1	12–4	12–11	13–6	14–0	14–7	15–1
3 × 10	35.7	165	15–5	16–2	16–11	17–7	18–3	18–11
3 × 12	52.7	297	18–9	19–8	20–6	21–4	22–2	22–11
4 × 4	7.15	12.5	6–11	7–3	7–7	7–10	8–2	8–5
4 × 6	17.6	48.5	10–10	11–4	11–10	12–4	12–10	13–3
4 × 8	30.7	111	14–4	15–0	15–8	16–4	16–11	17–6
4 × 10	49.9	231	18–3	19–2	20–0	20–10	21–7	22–4
4 × 12	73.8	415	22–2	23–3	24–4	25–3	26–3	27–2
			On-center spacing 48″					
3 × 4	5.1	8.9	4–1	4–4	4–6	4–8	4–11	5–1
3 × 6	12.6	34.7	6–6	6–10	7–1	7–5	7–8	7–11
3 × 8	22.7	82.1	8–8	9–1	9–6	9–11	10–4	10–8
3 × 10	35.7	165	10–11	11–5	11–11	12–5	12–11	13–4
3 × 12	52.7	297	13–3	13–11	14–6	15–1	15–8	16–3
4 × 4	7.1	12.5	4–11	5–1	5–4	5–7	5–9	6–0
4 × 6	17.6	48.5	7–8	8–0	8–5	8–9	9–1	9–5
4 × 8	30.7	111	10–1	10–7	11–1	11–6	12–0	12–5
4 × 10	49.9	231	12–11	13–6	14–2	14–8	15–3	15–10
4 × 12	73.8	415	15–8	16–5	17–2	17–11	18–7	19–3
6 × 6	27.7	76.3	9–7	10–1	10–6	10–11	11–4	11–9
6 × 8	48.2	175	12–8	13–4	13–11	14–5	15–0	15–6
6 × 10	78.4	363	16–2	16–11	17–9	18–5	19–2	19–10
6 × 12	116.0	653	19–8	20–7	21–6	22–5	23–3	24–1
			On-center spacing 96″					
6 × 6	27.7	76.3	6–10	7–2	7–5	7–9	8–0	8–4
6 × 8	48.2	175	9–0	9–5	9–10	10–3	10–7	11–0
6 × 10	78.4	363	11–5	12–0	12–6	13–0	13–6	14–0
6 × 12	116	653	13–11	14–7	15–3	15–10	16–5	17–0
8 × 8	63.5	230	10–3	10–9	11–3	11–9	12–2	12–7
8 × 10	103	478	13–1	13–9	14–4	14–11	15–6	16–1
8 × 12	153	860	16–0	16–9	17–6	18–2	18–11	19–7
10 × 10	132	610	14–10	15–7	16–3	16–11	17–7	18–2
10 × 12	195	1,098	18–0	18–11	19–9	20–7	21–4	22–1
12 × 12	237	1,335	19–10	20–10	21–9	22–8	23–6	24–4

Table 12. S4S Dimension Lumber Spans
(Total uniformly distributed load 60 psf)

b × d	S	I	f = 1,000 psi	1,100	1,200	1,300	1,400	1,500
			On-center spacing 16″					
2 × 4	3.1	5.4	5–1	5–4	5–6	5–9	6–0	6–2
2 × 6	7.6	20.8	7–11	8–4	8–8	9–1	9–5	9–9
2 × 8	13.1	47.6	10–5	10–11	11–5	11–11	12–4	12–10
2 × 10	21.4	98.9	13–4	14–0	14–8	15–3	15–10	16–4
2 × 12	31.6	178	16–3	17–0	17–9	18–6	19–2	19–10
3 × 4	5.1	8.9	6–6	6–10	7–2	7–5	7–9	8–0
3 × 6	12.6	34.7	10–3	10–9	11–3	11–8	12–1	12–7
3 × 8	22.7	82.1	13–9	14–5	15–1	15–8	16–3	16–10
3 × 10	35.7	165	17–3	18–1	18–11	19–8	20–5	21–1
3 × 12	52.7	297	20–11	22–0	22–11	23–11	24–10	25–8
			On-center spacing 24″					
2 × 4	3.1	5.4	4–1	4–4	4–6	4–8	4–11	5–1
2 × 6	7.6	20.8	6–6	6–10	7–1	7–5	7–8	7–11
2 × 8	13.1	47.6	8–6	8–11	9–4	9–9	10–1	10–5
2 × 10	21.4	98.9	10–11	11–5	11–11	12–5	12–11	13–4
2 × 12	31.6	178	13–3	13–11	14–6	15–1	15–8	16–3
3 × 4	5.1	8.9	5–4	5–7	5–10	6–1	6–4	6–6
3 × 6	12.6	34.7	8–4	8–9	9–2	9–6	9–11	10–3
3 × 8	22.7	82.1	11–3	11–9	12–4	12–10	13–3	13–9
3 × 10	35.7	165	14–1	14–9	15–5	16–1	16–8	17–3
3 × 12	52.7	297	17–1	17–11	18–9	19–6	20–3	20–11
4 × 4	7.15	12.5	6–4	6–7	6–11	7–2	7–5	7–9
4 × 6	17.6	48.5	9–11	10–4	10–10	11–3	11–8	12–1
4 × 8	30.7	111	13–1	13–8	14–4	14–11	15–5	16–0
4 × 10	49.9	231	16–8	17–6	18–3	19–0	19–8	20–5
4 × 12	73.8	415	20–3	21–3	22–2	23–1	23–11	24–10
			On-center spacing 48″					
3 × 4	5.1	8.9	3–9	3–11	4–1	4–3	4–5	4–7
3 × 6	12.6	34.7	5–11	6–2	6–6	6–9	7–0	7–3
3 × 8	22.7	82.1	7–11	8–4	8–8	9–1	9–5	9–9
3 × 10	35.7	165	9–11	10–5	10–11	11–4	11–9	12–2
3 × 12	52.7	297	12–1	12–8	13–3	13–10	14–4	14–10
4 × 4	7.1	12.5	4–5	4–8	4–11	5–1	5–3	5–5
4 × 6	17.6	48.5	7–0	7–4	7–8	8–0	8–3	8–7
4 × 8	30.7	111	9–3	9–8	10–1	10–6	10–11	11–4
4 × 10	49.9	231	11–9	12–4	12–11	13–5	13–11	14–5
4 × 12	73.8	415	14–4	15–0	15–8	16–4	16–11	17–6
6 × 6	27.7	76.3	8–9	9–2	9–7	10–0	10–5	10–9
6 × 8	48.2	175	11–7	12–2	12–8	13–2	13–8	14–2
6 × 10	78.4	363	14–9	15–6	16–2	16–10	17–6	18–1
6 × 12	116.0	653	17–11	18–10	19–8	20–6	21–3	22–0
			On-center spacing 96″					
6 × 6	27.7	76.3	6–2	6–6	6–10	7–1	7–4	7–7
6 × 8	48.2	175	8–2	8–7	9–0	9–4	9–8	10–0
6 × 10	78.4	363	10–5	10–11	11–5	11–11	12–4	12–9
6 × 12	116	653	12–8	13–4	13–11	14–6	15–0	15–7
8 × 8	63.5	230	9–5	9–10	10–3	10–8	11–1	11–6
8 × 10	103	478	12–0	12–7	13–1	13–8	14–2	14–8
8 × 12	153	860	14–7	15–3	16–0	16–7	17–3	17–10
10 × 10	132	610	13–6	14–2	14–10	15–5	16–0	16–7
10 × 12	195	1,098	16–5	17–3	18–0	18–9	19–6	20–2
12 × 12	237	1,335	18–2	19–0	19–10	20–8	21–6	22–3

Table 13. Spans Limited by Deflection
(Deflection = 1/360 at 40 psf live load)

$b \times d$	I, in.^{4}	o.c.	$E = 0.6 \times 10^6$	0.8×10^6	1.0×10^6	1.2×10^6	1.4×10^6	1.6×10^6	1.8×10^6
				Rough-sawn lumber					
2 × 6	36.0	12	9–4	10–2	11–0	11–8	12–4	12–11	13–5
		16	8–5	9–4	10–0	10–7	11–3	11–8	12–3
		24	7–5	8–1	8–7	9–4	9–9	10–3	10–7
2 × 8	85.3	12	12–4	13–8	14–8	15–7	16–4	17–2	17–9
		16	11–3	12–4	13–4	14–2	14–8	15–7	16–2
		24	9–9	10–10	11–8	12–4	13–4	13–8	14–2
2 × 10	166.7	12	15–5	16–1	18–4	19–6	20–6	21–5	22–4
		16	14–1	15–5	16–8	17–9	18–8	19–6	20–3
		24	12–4	13–6	14–6	15–5	16–1	17–1	17–9
2 × 12	288	12	18–7	20–5	22–0	23–4	24–8	25–6	26–9
		16	16–10	18–7	19–11	21–3	22–4	23–4	24–4
		24	14–9	16–3	17–6	18–7	19–7	20–5	21–3
				S4S lumber					
2 × 6 (1-1/2 × 5-1/2)	20.8	12	7–9	8–6	9–2	9–9	10–3	10–9	11–2
		16	7–0	7–9	8–4	8–10	9–4	9–9	10–2
		24	6–2	6–9	7–3	7–9	8–2	8–6	8–10
2 × 8 (1-1/2 × 7-1/4)	47.6	12	10–2	11–3	12–1	12–10	13–6	14–2	14–8
		16	9–3	10–2	11–0	11–8	12–3	12–10	13–4
		24	8–1	8–11	9–7	10–2	10–9	11–3	11–8
2 × 10 (1-1/2 × 9-1/4)	98.9	12	13–0	14–4	15–5	16–5	17–3	18–0	18–9
		16	11–10	13–0	14–0	14–11	15–8	16–5	17–0
		24	10–4	11–4	12–3	13–0	13–8	14–4	14–11
2 × 12 (1-1/2 × 11-1/4)	178	12	15–10	17–5	18–9	19–11	21–0	21–11	22–10
		16	14–4	15–10	17–0	18–1	19–1	19–11	20–9
		24	12–7	13–10	14–11	15–10	16–8	17–5	18–1

Example: What size rafter would be required if the on-center spacing were increased from 48″ to 72″?

Answer: This example demonstrates a hidden versatility in the span tables. Use your head and you will find that you rarely have to resort to calculation!

The secret lies in realizing the significance of the section modulus, $S = bd^2/6$. The section modulus of a beam varies directly with its breadth, b. Section modulus (S) is also a direct measure of the ability of a beam to hold up a load. Given identical clearspans (L) a beam of twice the section modulus will hold up twice the load (twice as wide a section of roof). In the example above, a 4″×12″ beam (S=96.0) was found sufficient to support a 48″ wide section of roof. Therefore a 6″×12″ beam (S=144) would be sufficient to support a 72″ section of roof.

5.

Framing Systems

We have seen in the previous chapter the various stresses to which building frames are subjected (also how to deal with each). Considering that these fundamental stresses are common to all building frames, it should not surprise you that the various American framing systems that have evolved over the past three centuries have quite a bit in common.

Figure 33 shows a building frame that I doubt will be recognized by any architectural historian. It is a frame that might have been built by an amateur from impressions gained while growing up around sheds and barns. In fact, it is my dog's house. I use it because it illustrates well the basic ingredients common to all of the frames. After a discussion of the basic elements, I will take you on a tour of the five classic framing systems used in this country from the seventeenth century to the present. Although regional permutations and variations on the basic themes developed, the odds are great that your house comes close to one of the five.

Dynamite's House (Illustration 33)

Begin at the beginning. Houses should be analyzed and designed not as they are of necessity built, but as the loads accumulate. The first loads are incurred at the roof—dead, snow, and wind loads. In most areas of the country the sum of these forces is large: 50 psf or more. Before the advent of trusses, large beams were required to carry the loads. Since the ability of a beam to carry a load varies inversely with the square of its clearspan, it is immediately apparent that the most economical system has the major roof beams running in the direction of the smaller dimension of the house. The main roof beams are called *rafters* and run in the direction of the roof slope. A *ridgeboard,* or ridgepole, serves primarily to tie the rafters together at the peak. Since the rafters commonly form two sides of a triangle, the vertical roof loads generate large outward thrusts at the rafter bottoms. This outward thrust is resisted by *ceiling joists* or attic-floor joists, which serve as the third side of the triangle. It is commonly thought that the horizontal collar ties often found tying rafter pairs together near the

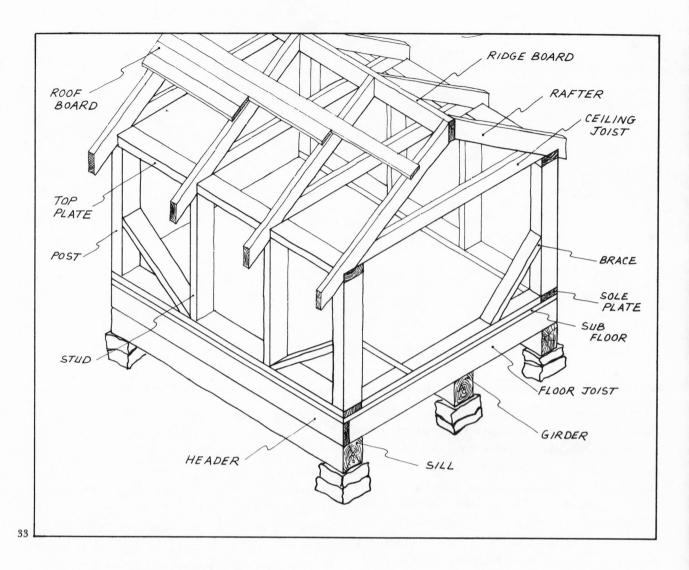

RIDGE BOARD

RAFTER

CEILING JOIST

ROOF BOARD

TOP PLATE

POST

BRACE

SOLE PLATE

SUB FLOOR

STUD

FLOOR JOIST

GIRDER

HEADER

SILL

33

peak serve the same function, but this is false. The primary reason for collar ties is to prevent the roof from flying apart at the ridge under wind-uplifting forces.

The intersection of rafter bottoms and wall is extremely important, as we've seen. At this junction the roof load is transferred to the wall. In a high wind this junction may also be called upon to provide the opposite force in holding the roof down. The *plate,* or wall *top plate,* facilitates the fastening of rafters to wall. Other plate functions include tying the wall together during framing, providing a third leg for bracing against racking, and fastening both exterior and interior sheathing. Originally the vertical load-carrying members of the wall were the *posts.* Later, smaller vertical members called *studs* were

used, not only to carry the vertical load, but to facilitate sheathing of the wall. Today the studs have assumed the load-bearing function as well. However, the term *post* is still used for the either solid or built-up members at the four corners of the building.

The exterior walls of a building are almost always built in a horizontal position and raised into place (hence, wall-raising). The *soleplate* facilitates the framing and raising as well as providing a solid nailing medium for the studs, braces, and interior wall surface. Bracing against racking is effected by creating triangles in the planes of the walls. These triangles are usually formed with the three legs: soleplate, post, and *brace* or, alternatively, top plate, post, and *brace.* In order not to interfere with window placement, smaller versions of both are sometimes used together. Lately, the same function is provided by diagonal sheathing or sheathing membranes such as plywood.

The subfloor may or may not be sandwiched between the wall and the floor and sill framing system. In any case, it serves as a convenient working platform during construction of the remaining building. The completion of the subfloor is a major milestone for the carpenter, especially in difficult terrain. *Floor joists* serve the same purpose for the floor as rafters in the roof: that is, they provide the bending strength. Their on-center spacing depends on the stiffness of the subfloor. A *header,* joist header, or box sill is used to prevent the joists from rotating from their

unstable vertical orientation, as well as providing support for the soleplate of the wall in the case of studs not falling directly over floor joists.

Finally the buck stops at the *sill.* Roof loads, wall loads, and floor loads are all ultimately transferred to this bottommost piece of wood. It is not only symbolic of the building process but the key member in the structural integrity of the building. It is to the wood frame building what the keystone is to the masonry arch. (In spite of its importance, however, it is often remarkably easy to replace.) When used on a pier-type foundation it is called upon to support loads in bending. With a continuous foundation, however, it provides no bending strength. Similar to the sill in

Table 14. Framing Terminology

blocking:	short pieces nailed between major framing members to act as fire-stops or to provide a nailing surface
brace:	a diagonal member fastened to major vertical and horizontal members to provide a rigid triangle resisting racking forces
bridging:	diagonal members that transfer and distribute concentrated loads from a floor joist to its neighbors
girder:	large beam supporting floor joists from below, usually at the same level as the sills
girts:	large horizontal beams supporting the ends of upper-story floor joists between posts
header:	a member that receives a set of repetitive members at right angles
joists:	repetitive members supporting the subfloor
ledgers:	small strips nailed to the bottom of larger members to support toe-nailed intersecting members
plates:	wall members connecting the ends of the studs and posts—usually the *top plate,* supporting the lower rafter ends, also the *soleplate,* resting on the subfloor and receiving the studs
posts:	large vertical members at the four corners of the building and at intersecting walls—may be solid or built up of smaller pieces
purlins:	members at right angles to rafters serving to break up the roof board clearspan
rafters:	main load-carrying members of the roof, usually running up and down the slope
ribbon or ribband:	a thin board let into the studs and supporting the second-story floor joists—replaces the girt in the balloon frame
ridgeboard:	member at the roof peak to which rafter pairs are nailed—more a convenience than a necessity
roofers:	roof boards nailed either to rafters or purlins
sheathing:	boards enclosing walls, nailed to studs and posts—may be nailed diagonally to eliminate requirement for braces
sill:	bottommost piece of wood; interfaces wood frame with foundation—may or may not support a load in bending
studs:	vertical wall members used between posts to support second-floor and roof loads and provide nailing for exterior and interior sheathing
subfloor:	first level of flooring over floor joists
trusses:	rafters, ceiling joists, and ties assembled in such a way as to span a greater distance than possible with the rafter alone

function but different in name is the *girder,* a heavy beam often running down the middle of the first floor and serving to break the clearspan of the floor joists. Load-bearing interior walls are usually placed directly over the girder.

Table 14 defines these terms and others which will be used in describing the classic framing systems.

Five Classic Framing Systems

POST-AND-GIRT *(Illustration 34)*

Post-and-girt, also called post-and-lintel and post-and-beam, came across the ocean from England with the first settlers. It is characterized by the use of large, widely spaced load-carrying timbers. Vertical loads are carried by posts at the corners and intersections of load-bearing walls. Plates and girts collect distributed roof and floor loads from rafters and joists and transfer them to the posts. Wall studs are reduced to a convenience for attaching wall sheathing. That many post-and-girt houses survive after several centuries may be attributed to the size of the timbers and their having been fastened by hardwood pegs rather than nails.

I don't wish to dash anyone's fantasy, but the post-and-girt system evolved, just as the FHA house evolved, for economic reasons. Several hundred years ago machine-cut nails and automatic circular sawmills didn't exist. It was simply less expensive to hand-hew the few large beams from trees felled in the immediate area and fasten

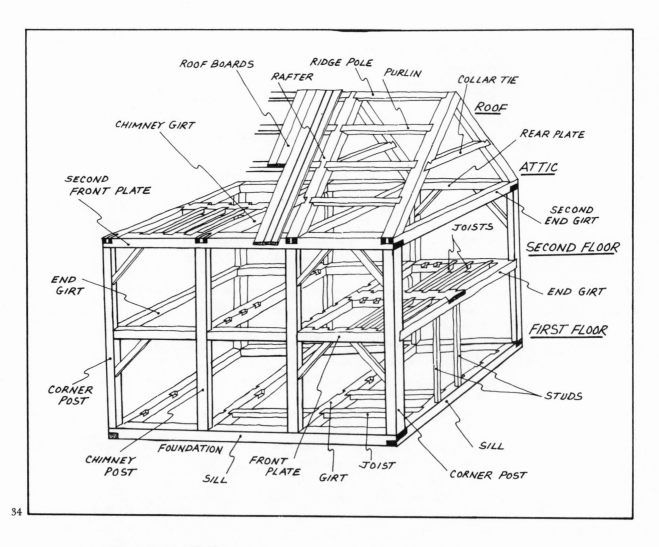

them together using elaborate mortise-and-tenon joints and hand-made pegs. Even the wall studs were sawn on two sides only. Often studs were made by sawing a plank and then splitting the plank into studs with an ax and wedges. First-floor joists and roof purlins required only one smooth and straight edge and so were hewn from small trees on one side only.

The rigidity of this building depended on close tolerance in the mortise-and-tenon joints. Every town had a framing carpenter whose specialty was making the joints and laying out and supervising the raising of the frame. Most of the remaining labor was commonly supplied by the owner, especially in rural areas. Very few boys grew up in rural America without acquiring basic carpentry skills. On my farm there still stands a workshop built by a twelve-year-old boy eighty years ago!

The post-and-girt frame is both easier and more difficult than others to repair. Easier, because few of the members support loads; more difficult because of the method of fastening those members which do support loads.

The post-and-girt frame enjoys a new popularity today, probably for several reasons. Revulsion for the throwaway mentality of our society has created a nostalgia for the past. In building, the present is characterized by the use of ever-smaller pieces of wood, fastened together with sheet metal devices by laborers who hate their jobs. The past is represented by the post-and-girt frame of

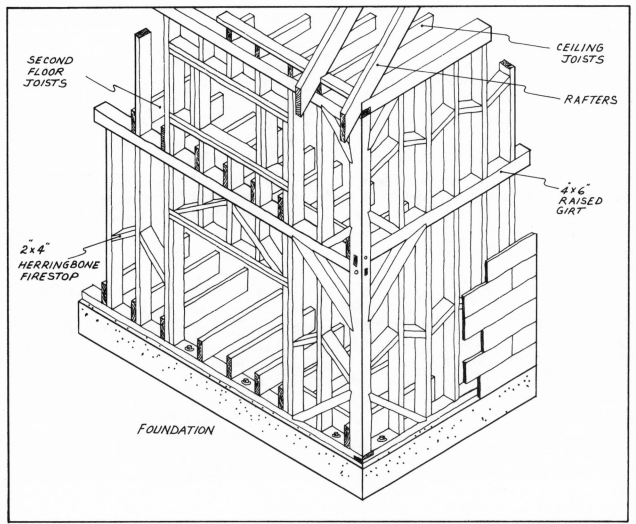

SECOND FLOOR JOISTS

CEILING JOISTS

RAFTERS

4"×6" RAISED GIRT

2"×4" HERRINGBONE FIRESTOP

FOUNDATION

35

hand-hewn timbers and pegs (organic), lovingly assembled by craftsmen who loved their work. Beyond nostalgia, however, is the unquestionable fact that the properly enclosed post-and-girt frame will outlast any of the more modern frames many times over.

THE EASTERN BRACED FRAME
(Illustration 35)

Given an increased availability of sawn lumber of small dimension, a decreased availability of long timber of large section, and less expensive machine-made nails and bolts, the Eastern braced frame represents a natural step. The basic frame retains the essential characteristics of the post-and-girt; the girts and plates are still fastened to the posts with pegged mortise-and-tenon joints. However, many subtle changes have taken place: smaller rafters of closer spacing eliminate the need for purlins; more of the roof load is now carried by the smaller plates, thus requiring the studs to bear loads; a greater number of repetitive members allows the spiking of joints since each joint is less critical; and the advent of the continuous concrete or brick foundation wall allows a smaller sill, bolted to the foundation for wind resistance. This latter point represents an important development. With the advent of the wood-burning stove, the massive central chimney fell into disfavor. Many a post-and-girt house has simply blown away after conversion from the central chimney to the smaller chimneys constructed to serve the stoves.

The herringbone blocking that so frustrates blown-in-insulation contractors is often said to have evolved as either a fire-stop or as bracing against racking. I don't believe either. I think it was because the carpenter involved in the transition wasn't comfortable with studs carrying the load. Because of the bracing and the blocking, this frame is the most difficult to insulate. In a two-story house many of the stud cavities are broken into eight different spaces, each one requiring a separate hole. If your house has this frame you'd be wise after insulating to obtain an infrared thermogram, which will spot empty cavities.

THE BALLOON FRAME (Illustration 36)

The balloon frame represents a giant step toward industrialization in the housing industry. Gone are the mortise-and-tenon joints; gone are the pegs; gone are the braces; in fact, there is no longer any member thicker than two inches! Milled lumber is cheaper; nails machine-cut from wire are cheaper; skilled labor is more expensive. Fewer sizes of wood and types of joint are put together by less skilled labor.

Plates, sills, and posts are built up from 2″ stock. The girt has been cleverly replaced by the ribband, a 1″×6″ or 1″×8″ board let into the studs as a support for the joists. Bracing is supplied, if at all, by applying the sheathing boards diagonally.

The balloon frame gets its name from the fact that the studs run as single pieces from sill to top plate, making the frame like a membrane. Both the major advantage and disadvantage derive from this fact. In drying from the "green" as-sawn state to the equilibrium state of dryness, lumber typically shrinks 6 to 8 percent in width but only 0.1 percent in length. The balloon frame is thus "Sanforized," its dimensions being controlled entirely by lengths of lumber. Prior to this development, much trouble was encountered with plaster and stucco walls.

The major disadvantage was the fluelike stud spaces, which extended as high as three stories. Much attention was supposed to be given to fire-stopping these cavities, since once a fire entered such a space it would be only a matter of minutes before the fire spread from basement to attic.

We think that we have discovered shoddy workmanship—that builders lost their pride just a few years back. If you gut your house you may be surprised to find that shoddy workmanship and a carelessness about detail go back a long time. The circa-1900 two-story balloon-framed house I presently live in is typical of its contemporaries; it lacks any semblance of fire-stopping from base-

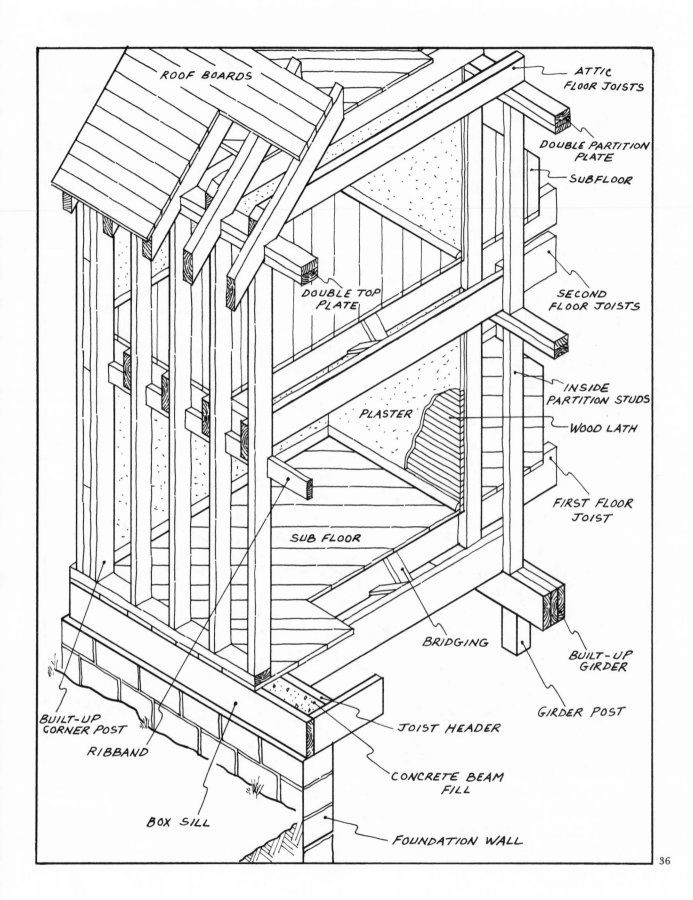

ROOF BOARDS

ATTIC FLOOR JOISTS

DOUBLE PARTITION PLATE

SUBFLOOR

SECOND FLOOR JOISTS

DOUBLE TOP PLATE

INSIDE PARTITION STUDS

WOOD LATH

PLASTER

FIRST FLOOR JOIST

SUB FLOOR

BRIDGING

BUILT-UP GIRDER

GIRDER POST

JOIST HEADER

BUILT-UP CORNER POST

RIBBAND

CONCRETE BEAM FILL

BOX SILL

FOUNDATION WALL

36

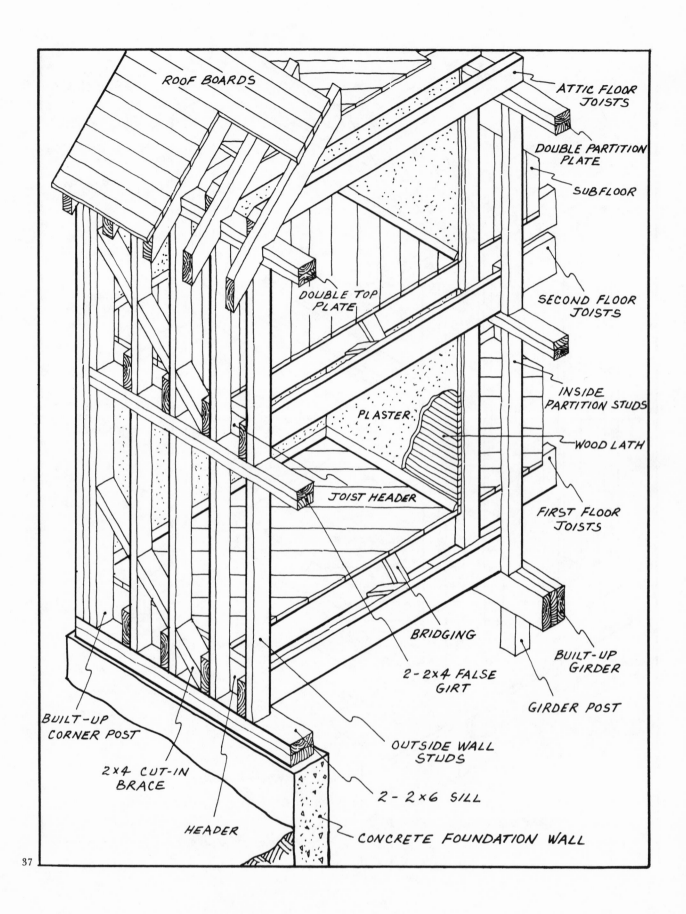

ROOF BOARDS

ATTIC FLOOR JOISTS

DOUBLE PARTITION PLATE

SUBFLOOR

DOUBLE TOP PLATE

SECOND FLOOR JOISTS

INSIDE PARTITION STUDS

PLASTER

WOOD LATH

JOIST HEADER

FIRST FLOOR JOISTS

BRIDGING

BUILT-UP GIRDER

2 - 2x4 FALSE GIRT

GIRDER POST

BUILT-UP CORNER POST

OUTSIDE WALL STUDS

2x4 CUT-IN BRACE

2 - 2x6 SILL

HEADER

CONCRETE FOUNDATION WALL

37

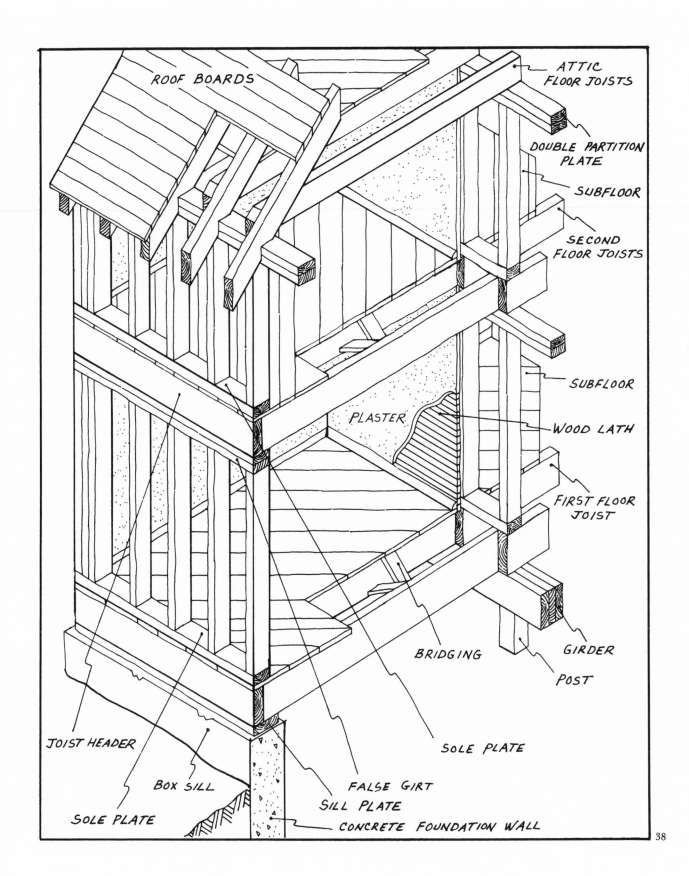

ATTIC
FLOOR JOISTS

ROOF BOARDS

DOUBLE PARTITION
PLATE

SUBFLOOR

SECOND
FLOOR JOISTS

SUBFLOOR

PLASTER

WOOD LATH

FIRST FLOOR
JOIST

BRIDGING

GIRDER

POST

SOLE PLATE

JOIST HEADER

BOX SILL

FALSE GIRT

SILL PLATE

SOLE PLATE

CONCRETE FOUNDATION WALL

38

ment to attic—or bracing, including diagonal sheathing. It was even easier in those days to build a poor house. Since the government didn't finance housing, no minimum property standards existed. Very few books were written on the subject; carpentry practices were simply handed down from master to apprentice, with the term *master* loosely applied.

THE MODERN BRACED FRAME
(Illustration 37)

The balloon frame had several strikes against it. The first was the fire-stopping problem, which gave fire inspectors cardiac arrest; the second was the increasing cost of the extremely long studs; the third was the difficulty of either raising or building in place two- and three-story walls. The modern braced frame brought back the girt (in the form of double 2×4's) as the solution to all of the above problems. It automatically provided a fire-stop; it eliminated studs longer than 8'; and it allowed fabrication of the wall on the deck.

THE PLATFORM FRAME (Illustration 38)

The platform, or Western, frame represents the last step toward industrialization, short of the factory-built modular house. Each story of the platform house is built upon a platform consisting of joists, box sill, and subfloor. Story builds upon story; after completion of the first-story walls, a second platform is built identical to the first as if the first-story walls were the foundation. This is the ultimate in standardization, requiring the lowest level of skill and the fewest standard sizes of framing material. The eight-foot $2'' \times 4''$ stud today is to the lumberyard what the chicken is to the supermarket.

The platform frame also standardized the use of the joist header and the soleplate. The soleplate and top plate of each wall automatically provided fire-stopping and nailing surfaces for exterior sheathing and interior drywall. The introduction of drywall made frame shrinkage less important. Bracing is now provided by either the exterior sheathing (diagonal boards, plywood, or other sheet material) or by $1'' \times 4''$ braces similar to the old style but let into the studs and nailed at plate, post, and stud crossing. Fire-stopping is rare in the platform-framed house.

Summary

This chapter should allow identification of the frame most closely resembling your own, thereby pointing out the function of the various frame members. The design procedures of the preceding chapter should provide you with the knowledge necessary to undertake any sort of structural alteration or repair.

6.

Changes

Introduction

Through the previous three chapters we have come to understand the nature of the forces on and within a house frame, how the various framing systems deal with these forces, the names of the members and their relationship to one another, and even how to find the required dimensions of each. We are now prepared to take the ultimate step—modify the frame.

A house is primarily a membrane separating an often harsh exterior environment from the inside controlled environment. Changing that outside envelope costs money—as much or more than constructing a new house. But changing interior spaces can be remarkably inexpensive. If you are in the majority, you bought or inherited your house secondhand. Even if you didn't, your family has changed since first moving in. When first built, the house probably fulfilled the definition of good design in being appropriate to its time, its place, and its expected function, but if there's anything certain in this life, it is that things change. Styles change; families change; needs change; even fuels change. After forty or more years of surrounding change, it would be sur-

prising indeed if the house remained optimal to its present owner's needs.

Most of us think that an old house cannot be changed, has never been changed, and should not be changed. In fact, however, change is the natural order of things. Pick up a hundred-year-old photograph of the main street of your town. Do you recognize anything? Not much, I'm sure. People a hundred years ago were much given to change; they cut houses in half, put houses together, moved houses and barns across town. They skidded houses down the frozen river—even floated houses to sea on barges. Part of the charm of the New England farm is its rambling nature. Shed after shed after shed was built until finally it was possible to walk from house to barn without shoveling snow. Most farms were not built this way originally. Country folks just have a hankering to be fussing with their houses.

To tell the truth, I think rebuilt houses are more exciting than new houses. Who has not been visually excited by a restaurant that was once a warehouse, or a house that was once a church? I hope you will someday add to your list "a house that was once a house," as I have. How can this be so universally so? I've given this a great deal of thought and think I have the answer.

The design of a house entails a million interconnecting decisions. Most of us have a difficult enough time picking coordinating colors for the living room. The complexity of a whole house design from the ground up is so vast that it simply overwhelms the mind. The number of architects who have handled it well can be counted on very few fingers. Design of a space *within the constraint of an existing shell,* however, eliminates some of the largest variables. With the elimination of each variable the mind is freed a degree.

The greatest difficulty most people encounter in house design is in picturing spaces. John Cole, my coauthor in *From the Ground Up,* recommends to the prospective owner-builder trying neighbors' and strangers' houses on like so many coats. Carry a tape measure with you, he says, and, upon finding yourself in an agreeable space, measure it up. I agree.

Rebuilding, then, is even easier than building new. The space you see is the space you've got. Sit in your 9' X 12' living room and, looking through the doorway into the kitchen, picture the connected spaces with just a counter between. Or stand at the foot of the stairs and picture the upstairs as a loft with a cathedral ceiling over your head. Knock out the walls between the living room, dining room, study, and front hall and picture a magnificent, nay stupendous, 20' X 30' living space with a nickel-plated wood stove, spiral staircase to your loft and a grand piano in the corner. Frank Lloyd Wright, eat your heart out!

O.K. We can picture the house of our dreams. How do we solve the practical problem of doing it? It's very easy, as I mean to show you; it's as simple as A, B, C. *A,* document what you presently have; *B,* document what you ultimately want; *C,* look at A and then B and, using the information in the three previous chapters, decide what needs to be done!

The ABC Process

I will describe the details of the process by using a typical example. Let's say the house you presently live in is a rather undistinguished, small two-story dwelling in a suburban community. You bought it twenty years ago because you had two small children and the house had three bedrooms and one and one-half baths and was situated in a good neighborhood. You long ago converted the coal furnace to oil, but now oil has gone up too. The furnace is forty years old and you don't know what to do. Buy a new oil burner—now? Some of your neighbors have been installing wood stoves and claiming, with obvious relish, great savings.

You and your wife rattle around in the house; the two front bedrooms are full of memorabilia that you've been meaning to give to the Salvation Army for several years now. The kitchen counter top is looking yucky and the bathroom fixtures look straight out of a late-night movie. In fact, you've been thinking of breaking out—making a new life for yourself; perhaps painting; maybe TM. Clearly, however, changing the slipcovers and wallpaper won't do the trick this time.

In other words, your house, although perfectly sound and in a neighborhood comfortable and familiar to you, no longer fits. It has three bedrooms; you need only one. It has no insulation; you obviously need some. It burns oil (rather inefficiently); you want to try wood. But most of all it's no fun; it doesn't mirror your new self; it is hindering rather than helping the new you. Let's see how this house can be turned into a new house—a house retrofitted for the future world and you—and within the limitations of your budget.

(A) DOCUMENTING WHAT YOU HAVE

Documenting the present house means working backward—instead of building the house from a set of plans, drawing a set of plans from the already built house. The usefulness of building plans is a function of their accuracy. With a little

T-SQUARE
TRIANGLE
DRAWING BOARD
24 x 36 SHEETS OF VELLUM
RESIDENTIAL TEMPLATE
ERASER
H, HB PENCILS
DRAFTING TAPE
FELT-TIP PEN
ROLL OF TRACING PAPER
ARCHITECT'S SCALE
CHEAP CIGARS

CORNERSTONES
Diploma

patience and the right tools, it is a simple matter to draw house plans accurate to a fraction of a real-world inch. The minimal tools required for this task are shown in Illustration 39. If the use of the tools isn't obvious once in hand, your local library has books on elementary architectural drafting.

Illustration 40 shows the drawings you'll need to make, floor plans for each level or floor of the house involved in the retrofit plus a structural

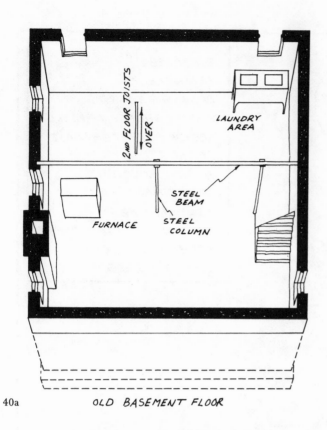

40a   OLD BASEMENT FLOOR

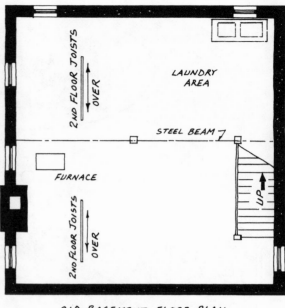

OLD BASEMENT FLOOR PLAN

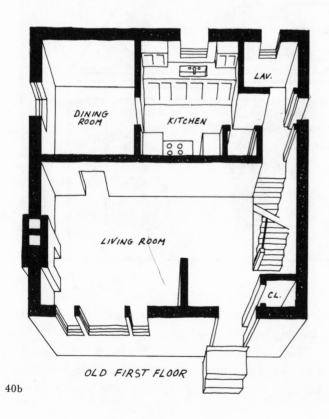

OLD FIRST FLOOR

40b

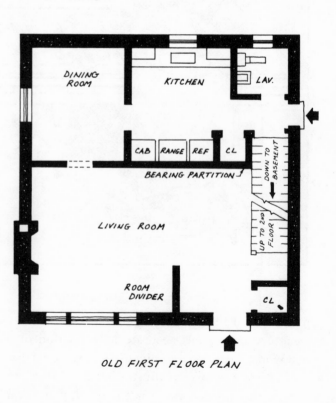

OLD FIRST FLOOR PLAN

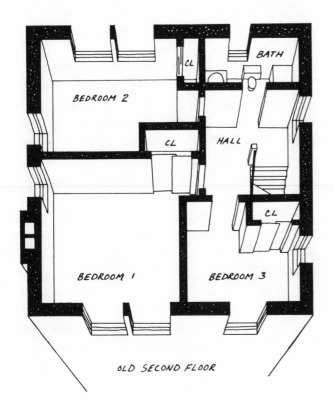

OLD SECOND FLOOR

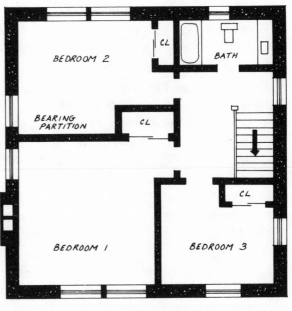

OLD SECOND FLOOR PLAN 40c

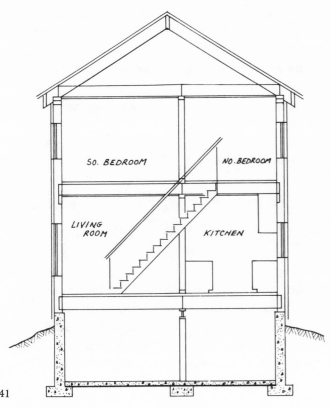

41

cross-section. If you plan to move walls, draw a plan of the basement as well, showing the location of girders and posts. The illustration shows how the floor plan corresponds to what you actually see. Plans are drawn as if a bird were looking down on the house sliced through at waist level. The scale of the drawing should be such that 1/4 inch on paper equals exactly 1 foot in the house. Draw everything as exactly as possible, including the thickness of the walls. Time spent in measuring and drawing will be repaid multifold. Illustration 40 doesn't show dimensions, but include them as well so that you won't have to keep measuring.

Next you'll need a typical section (Illustration 41). While the floor plan told us where things were, the section tells us how they were built. The typical section is a picture of what you'd see if the house were sliced by a great knife in a vertical plane parallel to the rafters and studs. It shows how the floor, wall, and roof are constructed and fastened so that an experienced carpenter could reproduce the house given only the floor plan and the section. Since the house is usually smaller vertically than horizontally and since detail is important, draw the typical section to the scale: 1/2 inch equals 1 foot. Both the floor plan and the section should be drawn on paper measuring 18″ × 24″ or 17″ × 22″.

The primary value of the section to you is in analysis of the structure. After reading the previous three chapters you should be able to identify your framing system and the function of each member in it. It doesn't require x-ray vision to sleuth the section; a surprising amount of information can be gained from visits to the basement and attic. Removal of electrical fixtures in the wall and ceiling plus a little probing will reveal the thickness of the wall studs and ceiling joists. Studs may also be located with a stud finder. Referring to the drawings of the classic framing systems will give you an almost x-ray vision of the house once you've obtained just a few clues.

In designing the new spaces, the existing structure is very important. Retrofitting within a limited budget requires utilization of the existing load-bearing structure to the greatest possible extent. Non-load-bearing walls can be removed with a wrecking bar and chain saw almost as easily and quickly as drawings can be with an eraser. However, removal of a load-bearing wall requires analysis and substitution. Generally, at least half of the walls of a house simply partition spaces and carry no loads at all. Load-bearing walls are easily recognized by the fact that the joists above are too small and too few to span the undivided distance otherwise. Many times a beam and one or two posts are all that are required, however, to replace a major load-bearing wall.

Poking around in your attic, we find that the roof rafters and attic joists form triangles running north and south. The ceiling joists are overlapped or spliced at the mid-point above the east-to-west wall. This tells us two things: (1) the east-west second-story wall is load-bearing and cannot be simply removed without remedial action; (2) the attic joists are in tension, holding the north and south wall top plates from bowing out, and therefore cannot be removed without further structural modifications. Since the remaining bedroom walls run in the same direction as the

attic joists, we know that they do not support loads.

Moving downstairs, we find with a tape measure that the first floor east-west wall separating the living room from the kitchen and dining room falls exactly under the load-bearing wall upstairs. Clearly, this wall is load-bearing and may be removed only after suitable structural alterations. Again, all of the north-south walls downstairs serve only to separate spaces.

Do the second-floor joists serve a similar function as the attic joists in tension? At first glance it may not appear so, but don't rush your analysis. A thorough consideration of every framing member will reveal that the 2 × 4 south wall studs are too small to span from sill to top plate unsupported. The second-floor joists serve to brace the south wall studs against wind pressure and cannot be entirely eliminated.

By now we should be anticipating what we indeed find in the basement — a load-bearing wall or member directly under the load-bearing walls of the first and second stories. It is a girder supported by the walls and two posts.

The only remaining question is whether the house is balloon or platform framed. Removing a baseboard from the south wall of one of the upstairs bedrooms will allow us to poke a hole in the plaster and spot either a ribband (balloon) or a plate (platform).

Draw up the floor plans and typical section using the information your detective work has yielded. Don't scrimp; an hour here is worth nine later as well as untold dollars.

(B) DOCUMENTING WHAT YOU WANT

A Shopping List. Next compile your shopping list. This is the most fun. Start a scrapbook for your project. Borrow or steal all the beautiful house magazines you can from friends; clip out the ideas that turn you on and paste them in your notebook; see what your local library has. There are also lots of picture books out now showing what people have created for next to nothing.

In doing this, however, remember that you

cannot exactly duplicate what you see. Who wants to copy, anyway? You're an artist at heart too, so do your own thing. Don't *just* paste the picture in your notebook; *analyze* the pictures. What is the *idea* behind the object that turns you on? Ideas can be executed in a number of ways, often for less money than in the picture. Trying to duplicate a picture exactly is not only artistically dishonest—it will blow your budget.

The details—the textures and colors, for instance—of your shopping list are not essential to this example. Important are those things that may impact the structure. Important items on your list are:

> insulation
> elimination of heat-losing windows
> some form of wood heat
> a dramatic open living space
> a larger kitchen
> a studio/sleeping loft.

Costs. It costs little to eliminate; it costs a lot to add. Strictly interpreted, this rule of building threatens the success of our project. Strict interpretation, however, contains the hidden assumption that more is better. In our case more is not better. Three bedrooms are not better than one studio/sleeping loft; one and one-half baths are not better than one bath plus a larger kitchen; separate small living and dining rooms are not better than one large social space. We are simply creating new spaces by the elimination of others.

In other respects, however, the strict interpretation of the rule is correct. It costs little to delete structural elements (where allowable); it costs a lot to add structure. It costs a great deal to add electrical wiring and plumbing; it costs virtually nothing to remove or terminate the use of such.

Armed with our shopping list, drawings, and the equally important rule of costs, we begin the process of creating the new from the old. Purchase a roll of tracing paper and a black felt-tip pen. Place the tracing paper over the floor plans and start sketching impulsively. Sketch whatever comes into your mind. Don't worry; the ink

won't go through the tracing paper and ruin your drawings, and each drawing is costing you about 2¢. "Jesus, this is fun! I think I'll become an architect." Tracing after tracing comes off the drawing boards. Wads of yellow paper cover the floor. The air is foul with cigar smoke.

But it happens. The long-dormant creativity once focused on tree-house design is born again; an exciting new space has been created from the old.

Illustration 42 shows the result of our creative labors. We have chosen to retain the second-story ceiling for a number of reasons: (1) the least expensive solution is always to do nothing at all; (2) the structural alternative to the attic joists is a very large and difficult ridge beam supporting the top ends of the rafters; (3) insulating an open attic is less expensive and more effective than creating an insulated cathedral ceiling; (4) the added height of a cathedral ceiling would make uniform heating more difficult.

The former north bedroom and full bathroom will become a master studio/sleeping/bathroom loft simply by removing the east-west bearing wall and rearranging the nonstructural closets. New, brightly colored bathroom fixtures replace the old white ones without replacing a single pipe (whew!). An indoor/outdoor carpet will cover the old linoleum tile. Between $500 and $1,000 can be saved by retaining the existing staircase, which will look simply smashing.

To create the open loft effect, the second story east-west bearing wall must be removed. Its structural function was limited to supporting the attic joists. Two solutions exist: support the joists from above, using $1'' \times 6''$ boards nailed from the centers of the joists to the rafters at the roof peak, or replace the wall with a $4'' \times 8''$ beam and posts. The first solution is chosen because it will prove easier to install the $1'' \times 6''$ boards before removing the wall than to install the $4'' \times 8''$ beam and posts after the bearing wall is removed.

Creation of the loft also requires elimination of the south bedrooms and their floors. Before we get carried away with the chain saw, however, note that repairs to a ceiling ultimately sixteen

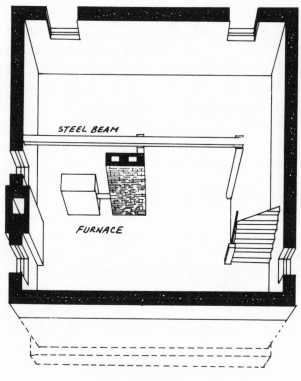

STEEL BEAM

FURNACE

42a   NEW BASEMENT FLOOR

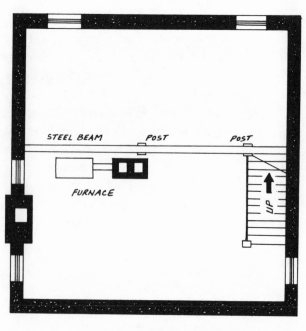

STEEL BEAM   POST   POST

FURNACE

UP

NEW BASEMENT FLOOR PLAN

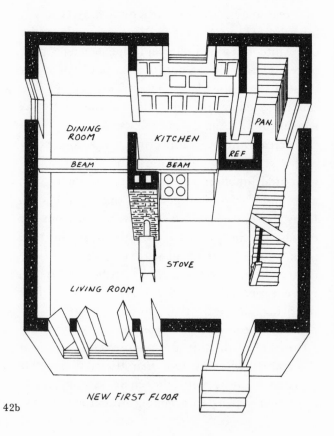

DINING
ROOM   KITCHEN   PAN.

REF

BEAM   BEAM

STOVE

LIVING ROOM

42b   NEW FIRST FLOOR

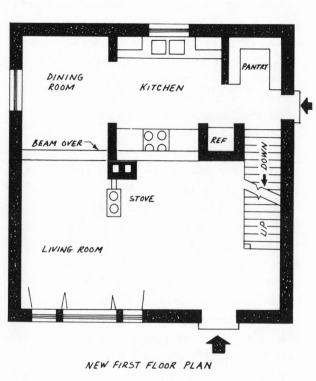

DINING
ROOM   KITCHEN   PANTRY

BEAM OVER   REF

STOVE   DOWN

LIVING ROOM   UP

NEW FIRST FLOOR PLAN

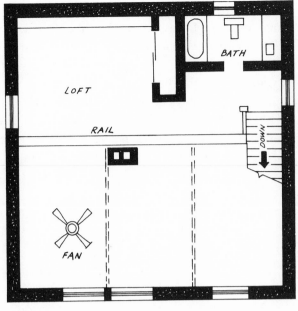

NEW SECOND FLOOR

NEW SECOND FLOOR PLAN   42c

feet above the first floor will be a hell of a lot simpler with the second floor still intact. Also, one of the structural functions of the second floor joists is to brace the south wall against the wind. Remembering that it costs more to add than to subtract, we elect to simply leave every third bedroom joist intact. The remaining joists spaced 48″ on-center will be turned to our aesthetic advantage by supporting Trac-lights and hanging plants.

Downstairs, the nonbearing wall between the kitchen and the dining room will be widened until it just encloses the cabinets and counters. The bearing wall between the living room and kitchen and dining room is very important and will be replaced by a 4″×10″ or 6″×8″ beam and three 4″×4″ or 6″×6″ posts, one at the west wall and the other two directly over the columns in the basement.

The kitchen will be enhanced and enlarged by substituting for the old half-bathroom an open pantry with floor-to-ceiling shelves. Elimination of the bearing wall down to counter level will also bring the kitchen into the social space, enlarging it psychologically. A new colorful enameled kitchen sink and new counter tops will provide new work surfaces. There is nothing physically wrong with the kitchen cabinets, so we plan to salvage them with paint remover, a belt sander, stain, and polyurethane varnish. We will find, upon ripping up the old linoleum, a beautiful unfinished hardwood floor, which we will sand, stain, and polyurethane. The plumber and electrician won't be sending any bills because we've done nothing but *remove* fixtures.

Now for energy. After reading *From the Walls In* we realize that north windows do little but lose heat; east and west windows represent a virtual draw between gains and losses; south windows always gain heat. Our plans therefore call for eliminating all of the north windows except those in the bathroom and kitchen. These we keep for ventilation. All of the south windows will be retained for their passive solar heat gain. All of the windows will be outfitted with decorative interior insulating shutters. Since the west and east windows in the doomed south bedrooms will be above our reach, we may eliminate them. An option is to leave just enough floor around the perimeter to serve as a three-to-four-foot-wide catwalk above the living room from which the upper windows and shutters can be operated.

The fireplace and outside chimney are a bad combination. A fireplace is not an efficient heater and simply blocking up the fireplace and installing a wood stove is less than optimal for a number of reasons: (1) the masonry loses heat to the outside as rapidly as a glass window does; (2) the draft in an outside chimney is not good; (3) so much heat is lost by the outside chimney that severe creosote buildup will result from wood stove operation. Our plans therefore call for removal of the existing chimney and fireplace down to the sill line and building a two-flue

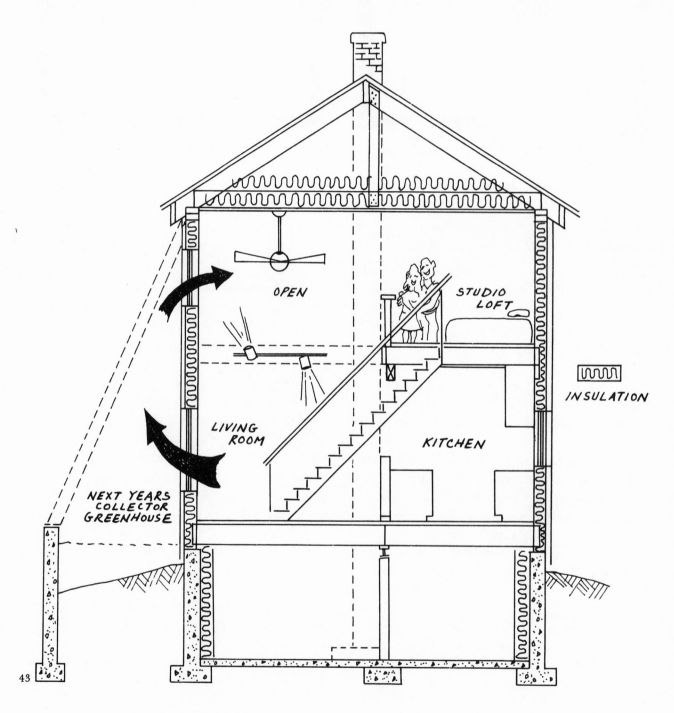

concrete block chimney up through the center of the house. One flue is for an airtight wood stove which will heat the entire house from its central position in the living room; the other is for a wood/oil combination furnace, which we may install in the basement sometime in the future.

Unless we prevent it from doing so, the warm air generated from the wood stove will rise straight up to the ceiling sixteen feet above the social space and overheat the loft while leaving the first floor cool. A slowly turning ceiling fan (Sears, Roebuck Catalogue Number 34H9055C, $128), reminiscent of Humphrey Bogart and *Casablanca,* will push this air down again, and result in uniform heating throughout the house, as well as envious comments from your guests (Illustration 43).

Finally, we must insulate all exterior surfaces. The attic will be insulated between the ceiling joists, using the optimum amount of fiberglass blanket or loose-fill cellulose. Cellulose will be blown into the walls from the inside since we have a lot of patching to do anyway. The cellar walls will be studded up and insulated to provide a warm workshop (which will be used as a base of operations for this project). There are many surface repairs to make; there are too many layers of wallpaper; and we want an effective vapor barrier. Therefore, we will apply 3/8″ sheetrock over a continuous 6 mil polyethylene vapor barrier to all walls and the upper ceiling.

(C) GETTING FROM A TO B

The point made above about working on a ceiling eight feet rather than sixteen feet above a floor illustrates the importance of a step-by-step analysis of the A-to-B procedure. What you need is a game plan—the sequence of operations that will make the job simplest. To generate such a plan, simply list every task that has to be done. One by one, *imagine* doing each of the tasks. Ask yourself, "What other things have to be done before I can do this thing?" After each task has been examined thus, simply arrange the tasks in the logical order.

I don't want to steal all of your fun and so will terminate this chapter posthaste.

P.S. I prefer "Swisher Sweets" cigars while playing architect.

Buttoning Up

7.

Heat Losses

The highest-technology insulation in the world, improperly installed, will not stop the heat loss from your house. On the other hand, good results can be achieved with remarkably inexpensive materials when they are installed with care and understanding. Understanding is the key; understanding *what* heat is, and *how* and *why* it flows from one point to another is the secret to effective insulation.

What Is Heat?

Heat is a form of energy. It is the kinetic energy or energy of motion of the atoms and molecules that make up our world. The second law of thermodynamics states formally what many of us have suspected all along: that order degenerates into disorder; that higher, more concentrated forms of energy ultimately degenerate into mere jiggling and running about. Heat is at the bottom, the lowest, most degraded form of energy. Electricity is among the highest, most capable forms of energy. That is why it is degenerate to turn electricity directly into heat without first getting some useful work out of it.

Anyway, all of these atoms and molecules are pushing, pulling, bumping, gyrating, and vibrating. A measure of their state of agitation is called temperature. The more agitated they are, the more space they require. That is the physical basis for all instruments which measure what we call temperature.

Temperature scales are defined by points at which certain physical phenomena occur. Both the Fahrenheit and Celsius scales are defined by the melting and boiling points of water. At very low temperatures water is in its solid state, ice. Attractive forces exist between the molecules. At very low temperatures, water molecules have insufficient energy of motion to break free from these forces. They are, in effect, in a crowded elevator. They may jiggle and push, but they simply can't get away from their neighbors. At the melting temperature they have acquired just enough energy to break the rigid bonds and move relative to their neighbors. They still don't have enough energy to leave the group as a whole, but at least they have enough energy to move about the container. At the boiling temperature the molecules achieve a significant new freedom; they have gotten up enough steam (pun intended) to venture forth on their own and escape the group.

The difference in energy levels between the freezing and boiling points of water is arbitrarily divided into 100 parts (Celsius) or 180 parts (Fahrenheit). (Fahrenheit must have been a rather perverse fellow!)

Heat is important to human beings because we consist largely of water! Obviously, if we were to freeze solid we would not be very lively. At the other end, if we were to boil we would be in Humpty Dumpty's situation: there would simply be no getting us together again. Seriously, though, the ongoing complex chemical reaction that we call human life proceeds in a balanced fashion over a very limited temperature range centered about 98.6° F. When our bodies fail to maintain that precise internal temperature for a significant length of time, we are in big trouble. Our ongoing chemical reaction produces a lot of waste heat. The waste-heat generation of even a sedentary adult is equivalent to that of a 100-watt light bulb. Like a nuclear power plant, we must find a way of disposing of this waste heat or suffer the consequences of overheating. Ordinarily, we dispose of the heat by simply immersing ourselves in an environment of slightly lower temperature. Depending on how much insulative material we cover ourselves with and the rate of waste-heat generation, an air temperature in the range of 50–80° F works quite well. Maintaining an artificial inside environment in this temperature range easily and economically is what insulation is all about.

How Does Heat Flow?

As stated by the second law of thermodynamics, the natural order of things is for concentrations of energy to dissipate, or simply for heat to flow from warmer to cooler regions. There are three different natural physical processes by which heat energy flows from warmer to cooler: *conduction, convection,* and *radiation.*

Conduction is the mechanism by which the frying pan handle gets hot. The handle is not in the flame, yet the handle gets hot. The frying pan is iron in its solid state. The iron molecules are not free to get up and move relative to each other. The only way in which they can transfer energy is by passing it on to their neighbors, as in the game "hot potato." All materials conduct heat, but some do it better than others. We call those that do it very well "conductors" and those that do it poorly "insulators." About the poorest conductor of heat is dead air (air that is not moving except on a molecular level). As it turns out, most commercial insulation products are nothing more than attempts to stop air from moving.

Human skin is a sensitive instrument for measuring conductivity, although indirectly. We are all aware of the sense of warm *versus* cool. Actually, what our skin is telling us when we touch an object is not the temperature of the object alone, but how rapidly heat is flowing into or out of our skin. We know that the rate at which heat is conducted toward or away from a body depends not only upon the temperature of the object, but also upon its conductivity. If you are experimentally minded, try this. Allow a wide variety of objects come to identical temperatures by setting them for several hours in a constant temperature room. Although they are all at the same temperature, the "conductors" (metal, stone, glass, water, and so on) will seem cool to the touch, while the "insulators" (wool clothing, carpet, fiberglass insulation, plastic foam, and even wood) will seem warm to the touch. Yet all of the materials are at a lower temperature than the body.

Convection is totally unlike conduction. In this case the molecules of a fluid (either liquid or gas) pick up heat energy from a warm surface, carry it with them over a great distance (relative to their own size), and drop the energy at a cooler surface. If the cool molecules return for a second trip, we have a convection cell. Note that the transfer of energy at the warm and cool surfaces is by conduction.

While conduction is intuitive and simple to grasp, convection is more subtle. To understand

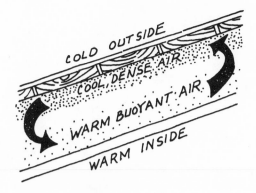

A ROOF AND CEILING CONVECTION

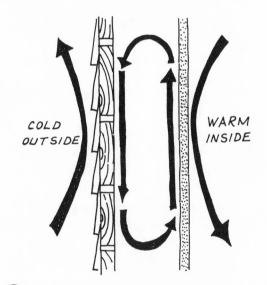

B WALL CAVITY CONVECTION

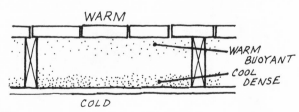

44 C FLOOR CONVECTION

heat flow by convection, we first must understand why fluid molecules would want to convect in the first place. The reason is simple. Warmer fluid molecules, having more energy, require more "personal space." Upon warming, therefore, fluids expand and become less dense. Like hot-air balloons or logs in the water, they rise. On the other hand, cooling fluids become more dense and sink. "Hot air rises; cold air falls." It's as simple as that.

If warm air is rising in one place and cool air is falling in another, it's obvious that horizontal transfer is required to fill the vacated spaces. Thus a convection cell is born. Understanding this, we can now see that the relative value of air as an insulator depends upon its stability. Illustration 44 shows three different air spaces. Space A is a ceiling. Air immediately above the plaster ceiling is warmed by conduction from below, while the air touching the bottom of the roof boards is cooled by conduction. The relative buoyancy of the two layers is unnatural, and the air moves to become more stable. The process is continuous and develops into a convection cell. Heat loss through a ceiling in winter is largely through this convection.

Space B is an empty wall cavity. Warm air is continuously generated by conduction at the warm side, while cool air is generated at the cold side. In response to gravity the warm air rises and the cool air falls. A circular pattern evolves, with the same molecules making the round trip: pick up heat at the warm side; rise to the top; drop heat on the cool side; fall to the bottom. The air in the wall cavity is like a conveyor belt transporting heat from inside to outside. The heat loss by convection in a wall is nearly as great as in a ceiling.

Space C is a floor joist cavity between the warm inside space and the cold crawl space. It looks the same as space A but is remarkably different. Both the warm air layer generated at the top and the cold layer at the bottom are happy in their positions and so don't move. If we could stop the wind from blowing into the cavity from outside we would have a true dead air space and good insulation—a rare case of getting something for nothing!

Air spaces are not the only air-type insulation. Because of fluid friction, the air immediately adjacent to wall, floor, and ceiling surfaces is only slowly moving and so has some insulative effect. The insulation value of a pane of glass in fact consists almost entirely of the insulative effect of the air on either side. Thus whether the glass is 0.5″ or .001″ thick makes very little difference to the insulation value.

Radiation is even stronger. Yet it too generally follows the rule that heat is transferred from warmer to cooler. All molecules, always, everywhere, are radiating energy much like miniature radio stations. The only difference is in their frequencies of transmission (Illustration 45). Using visible radiation as a reference point, heat radiation is infrared (below the lowest visible frequency: red). The frequency at which the greatest radiation occurs increases with temperature. Thus, as you stoke the stove, the radiation creeps into the visible red region. The sun obeys the same principle; its 10,000° F surface temperature is so high that most of its radiation is at the visible yellow frequency.

The rate at which a body radiates energy is proportional to:

$$A\epsilon\sigma T^4$$
where A = *area of the body surface*
ϵ = *emissivity of the body surface*
σ = *Stefan-Boltzmann constant*
T^4 = *absolute temperature of the body raised to the fourth power*

Absolute temperature is a temperature scale used only in the sciences. Recall that temperature is a measure of the energy of motion of atoms and molecules. Absolute zero is the temperature at which all motion ceases. Zero on the absolute scale corresponds to –273° Celsius and –459° Fahrenheit (and you thought last winter was cold!).

Emissivity, ϵ, refers to the relative ability of the surface of a body to give off radiation. A black body (a dark hole drilled in a cube of carbon

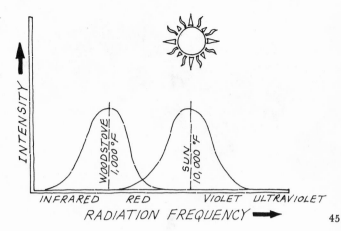

45

down at the National Bureau of Standards) is defined as being the blackest thing around and having a perfect emissivity of 1.00. All other surfaces have emissivities of less than 1. Among common materials, the emissivity of flat black paint is around 0.95, while the emissivity of polished aluminum foil (brighter even than Reynolds Wrap) is only 0.05.

In the transfer of heat to and from bodies we also have to consider absorptivity, α. Absorptivity is again defined as the ability of a body to absorb radiation beamed at it relative to the absorptivity of the black body of 1.00. Fortunately, in common materials, α is nearly equal to ϵ. A body having high α and low ϵ would spontaneously rise in temperature relative to its surroundings. You can well imagine the amount of money industry is spending developing for solar collectors "selective surfaces" having high α and low ϵ.

Aside from such artificial surfaces, Illustration 46 shows that when two bodies of equal emis-

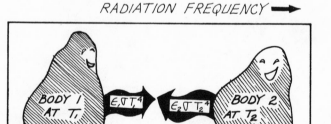

46

DARK
$\epsilon = \propto = 0.9$

SHINY
$\epsilon = \propto = 0.05$

47

Calculating Heat Loss

You may have concluded by now that calculating the heat loss of a house is a very exacting task. This is not at all true, as I mean to demonstrate now. Illustration 48 shows heat loss through a solid uniform slab of material. The exact equation for the conduction of heat through such a slab (called the heat flow equation) is

Equation 3.1

$$H_{hour} = \frac{A \times \Delta T}{R}$$

where H_{hour} = Btu's lost per hour. A Btu is the amount of heat energy required to raise one lb. of water one F°.
A = face area of the slab in square feet
$\Delta T = T_{inside} - T_{outside}$, or difference in temperature between the two sides in F°
R = total thermal resistance of the slab

Thermal resistance, R, is actually defined by this equation. In the laboratory the two faces of a slab of insulative material are maintained ΔT degrees apart, the amount of energy per hour required to maintain ΔT is measured, and R calculated as a result. Of course no house consists entirely of solid uniform slabs of material. More typically a wall consists of various layers of

sivity and absorptivity face each other, the net transfer of energy is from higher to lower temperature. Sit by a wood stove and feel the strong net radiative transfer from the stove to you. It's hard to believe that your body is at the same time radiating back toward the stove. On the other hand, stand in front of an open refrigerator (this works best at midnight while you're naked and groping for snacks). Aside from the cold air falling out onto your feet, feel the net radiative transfer from your body to the refrigerator.

Radiation can be blocked by solid material. As a rule of thumb, if you can't see through it, then neither can heat radiation. Illustration 47 shows two different types of blockage. In case A the heat radiation is absorbed by the dark material and subsequently reradiated by the other side. Although the radiation was stopped momentarily, the heat is transferred through the material by conduction and subsequently sent on its way again. In case B the surfaces of the material have very low emissivity (and absorptivity). Most of the radiation is not absorbed but reflected back toward the radiator; and what small percentage is absorbed is not readily reradiated by the other side because of its low emissivity.

The conclusion I mean to implant is that *polished foils act as insulators (heat flow retarders) when facing air*. If they actually touch another material, however, the benefit is lost because heat flows by conduction instead.

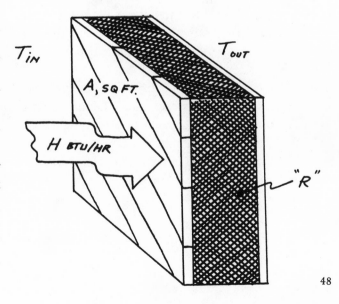

48

boards and plaster enclosing a cavity containing either air or a fibrous insulating material. To complicate the picture further, there may be four surfaces facing air, each of different emissivity! How do we calculate the total thermal resistance of such a hodgepodge? Here it is worth noting the difference between an engineer and a physicist. The physicist wishes to "understand" physical processes. This has led him from being a philosopher of nature (knowing a little about everything) through the process of specialization (knowing more and more about less and less), to his logical end (someone who knows everything about nothing). On the other hand, the engineer typically cares not a whit for why something happens, only how to assign a number to it. Results are what counts! Thank God for engineers.

Here's how the engineer does it. First he builds a sample wall, roof, or floor construction. Then he says, "I don't care whether heat is flowing through that thing by conduction, convection, or radiation or all three at once. The simplest formula I have is for conduction alone, so I'll use it." He then performs the conduction experiment (Illustration 48), turns the calculator crank, and out comes apparent total thermal resistance, R.

After performing this experiment dozens of times with different assemblies of material and air spaces he can sort out the apparent thermal resistance contributions of air surfaces, air spaces, and solid materials. Reversing the procedure, he can then predict the total thermal resistance of any proposed construction by adding the thermal resistances of each of the component parts. And it works!

Tables 15, 16, and 17 list the thermal resistances of surfaces, air spaces, and solid materials as discovered by the engineers. Before using Tables 15 and 16 for the thermal resistances of surfaces and air spaces, we must first specify the emissivity of the surface or space concerned. Get that from Table 18.

SURFACES, TABLE 15

Each building section has two surfaces, one inside the building and one outside. The effective thermal resistance of the inside surface is determined by the thin boundary layer of dead air created along the surface by friction and the emissivity of that surface. The outside surface is exposed to wind, making that boundary layer much smaller and less effective.

AIR SPACES, TABLE 16

Heat is actually transferred across air spaces within building sections by all three processes. The relative contribution of each process is a function of the thickness of the air space (conduction and convection), orientation of the air space relative to the direction of heat flow (convection), and emissivity of the combination of bounding surfaces (radiation).

BUILDING AND INSULATING MATERIALS, TABLE 17

Heat is transferred through building materials almost entirely by conduction. Table 17 lists most of the conventional building and insulating materials. Some of the items are listed as total thermal resistance: for example, a carpet. Most, however, are listed as thermal resistance per inch of thickness, since they come in a variety of thicknesses. To get the total thermal resistance of such an item, simply multiply the resistance per inch by the thickness in inches.

Table 15. Thermal Resistance of Surfaces, R

nature of single surface	direction of heat	emissivity, ϵ		
		0.05	0.20	0.90
Inside wall	Horizontal	1.70	1.35	0.68
Inside ceiling	Upward	1.32	1.10	0.61
Inside floor	Downward	4.55	2.70	0.92
Outside surface, 15 mph	Any	—	—	0.17
Outside surface, 7-1/2 mph	Any	—	—	0.25

Table 16. Thermal Resistance of Air Spaces @ $T_{ave} = 50°F$, $\Delta T = 30 F°$

air space location	direction of heat flow	air space (in.)	emissivity, ϵ			
			0.03	0.05	0.20	0.82
Horizontal	Upward	3/4	1.72	1.67	1.37	0.78
ex. ceiling		1-1/2	1.82	1.76	1.43	0.80
		4	2.14	2.06	1.62	0.85
Horizontal	Downward	3/4	3.80	3.55	2.39	1.02
ex. floor		1-1/2	6.41	5.74	3.21	1.14
		4	10.70	8.94	4.02	1.23
Vertical	Horizontal	3/4	2.95	2.80	2.04	0.96
ex. wall		1-1/2	2.90	2.76	2.02	0.96
		4	2.74	2.63	1.94	0.94
Pitched 45°	Upward	3/4	2.02	1.95	1.54	0.83
ex. roof		1-1/2	2.09	2.01	1.58	0.84
in winter		4	2.32	2.22	1.71	0.88
Pitched 45°	Downward	3/4	3.47	3.27	2.27	1.01
ex. roof		1-1/2	3.50	3.30	2.29	1.01
in summer		4	3.61	3.39	2.33	1.02

Table 17. Thermal Resistances of Building and Insulating Materials at $50°F$ T_{ave} and $30 F°$ ΔT

material	R (per inch)	R (total)
Softwoods	1.25	—
Hardwoods	0.91	—
Plywood	1.25	—
Poly vapor barrier	—	0.00
Sheetrock	0.90	—
Stone or concrete	0.08	—
Plaster or bricks	0.20	—
8-inch concrete block	—	1.11
1/8-inch cork tile	—	0.28
Cork board, average	3.50	—
Carpet with rubber pad	—	1.20
Carpet with fiber pad	—	2.1
Asphalt roll roofing	—	0.15
Asphalt selvage	—	0.30
Asphalt shingles	—	0.44
Standard exterior door	—	2.00
Insulating glass, 1/4-inch space	—	1.50
Insulating glass, 1-inch space	—	2.00
Cellulose, 2.2 lb./cu. ft.		
Fiberglass blanket or batt	3.15	—
Fiberglass loose fill	2.2	—
Vermiculite loose fill	2.2	—
Polyurethane, 2 lb./cu. ft.	6.25–7.50	—
Polystyrene, blown	4.06–5.50	—
Polystyrene, bead board	3.70–4.25	—
Urea formaldehyde, Rapcofoam	4.2	—

Example: for a full 6-inch fiberglass batt: $R = 3.2 \times 6 = 19.2$ Note, however, that when insulation is placed between framing members, the framing members present alternate heat paths of lower R value. To account for the greater heat loss, we make use of the effective R value, R_{eff}, which varies with the situation. The calculation of effective R values is described in Chapter 10 and listed in Table 23.

Finding the Total Thermal Resistance

To find the total thermal resistance of a floor, wall, or roof, simply draw a picture of the construction so that you can identify all of the dif-

Table 18. Emissivity of Various Surfaces

nature of surface(s)	emissivity, ϵ
Ordinary boards, one surface	0.90
Ordinary boards, two facing surfaces	0.82
Galvanized steel, white or aluminum painted paper, one or two facing surfaces, average	0.20
Builder's foil, highly reflective, one surface	0.05
Builders' foil, highly reflective, two facing surfaces	0.03

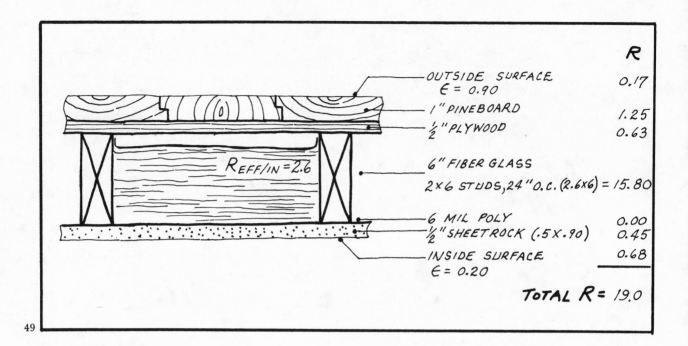

	R
OUTSIDE SURFACE $\epsilon = 0.90$	0.17
1" PINEBOARD	1.25
$\frac{1}{2}$" PLYWOOD	0.63
6" FIBER GLASS 2×6 STUDS, 24" O.C. (2.6×6)	= 15.80
6 MIL POLY	0.00
$\frac{1}{2}$" SHEETROCK (.5×.90)	0.45
INSIDE SURFACE $\epsilon = 0.20$	0.68
TOTAL R	= 19.0

$R_{EFF/IN} = 2.6$

49

ferent resistive elements; list each element and its thermal contribution; add all of the contributions in the column to find the total resistance (see Illustration 49). The total resistance found will be used in the conduction formula to predict heat loss through the floor, wall, or roof.

We can adapt the heat flow equation to calculate not only heat loss per hour through any exterior surface of the house but also the annual heat loss through that surface.

First we need the concept of the *degree day* (here abbreviated DD). The number of degree days in one day is the difference between the average temperature for that day and 65° F. The accumulated number of degree days during the heating season is kept by the weather bureau as an indication of the amount of fuel consumed. A similar concept is *cooling degree days,* the difference between the average temperature and 78° F. Illustrations 50 and 51 show heating degree days and cooling degree days for the U.S.

Now the heat flow equation gives heat loss per hour at a given ΔT. To convert the hourly loss to the annual loss we simply multiply by the number of hours in the heating season, 24 × heating days. The ΔT in the equation refers to the precise ΔT at each hour and A is the area of the surface through which heat is flowing.

$$H_{annual} = \frac{A \times \Delta T \times 24 \times heating\ days}{R}$$

Do you recognize anything familiar? The factor ΔT × heating days is what we have just called degree days. Therefore

Equation 3.2

$$H_{annual} = \frac{24 \times A \times DD}{R}$$

We will have use for both the hourly form and this annual form in Chapter 9 when we calculate the annual fuel bill.

Heat Loss by Infiltration

Infiltration is a special case of convection. It is the physical replacement of warm inside air by cold outside air (or the reverse in the summer). Since heat must be added to the incoming air continually in order to maintain the house tempera-

MEAN ANNUAL TOTAL HEATING DEGREE DAYS
(Base 65°F)

SCALE OF SHADES

0 — 2000

2000 — 4000

4000 — 6000

6000 — 8000

8000 — 10000

Over 10000

NOTE.--CAUTION SHOULD BE USED IN INTERPOLATING ON THESE GENERALIZED MAPS. SHARP CHANGES MAY OCCUR IN SHORT DISTANCES, PARTICULARLY IN MOUNTAINOUS AREAS, DUE TO DIFFERENCES IN ALTITUDE, SLOPE OF LAND, TYPE OF SOIL, VEGETATIVE COVER, BODIES OF WATER, AIR DRAINAGE, URBAN HEAT EFFECTS, ETC.

THESE SMOOTHED CHARTS ARE BASED ON THE PERIOD 1931-60

PUERTO RICO AND VIRGIN ISLANDS

50

MEAN ANNUAL TOTAL COOLING DEGREE DAYS
(Base 65°F)

SCALE OF SHADES

0 — 500

500 — 1000

1000 — 2000

2000 — 3000

3000 — 4000

Over 4000

NOTE.--CAUTION SHOULD BE USED IN INTERPOLATING ON THESE GENERALIZED MAPS. SHARP CHANGES MAY OCCUR IN SHORT DISTANCES, PARTICULARLY IN MOUNTAINOUS AREAS, DUE TO DIFFERENCES IN ALTITUDE, SLOPE OF LAND, TYPE OF SOIL, VEGETATIVE COVER, BODIES OF WATER, AIR DRAINAGE, URBAN HEAT EFFECTS, ETC.

BASED ON 30-YEAR PERIOD, 1931-60.

PUERTO RICO AND VIRGIN ISLANDS

51

HEAT LOSSES / 83

ture, infiltration amounts to a rate of heat loss. Infiltration is usually quantified in either cubic feet of air per minute or total house volume air exchanges per hour. The former is useful in tight new construction, where a certain ventilation rate per occupant is desired in order to maintain air quality. Ten cubic feet per minute (cfm) per person is the usual standard, although conservationists are promoting 5 cfm. Total air exchanges per hour are more useful in older buildings where the infiltration unfortunately far exceeds minimum ventilation standards! An old weather-beaten wood frame building having windows that rattle in the wind will totally change its air anywhere from two to ten times per hour depending on condition and exposure to wind. New houses of average workmanship have an air exchange rate of about one air exchange per hour, while it is quite possible, by attention to detail, either to build a new structure or to retrofit an older building to a standard of only a half air exchange per hour.

The hourly rate of heat loss by infiltration is

Equation 3.3

$$H_{hour} = 0.0182\, Q\Delta T$$

where H = Btu per hour
Q = cu. ft. per hour (air exchange rate × volume of structure)
ΔT = inside temperature outside temperature, F°
.0182 = weight of 1 cu. ft. of air × specific heat of air

Just as with heat loss by conduction, the infiltration equation can be put into an annual form by multiplying by the number of hours in the heating season and equating the product of heating days and ΔT to the annual degree days.

Equation 3.4

$$H_{annual} = 0.437\, Q \times DD$$

8.

Heat Gains

In Chapter 7, I had the depressing task of describing how heat is lost from your house. But have heart; I bring glad tidings. All is not lost! There are in fact three sources of incidental heat gain which you may never have considered: *animal, utility,* and *passive solar.* Compared to the heat loss of a large, old, uninsulated, drafty house, these gains are but small change. Compared to the heat loss from a small, tight, optimally insulated house, however, they are significant. In fact, they constitute the entire source of heat in the so-called zero-energy houses in Europe and Scandinavia.

Animal Heat Gain

Human beings run at an average body temperature of 98.6° F. This temperature is about 30F° higher than the inside house temperature. That is, in terms of the heat flow equation, our personal ΔT is 30F°. The heat dissipated by our bodies to our surroundings is waste heat due to the imperfect transformation of food (chemical) energy into activity (mechanical) energy. This waste heat

amounts to 340 Btu/hr.$^{-1}$ for an average sedentary person.

The average family consists of 3-1/2 people and 1/2-person-equivalent critters. The average percentage of time spent in the home is about 50 percent. Therefore,

$$H_{animal} = 340 \, Btu/hr.^{-1} \, person^{-1} \times 4 \, people \times 0.50 = 680 \, Btu/hr.^{-1}$$

If you are blessed with either a larger or smaller family, the number to use is simply 170 Btu/hr.$^{-1}$ person^{-1}.

Since you probably laughed at the 1/2-critter figure in my calculations, I should like to point out that critters are not taken so lightly in other societies. The rock group "Three Dog Night" takes its name from the Australian aborigine practice of sleeping with dogs at night. A three-dog night is the equivalent of our design-minimum-temperature.

The aborigines represent low technology, however, compared to those Austrian farmers who incorporated barns into their houses. With 10 good-sized cows producing heat below and a hay ceiling above, those fellows had the energy crisis licked as long as the cows stayed out of the garlic patch.

Utility Heat Gain

Utility heat gain represents the heat gain from purchased energy other than what we commonly think of as heating fuel. Most of the energy coming into the house to power lights and appliances ultimately turns into heat. The ordinary incandescent light bulb is only 5 percent efficient at producing visible light. Ninety-five percent of the electrical energy is directly converted to heat, while the 5 percent in light turns into heat upon striking an object. The major wastes of utility heat are the hot water discharged down the drain, and the clothes dryer, if vented to the outside. An electric (though not a gas) dryer can be vented to the inside during the heating season, provided the house has an adequate vapor barrier. A remarkable amount of heat can be recovered from a shower or bath if the water is held until it drops to room temperature. Any animal heat gained while scrubbing the resulting ring around the tub is a bonus.

Assuming the dryer is vented inside and the tub water held after bathing, about 70 percent, or 530 kwh (kilowatt hours) of the estimated 760 kwh total monthly utility energy is retained by the house as utility heat gain. This amounts to about 630 Btu per hr.$^{-1}$ per person^{-1}.

The total of animal and utility heat gains per person due to ordinary household activities is thus seen to be

Equation 8.1

$$H_{animal+utility} = 800 \, Btu/hr.^{-1} \, person^{-1}$$

Passive Solar Gain

Passive solar heat gain is the amount of solar radiation that passes into the windows of a building during the heating season. It is "passive" because the building's role is limited to simply sitting there and soaking it up. "But a window loses more heat than it gains during the winter," you say. True enough, in most cases, but we have already accounted for the window's loss by assigning the window an R (total thermal resistance) value in the heat-loss equation. If we're calculating the heat loss, we must also calculate the heat gain. The important figure is the *net* loss, or the difference between loss and gain.

The number of Btu per sq. ft.$^{-1}$ received through a window during the heating season is given by

Equation 8.2

$$H_{solar} = A \times SC \times 24 \times HD \times SF \times Y / 1,550$$

where

> *where H = the total number of Btu's*
> *through the window during*
> *the heating season*
> *A = area of window in sq. ft.*
> *SC = shading coefficient*
> *24 = number of hours per day*
> *HD = number of heating days per year*
> *SF = solar factor*
> *Y = climatic factor*

Note that H is the number of Btu's that get all the way through the window to heat the house, not the number striking the exterior.

The *area,* A, is taken to be the sash area, of which 80 percent is assumed to be glass and 20 percent wood.

The *shading coefficient,* SC, is defined as the ratio of radiation through the window in question to that through a single-glazed window exposed to the sun from sunrise to sunset. Since each layer of glass absorbs or reflects about 10 percent of the radiation striking it, SC for the case of no sky shading is: single glazed 1.0, double-glazed 0.9, triple-glazed 0.8. These factors

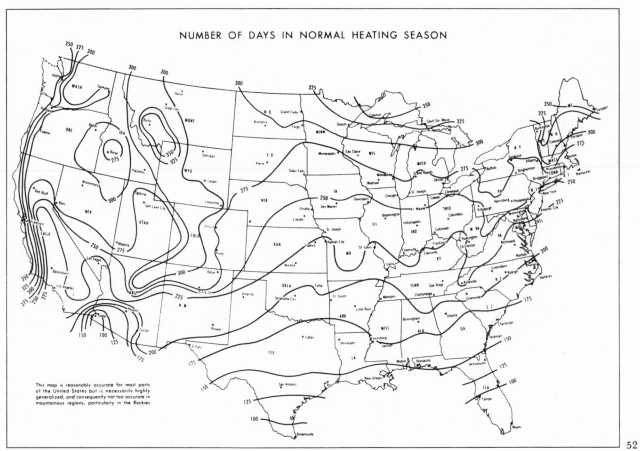

NUMBER OF DAYS IN NORMAL HEATING SEASON

This map is reasonably accurate for most parts of the United States but is necessarily highly generalized, and consequently not too accurate in mountainous regions, particularly in the Rockies

52

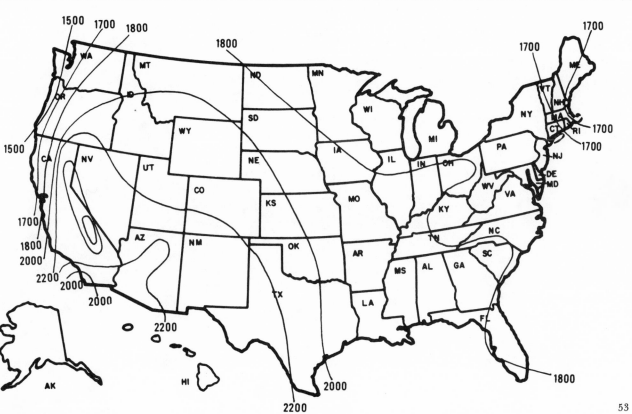

53

should then be multiplied by the percentage of the sun's path blocked. Thus a south-facing double-glazed window that is in shade 50 percent of the day would have an SC of about $0.9 \times 0.5 = 0.45$.

Heating days, HD, are the number of days in the year during which the combined animal and utility heat gain is not sufficient to heat the house. In other words, HD represents the number of days in a year during which solar gain is useful in heating the house and thus preventing the furnace from coming on. Illustration 52 shows the normal number of heating days in a season, assuming an interior temperature of about 70° F. To correct for an interior temperature different from 70° F, deduct 6 HD for each degree F lowered thermostat setting.

The *solar factor,* SF, is read from Table 19. It accounts for all of the geometric effects in received solar radiation, including the sun's altitude, azimuth, latitude, and ratio of direct to diffuse radiation. Note that the solar geometry is symmetric about true south: that is, SF is identical for east- and west-facing windows.

Finally, Y (Illustration 53) accounts for solar

Table 19. Window Solar Factors

Window Orientation	Latitude			
	24°	32°	40°	48°
N	9	8	7	6
NE, NW	16	14	11	9
E, W	37	33	29	25
SE, SW	51	51	50	46
S	55	59	62	59

weather or regional differences in cloudiness and clearness of the sky.

In summary, the equation allows us to calculate the annual amount of solar gain through ordinary windows that may be deducted from the annual heat loss when predicting the annual fuel bill. Before proceeding, a word of caution is in order. Use of this equation assumes a normal percentage of window area. Window areas in excess of the normal 15 percent of wall area may result in solar overheating and subsequent necessary venting of excess heat. Therefore, the equation assumes either:

(1) a clear-day total solar gain not exceeding the total daytime heat losses, or
(2) a heat storage system capable of absorbing excess daytime gain for night release.

9.

The Fuel Bill = Losses - Gains

Having discovered the equations of heat loss (Chapter 7) and the equations of heat gain (Chapter 8), we are in a position to consider the balance between the two. The results will be (a) the maximum hourly heat loss, or the size of the burner needed to keep the house toasty on the coldest nights of the year, and (b) the net annual heat loss, which translates into your annual fuel bill.

To start, let's bring the heat loss equations once again front and center:

method of heat loss	*Btu per hr.*$^{-1}$	*Btu per yr.*$^{-1}$
Conduction	$H = \dfrac{A \times \Delta T}{R}$	$H = \dfrac{24 \times A \times DD}{R}$
Infiltration	$H = .0182Q \times \Delta T$	$H = 0.437Q \times DD$

where

H = heat loss in Btu per unit of time
A = area of section in sq. ft.
ΔT = temperature inside – temperature outside, in F degrees
DD = number of degree days for site
R = total thermal resistance of building section
Q = cubic feet per hour of air exchange

While even the simplest building loses heat through half a dozen different surfaces, the calculation can be remarkably simple—provided we go about it in an organized way. I suggest you use a heat flow ledger much the same as an accountant's money ledger. You will be keeping track of heat debits and heat credits. I will illustrate the use of the heat ledger by an example. The same example house will be used throughout subsequent chapters, so learn it well!

Example: The example house is the two-story wooden frame poor-man's Greek Revival farmhouse so common in New England. It is located at 44° north latitude at a site having 8,000 degree days per year. Upon investigation we find that this retrofit candidate has no storm windows or doors, no wall cavity insulation, and a token 2 inches of rock wool in the attic. We guess by rattling the double-hung windows and inspecting the doors and basement walls that the house is of average tightness, having an infiltration rate of 2 air exchanges per hour. Illustration 54 shows the house.

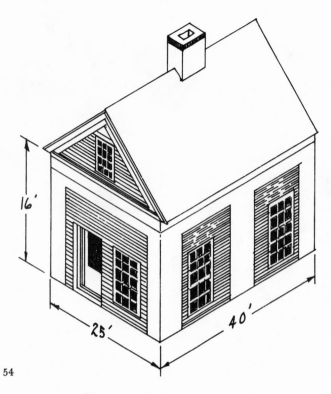

CLIMATIC DATA:
Design (probable) minimum temperature = –15° F
Degree Days = 8,000
Heating Days = 275
Latitude = 44° N

BUILDING DATA:
Floor 1000 sq. ft., R=10
Ceiling 1000 sq. ft., R=8
Doors 40 sq. ft., R=2.5
Windows 312 sq. ft., R=1.0
(No. 96, So. 96, E. 60, W. 60)

Solid Wall, 1,728 sq. ft.

Volume heated = 16,000 cu. ft.

54

I	II	III	IV	V	VI	VII	VIII	IX	X
			before retrofit					*after retrofit*	
Section	A	R_1	$\dfrac{A}{R_1}$	$\dfrac{24A \times DD}{R_1}$	Percentage of total loss	R_2	$\dfrac{A}{R_2}$	$\dfrac{24A \times DD}{R_2}$	Percentage of total loss
Floor	1000	10	100	192×10^5	6	41	24.4	47×10^5	4
Wall	1728	3.9	443	850×10^5	28	14	123.4	237×10^5	19
Ceiling	1000	8	125	240×10^5	8	33	30.3	58×10^5	5
Doors	40	2.5	16	31×10^5	1	4.0	10	19×10^5	2
Windows	312	1.0	312	599×10^5	20	2.0	156	300×10^5	24
Infiltration	.0182Q	=	582	$1,117 \times 10^5$	37	.0182Q =	291	559×10^5	46
Total Heat Loss			1,578	$3,029 \times 10^5$	100		635	1220×10^5	100
Annual Plus Utility Gain				288×10^5				288×10^5	
Passive Solar Gain				313×10^5				282×10^5	
Net Annual Heat Loss				$2,428 \times 10^5$ Btu/yr.				650×10^5 Btu/yr.	

Legend
A = area (sq. ft.)
R_1 = thermal resistance before retrofit
R_2 = thermal resistance after retrofit
DD = degree days

Losses

Start the ledger by listing in column 1 each of the building sections through which heat is lost by conduction. Enter infiltration as the last item in the column, not because it is a section, but because we can treat it in much the same way. Next enter the surface area of each section in square feet. Note that if the building had one exterior wall insulated and the remainder not, both types of wall would have to be entered, reflecting the different heat-loss characteristics. The same is true of all the other sections.

In column III enter the total thermal resistance, R, of each section. Chapter 7 showed how to calculate R. We now have enough information to calculate area divided by thermal resistance (A/R) for each section. If we total all of the A/R's along with an appropriate infiltration figure, we have the "heat loss coefficient" of the building, in the example case 1,578 Btu hr.$^{-1}$ F$^{\circ-1}$. The units Btu hr.$^{-1}$ F$^{\circ-1}$ indicate the significance: the number of Btu's per hour that must be supplied by the furnace for each degree F difference between inside and outside temperatures. If we wish to maintain an inside temperature of +65° F when the outside temperature is at the design minimum of –15° F, our furnace would have to supply heat at the rate

$$1{,}578 \; Btu \; hr.^{-1} \; F^{\circ-1} \times 80F^{\circ}$$
$$or \; 126{,}240 \; Btu \; hr.^{-1}$$

Where do we get the appropriate infiltration figure? Referring to both Equation 5.1 and Equation 5.3 we see that the infiltration equivalent of A/R is .0182Q.

Fortunately, the outside temperature is not –15° F very often. (If it remained there all winter we would burn about 8,000 gallons of oil per year in this house!) To calculate the annual heat loss, first through each section and then from the entire house, Equation 5.2 tells us to simply multiply the figures in column IV by 24 and then by the number of degree days (8,000 in this case). Because the resulting numbers are so outlandish, we also divide by the number 10^5 (100,000) before entering them in column V. We see, for example, that we are losing 192×10^5 Btu per year^{-1} through the floor. The quantity 10^5 Btu has a name: the *therm*. To those of us who grew up with oil heat the therm has a particular significance. One gallon of #2 fuel oil contains a potential heating value of 140,000 Btu. When this oil is burned in a furnace at 70 percent efficiency, 100,000 Btu (140,000×.70) is delivered to the house. Therefore, roughly speaking, 1 therm=1 gallon of oil. Totaling the annual heat losses in column V, we get a staggering 3,029 therms! It's a good thing we were already planning to retrofit this house.

Column VI lists the percentages of the total heat lost by each section, including infiltration. This has no particular significance, but some of the figures will probably surprise you. The heat loss through the door is only 1 percent of the total, whereas you probably had the impression that the door was one of the bigger losers. The discrepancy is partly due to the form. Most of the heat loss through a door is due to infiltration rather than conduction. In fact, if a door is already well sealed against infiltration, it usually doesn't pay to add a storm door in order to cut conductive losses!

The 8 percent loss through the ceiling is surprising also because we have all read innumerable times that most of the heat is lost through the attic or roof. In an uninsulated one-story house, it is true that most of the conductive heat loss is through the ceiling, but this ceiling is already insulated (although to a much earlier standard!). Adding a single inch of insulation to a previously uninsulated attic typically cuts its heat loss by a factor of two. We will see in Chapter 10 that it will pay us to add insulation to the existing 2″ of rock wool, but as it now stands, the attic is not the biggest problem.

After Retrofit

Chapter 10 will show how to determine how much of which insulation should be added to our house. For now, however, let's assume we have added: 6″ of fiberglass to the first-floor joists, 4″ of cellulose to the empty exterior wall, and 9″ of fiberglass to the existing 2″ of rock wool in the attic. In addition, we have installed storm windows and doors. Using the effective R values per inch in Table 23, we calculate the new R values (R_2) listed in column VII. By weatherstripping the windows and doors and caulking the building joints and electrical outlets, we have reduced infiltration by half to 1 air exchange per hour. Columns VIII to X are formed just as columns IV to VI were, but using this time the new values, R_2.

Summing the entries in column VIII and multiplying by the design ΔT of $80\,F°$, we find a new maximum hourly heat loss of 50,800 Btu per hr. versus the previous maximum of 126,000 Btu per hr.

Column IX now totals to 1,220 therms per yr., which we translate roughly into 1,200 gallons of oil. Not bad! We have, simply by insulating and weatherstripping, reduced our losses by 60 percent. But if you think that's good news, hold on. So far we have calculated only the losses. Here come the gains.

GAINS

There are three sources of incidental heat gain in a residence: animal, utility, and solar. These were discussed in detail in Chapter 8. Using the methods presented there, we will calculate the gains for the example house which will be used to offset the losses in the final fuel calculation.

Animal and Utility Gain: We found before that the sum of animal and utility heat gains for an occupant of average habits could be calculated on the basis of

$$H_{animal\,+\,utility} = 800\ Btu/hr./person$$

Since this incidental heat is of use only on days when the furnace would ordinarily run (days with an average outdoor temperature of less than $65°\,F$), we calculate the heat gain only over the heating season. Therefore, for a family of four and a heating season of 275 heating days:

$$animal + utility\ gain\ per\ heating\ season$$
$$= 800\ Btu/hr./person \times 4\ people$$
$$\times 24\ hrs. \times 275\ days$$
$$= 288 \times 10^5\ Btu/yr.$$

Passive Solar Gain: Chapter 8 also presented a method for calculating the passive solar gain through ordinary windows. A restriction on the method was that the window area not exceed the ordinary 15 percent of the total exterior wall area for fear of overheating and subsequent venting of excess heat, making the calculation invalid.

First check the window ratio. The total window area in the example house is 312 square feet. The gross wall area (opaque wall plus doors plus windows) is 2,080 square feet. The percentage of window is therefore 312/2,080=15 percent.

Next, calculate the heating season solar gains for each of the window orientations, using Table 19, Illustration 52 and Equation 4.3.

In the example, the north and east windows are assigned shading coefficients of 0.9 since they are double-glazed (each with the addition of a storm window) and are never shaded by trees or other buildings. I have used a shading coefficient of 0.8 for the south and west windows because of their being shaded an estimated 10 percent by deciduous trees in addition to being double-glazed (0.9 × 0.9 = 0.8). The value of 825 for Y was interpolated from Illustration 52.

Deducting the animal, utility, and solar gains from the annual heat losses, we find the previous *net* heat loss to be 2428 therms per year and the new *net* heat loss to be 650 therms per year. These figures represent the heat losses that must be made up by our heating system before and after retrofit.

It has been customary in the past to calculate only heat loss. Animal, utility, and passive solar heat gains were simply assumed to push the house

Table 19. Heating Season Solar Gains

solar gain =	area	X	shading coefficient	X	24 hr.	X	heating days	X	solar factor	X	y ÷ 1550 =	
North	96	X	0.9	X	24	X	275	X	6.5	X	825/1550 = 19.7 × 10^5	$\frac{Btu}{yr}$
South	96	X	0.8	X	24	X	275	X	61.6	X	825/1550 = 166.2	"
East	60	X	0.9	X	24	X	275	X	27.0	X	825/1550 = 51.2	
West	60	X	0.8	X	24	X	275	X	27.0	X	825/1550 = 45.5	
Total solar gain											= 282 × 10^5 $\frac{Btu}{yr}$	

temperature up from 65°F to the thermostat temperature, 72°F. We can see from the example that this was not a bad assumption. Dividing the total-heating-season animal, utility, and solar heat gain of 570 therms by the number of hours in the heating season, 24 × 275, we get an hourly average contribution of 8,636 Btu/hr. Before retrofitting, our heat loss coefficient was 1,578 Btu/hr.$^{-1}$ F°; that is, we lost 1,578 Btu per hr. for each degree Fahrenheit difference between inside and outside temperatures. Turning this around, we see that the incidental heat gain alone would therefore have raised the house temperature by 8,636 Btu/hr.÷1,578 Btu/hr. F° = 5-1/2 F°.

Applying the same rule to the retrofitted house, however, we get an unassisted temperature boost of 8,636 Btu/hr.÷635 Btu/hr. F°, or 13.6°F! In addition, the post-oil embargo average thermostat setting is nearer 65°F than 72°F. Obviously, the combination of these two factors will require in the future that heat loss calculations take into account heat gains as well as losses.

The Zero-Energy House

The annual heat balance of the example house is striking. In a climate with 8,000 degree days we have found that incidental heat gain makes up nearly 50 percent of the annual heat loss. I'm sure you have also noticed that this house is far from optimal. The windows are uniformly distributed rather than concentrated on the south wall; no insulated curtains or shutters are used; the R values are less than optimal; the infiltration rate is about twice what could be achieved in new construction or extensive retrofit. Incorporating these improvements brings one ever closer to the "zero-energy house."

As one approaches a zero net annual energy figure, however, the question of economic justification should be kept in mind. It becomes more and more expensive to capture those last few Btu's of solar energy, the reason being that solar energy is not received at a constant usable rate but in bursts. We cannot, without incorporating expensive heat storage systems, simply increase the area of glass, because the house will overheat. On the other hand, there are strings of days when only 10 percent of clear-day radiation is received. The economically justified zero-energy house is likely to remain as elusive in the twentieth century as was the perpetual-motion machine in the nineteenth. But expect some damn easy-to-heat houses to result from the quest!

10.

Insulation

Introduction

Insulating a house properly entails much more than simply stuffing pink fluffy material between the studs and rafters. Even after one understands how heat flows there are many questions needing answers: Which insulation is a better buy? Which will last longest? What thickness will pay for itself? What about the heat loss through the framing? What if I heat with wood that I myself cut?

I hope this chapter will answer these questions. The reasoning behind the answers is presented for those who desire to understand. For those seeking only the answers, the results are given in tables and graphs.

First we will compare the most common commercial insulating materials: their strengths, their weaknesses, the truth behind the manufacturers' claims. Second, we will consider the difference between the *nominal* or laboratory R factor (thermal resistance), and the *effective* R factor as installed in a house. Third, we will learn to determine the thickness of each insulation that will result in the lowest lifetime operating cost for your house, regardless of your geographic location or fuel source.

The Commercial Insulations

Commercial insulations are for the most part nothing more than attempts to stop air from moving. This fact can be seen by comparing the thermal resistance (R) of a 3/4-inch-thick horizontal, low-emissivity air space to 3/4 inch of the insulators.

Each of the insulations has strong and weak points. Thermal resistance per inch is important when only a limited space is available. In unlimited spaces, such as open attics, R value per dollar is more important. Table 20 lists the common insulations, their R factors per inch, cost per board foot (1 sq. ft. X 1 in.), and cost per R. The R values are taken either from American Society of Heating and Ventilating Engineers (ASHRAE) published values or from National Bureau of Standards tests. The costs are based upon June 1977 national averages.

The relative costs in Table 20 are for the materials themselves. Installed costs may be different. Since all of the blown materials are contractor installed, the costs listed are installed cost for the simplest situation. For the nonblown materials, add your own labor or the hired labor cost of installing the material.

Table 20. Comparative Values of Insulating Materials

	R per inch	dollars per board foot	cents per R	R per dollar
Blown fiberglass (attic)	2.2	.0275	1.3	80
Fiberglass blanket or batt	3.15	.033	1.0	95
Blown cellulose (attic)	3.7	.055	1.5	67
Blown cellulose (wall)	3.3	.07	2.1	47
Polystyrene "Beadboard"	3.9	.10	2.6	39
Extruded styrene "Styrofoam"	5.25	.24	4.6	22
Blown urea formaldehyde (walls)	4.2	.18	4.3	23
Urethane	6.25	.35	5.6	18
Vermiculite	2.2	.11	5.0	20
Blown Rockwool	3.3	.07	2.3	44

Table 21. Cost Multipliers for 3-1/2"-4" Wall Cavities, Blown-in Insulation

insulation blown in behind:	multiply costs in Table 20 by:
Gypsum drywall	1.0
Poly vapor barrier	1.0
Shingle or shake	1.0
New clapboard	1.0
Plywood	1.0
Board and batten	1.0
Asphalt shingle	1.15
Old clapboards	1.25
Vinyl siding	1.25
Cedar or redwood siding	1.35
Asbestos shingle	1.5
Aluminum siding	1.5
Horizontal painted shiplap boards	1.5
Brick	(Add $1/sq. ft.)
Steel	(Won't touch)
Stucco	(Won't touch unless owner contracts stucco mason for repair.)

Obviously, for blown-in insulations, knocking holes in brick is a lot more expensive than drilling holes in clapboards. Removing vinyl and aluminum sidings results in a lot of cracked and dented siding, for which the contractor is ordinarily responsible. Table 21 shows the factor by which an insulation contractor might multiply the base cost in Table 20 for various wall materials. Once again, the bottom line is the estimate from the contractor himself. If you have a difficult situation, ask for a separate bid with you making and repairing the holes.

Pros and Cons of the Most Popular Insulations

FIBERGLASS BLANKET AND BATT

Fiberglass is by far the most common commercial insulation. Its use in new wood-frame construction is standard. The product consists of long filaments of spun glass loosely woven and cut into batts 48" and 96" long and blankets of up to 100' in length.

Table 22 lists the standard manufactured sizes of fiberglass products. Most of the standard widths and thicknesses can be obtained with aluminum foil facing, asphalt-laminated kraft paper facing, plain kraft paper facing, or unfaced. For use under first floors, where the vapor barrier must face up, a reverse-flange facing is available. Local lumberyards stock only a few of the listed sizes, so check local availability long before starting an insulation job. In general, a person would have to be either very lazy or allergic to the material not to install it himself. Fiberglass has a reputation for being non-flammable. This is not strictly true, since the resins which bind the fibers into a matt will burn when the surrounding wall materials provide a hot enough fire. However, it is safe to say that fiberglass does not represent an unusual fire danger.

Strong points: low cost per R factor, ease of installation, relatively nonflammable, resistant to water damage, nonsettling. *Weak points:* cannot be blown into a cavity.

Table 22. Fiberglass Insulation Sizes Available

kraft paper faced

R-30	9" × 16" × 48" batt
R-30	9" × 24" × 48" batt
R-26	8-1/4" × 16" × 48" batt
R-22	6-1/2" × 15" or 23" × 48" batt
R-19	6" × 15" or 23" × 48" batt
R-11	3-1/2" × 15" or 23" × 56' roll
R-11	3-1/2" × 15" or 23" × 48" batt
R-11	3-1/2" × 15" × 93" or 96" batt
R-11	3-1/2" × 11" × 48" batt

kraft flush with edges

R-19	6" × 24" × 48"
R-11	3-1/2" × 24" × 48"

unfaced friction-fit

R-30	9" × 16" × 48" batt
R-30	9" × 24" × 48" batt
R-26	8-1/4" × 16" × 48" batt
R-26	8-1/4" × 24" × 48" batt
R-22	6-1/2" × 15-1/4" × 48" batt
R-19	6" × 15-1/4" or 23-1/4" × 48" batt
R-19	6" × 15-1/4" or 23-1/4" × 48" batt
R-13	3" × 15-1/4" × 47" batt
R-11	3-1/2" × 15-1/4" × 93" or 96" batt
R-11	3-1/2" × 23-1/4" × 48" batt

foil-faced

R-19	6" × 15" or 23" × 32' roll
R-19	6" × 15" or 23" × 48" batt
R-11	3-1/2" × 15" or 23" × 56' roll

flame-resistant foil-faced

R-19	6" × 15" or 23" × 48" batt
R-11	3-1/2" × 15" or 23" × 48" batt
R-19	6" × 24" × 48" batt
R-11	3-1/2" × 24" × 48" batt

noise barrier

R-11	3-1/2" × 16" or 24" × 96" batt
R-8	2-1/2" × 16" or 24" × 96" batt

for inside masonry wall

R-3.5	1" × 15" or 23" × 96" batt

rigid form board

R-4.3	1" × 24" × 48"

sill-sealer

1" × 6" × 50' roll

blowing wool

R-2.2	per in. of thickness; BAGS

CELLULOSE

Cellulosic fiber is rapidly gaining favor as a retrofit insulating material. It consists basically of newspapers recycled into very fine fiber. It looks like an old mouse nest. On the site, bags of cellulose are poured into the hopper of a machine that separates the fiber and blows it through a hose into the attic or wall cavity. Like urea formaldehyde (see below), it is an excellent insulation if installed properly. When treated with fire-retardant chemicals, cellulose is no more flammable than fiberglass or urea formaldehyde. Untreated cellulose, however, is nearly explosive in a fire. Several fire-retardant chemicals have been used, but to date only boric acid has proven acceptable. Look on the bags or get in writing from the contractor the assurance that the cellulose to be installed is "nonstarch," "noncorrosive," and of fire-retardant class I or II. The bags may also give the recommended square-foot coverage of each bag at recommended densities. If you feel that there is any question, *save the bags.*

The material should be installed by a professional. Although blowing machines are generally available through tool rental companies, doing it yourself may prove false economy. For best performance the cellulose must first be finely dispersed and then installed at its proper density. If installed at too low a density, the material will ultimately settle, possibly leaving a significant uninsulated void at the top of each wall cavity. The effect of such voids on the insulation effectiveness is surprisingly great (see *Effective versus Nominal R Values,* below). Proper cellulose installed densities are: 2.6 lb. cu. ft. in the attic and 3.5-4.5 lb./cu. ft. in the wall, increasing with the unblocked wall cavity height. Most walls have blocking, bracing, and fire-stops, requiring more than one hole to be drilled. The professional has the experience to find these.

In blowing cellulose into an attic, it is difficult to avoid blocking soffit ventilation inlets. Make sure the installer clears these vents and installs baffles if necessary before he leaves the job.

Strong points: fine particles are easily blown into small spaces; in an old house with uneven joist and stud spacing, all voids are automatically filled; low cost per R; recycled material. *Weak points:* simplicity of equipment and availability of raw material make cellulose a prime target for fly-by-night operators; running water in the wall cavity caused by driven rain or ice dams can result in wetting and subsequent collapse of the cellulose. Once saturated, cellulose dries to a papier mâché consistency with little insulating value.

UREA FORMALDEHYDE

UF foam, sold under the trade names of Rapco Foam, Insulspray, and Celsius Foam among others, is another popular blown-in insulation. Developed in Germany in the 1930s, it has been widely used in Europe, and its use is rapidly spreading in the United States. Because of certain peculiarities, it is the most controversial of all the insulations.

Under ideal conditions in the laboratory, and after curing, the foam has been tested to have an R rating of as high as 5.5/in., the value initially advertised by Rapco. Rapco and Insulspray now advertise 4.8/in. The R value obtained by averaging non-manufacturer-reported values on thirty-five separate samples is only 4.4. A value of 4.2 appears to be temporarily accepted by the National Bureau of Standards. The reason for the large discrepancies in reported urea formaldehyde R values is shrinkage during curing. A number of factors may lead to excessive shrinkage: out-of-date chemicals, improper ratio of chemicals, improper temperature of chemicals, and too rapid a cure. One manufacturer claims normal shrinkage of from 1 percent to 3 percent linear; another claims 2 percent to 6 percent linear: i.e., cracks totaling up to 1″ over a 16″ wide stud space. Much controversy surrounds the extent to which cracks in the insulation constitute heat short circuits in parallel with the foam. The result of these short circuits is a lowering of the total cavity effective R by a factor much greater than the shrinkage ratio. In addition, cracks between the foam and studs allow greater infiltration. Effective versus nominal R values will be discussed in greater detail below. Unfortunately, once a rigid foam is in place, nothing can be done to rectify a bad job other than opening the wall—an expensive solution! Because of the adverse publicity generated by a few improper installations, the major suppliers of UF chemicals are intensifying their training and quality-control programs, as well as their research on shrinkage during curing.

UF should not be used in attics or between rafters. It has been found not to perform well under a combination of high temperature and humidity conditions. Because of its temperature and humidity sensitivity, its use in southern states is increasingly being questioned. Because of its relative high cost per R factor, it competes economically with fiberglass and cellulose only in wall cavities, anyway.

As you will see after reading the chapter on condensation and vapor barriers, it would be wonderful if UF were a vapor barrier, but it is not. While UF is not damaged by passage, accumulation, or freezing of water, it consists of 40 percent open cells, and thus has a high vapor permeability. In fact, there is little difference between fiberglass, cellulose, and UF in ability to retard the passage or condensation of water vapor.

On the other hand, uniquely among the blown insulations, UF will not be permanently damaged by standing, driven, or running water. It, like virtually every other man-made material, is technically flammable. However, its fuel contribution rating and toxicity are low enough to gain its acceptance by the New York City Building Code. It is also a good sound absorber and is often used in interior motel walls for this quality. Properly installed, it probably has about the same total R value in a wall cavity as fiberglass and cellulose.

Strong points: high R if properly installed; does not contribute fuel to fire; its smoke is less toxic than that of plywood; nonsettling; not damaged by water; flows well. *Weak points:* expensive; excessive shrinkage may result in lower effective R than either cellulose or fiberglass; it is difficult to detect and virtually impossible to rectify a bad installation.

BLOWN FIBERGLASS

Blown fiberglass consists of small clumps of fiberglass "wool," blown into cavities and attic spaces in the same manner as cellulose. Proper settled density is therefore important for the same reasons. It is cheaper than cellulose and less prone to water damage. However, its R factor is quite a bit lower. It's losing ground to the other blown-ins because of its low R factor and the belief that the glass fibers are harmful if inhaled. I certainly don't like the idea of billions of tiny glass fibers in my house.

Strong point: cheap. *Weak points:* nasty stuff; low R value per inch.

POLYSTYRENE "BEADBOARD"

Beadboard is a rigid board of molded polystyrene beads. Children's surfboards are often made of it. If it's a foam board and white, it's probably beadboard. It is available in thicknesses of 3/4", 1", 1-1/2", 2", 4", and 6" and widths of 16", 24", and 48". As with fiberglass, check local suppliers before counting your chickens, however. It is easily cut by knife or saw. It's not damaged by water, but the tiny passages between the beads make it quite permeable to water vapor. It should not be exposed on the inside of the house, as it burns readily with a toxic smoke. Three good applications are insulating between irregularly spaced rafters when finishing off an attic, insulating outside the wall sheathing, insulating inside concrete cellar walls.

Strong points: cheapest foam; easy to use. *Weak points:* not a vapor barrier; lowest R value of the foams; relatively flammable.

STYROFOAM

Styrofoam is the trade name of extruded polystyrene made by Dow Chemical Company. Compared to bead board it is stronger, heavier, more expensive, and of higher R value. It is also completely waterproof and a vapor barrier. It too burns with a toxic smoke, and so should be covered with a minimum of 1/2" gypsum drywall for inside applications. It is most commonly used to insulate the outside of foundation walls, under concrete slabs, under roofing on cathedral ceilings, and as exterior wall sheathing.

Strong points: waterproof, vapor barrier; high R factor. *Weak points:* expensive; burns.

URETHANE

Called urethane, U-thane, and polyurethane, this foam is relatively exotic. It is the most expensive, has the highest R factor, is the most water-resistant, and is the most dangerous of all the foams in a fire. The high R factor (claimed to be as high as 9.0/in. by some manufacturers) is due to its cells being filled with low conductivity gas. When and if the gas exchanges with air, the R factor drops to 5.6–6.25/in. It is often claimed that 1 inch of urethane insulates as well as 6 inches of fiberglass. The truth is that 1 inch of urethane equals 2 of fiberglass but at 10 times the cost. Its flammability is compounded by the generation of cyanide gas, a deadly combination, which has led to a building code ban in New York City. I personally believe its use should be limited to insulating concrete, roof decks, picnic coolers, and thermos jugs.

Many other insulations find application in particular circumstances. However, the basic choice is among these seven, and in particular among the first three. Based upon cost, performance, and ease of installation, my personal preferences are:

(1) In any space that is accessible (open stud space or open attic), I would install fiberglass blanket or batt myself because it's the most cost-effective and has no major aging problems. If the attic joists are not spaced 16″ or 24″ on-center, I would use loose cellulose to fill the gaps. If you don't wish to do the work yourself, or if the attic has a floor, but you don't wish to convert the attic to living space, have cellulose blown under the floorboards between the ceiling joists.

(2) In a closed wall having no danger of running water, cellulose is likely to achieve as great an effective R value as urea formaldehyde and at lower cost. If there is a history of rainwater driving through the walls or ice dams resulting in water running down the walls, either solve the problem or install urea formaldehyde.

(3) Under a crawl space or unheated basement floor, I would install unfaced fiberglass between the joists, held up by a permeable, cheap material. Consider 1″ beadboard; it's cheaper than plywood, breathes well, and adds its own insulation value to that of the fiberglass.

Effective versus Nominal R Values

It is usually assumed in heat loss calculations that the floor, wall, or roof has a total R (thermal resistance) value consisting of the uninsulated R value of the section plus the R value of the thickness of insulation installed. Intuition tells us that the solid wood portion of a wall consisting of 2×4 studs (1-1/2″×3-1/2″) spaced 16″ on-center is 1-1/2″÷16″, or 10 percent of the total. Moreover, the stud itself has a moderate insulating value. Therefore the heat loss through the entire wall should be within a few percent of that, calculated on the simple assumption that the wall consists of insulation alone. This assumption is incorrect.

Heat paths through areas of low R value act as heat short circuits. A simple example will demonstrate the effect. Illustration 55 shows a wall panel consisting of two slabs of equal area, the first having an R value of 1.0 and the second an R value of infinity. Let the area of each be 1 sq. ft. and the ΔT across the slabs be 1F°. By the conduction equation we find the rate of heat flow through the first slab to be 1 Btu/hr.$^{-1}$ and the rate through the second slab to be 0 Btu/hr.$^{-1}$ (any number divided by infinity equals zero). Then the heat loss of the combined slab is as though the slab-effective R value were 2.0. In other words, given the ratio of areas in the example, no matter how well we insulate one side, the *effective R value* of the total section will never exceed twice the R value of the other side.

Ordinary construction consists of fiberglass batts placed between 1-1/2″ thick wooden studs, joists, or rafters. The effect we have just seen is to lower the effective R value of the section by 15 to 18 percent—not a serious consequence. However, in retrofitting, we often face a choice of blown-in cellulose or urea formaldehyde. Each of these materials, through different mechanisms, raises the possibility of a much more dramatic short circuit—the air space. Cellulose may settle in a wall cavity if either installed at too low a density to support its own weight or saturated by

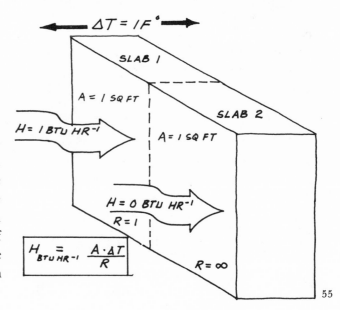

55

abnormal amounts of moisture. Urea formaldehyde will not settle, but is acknowledged to shrink upon curing anywhere from 1 to 6 percent linear. Since the R value of a large wall cavity air space is only 0.92 regardless of thickness, you can see that large air spaces may constitute very effective short circuits.

Assuming that the R value of the air space is nearly independent of its thickness, the R value *per inch* of the air space decreases as the thickness of the wall cavity increases. Thus we find that in the presence of significant cavity air spaces, little benefit results from increasing the thickness of the insulation.

Illustration 56 shows a wall section consisting of three heat paths: through the insulation, through the wood framing, through air spaces. The formula for the effective R value of the entire section is easily derived. First, the heat loss through each of the different heat paths is found, using the conduction formula and the appropriate areas and R's of each. The total heat loss can be calculated either as the sum of the three separate heat losses or alternatively as if the section were uniform, having an R value which we call the *effective R value*.

Table 23 shows the results of applying Equation 6.1 to the four most common wall framing systems and the three most common retrofit insulating materials. R_{nom} is the nominal insulating value, obtained by simply multiplying the advertised insulation R value per inch by the wall cavity thickness. $R_{eff/in.}$ is R_{eff} divided by the wall cavity thickness. It is important to note that *the house will lose heat as if the wall cavity had an average R value of R_{eff} and an insulation R value per inch of $R_{eff/in}$*. The results are quite simply astounding. As noted before, with no air space at all R_{eff} is between 82 and 85 percent of R_{nom} with the common framing systems. With the air spaces shown, however, R_{eff} may be less than 50 percent of R_{nom}. Table 23 also shows that the percentage effect increases with the thickness of the insulation. For example, with insulation shrinkage of 3 percent linear, the theoretical gain in R_{eff} from increasing the wall thickness from 4″ to 6″ is only 1.7, less than 1.0 per inch!

A critical assumption in the calculation is that the R value of an air space is 0.92, regardless of the shape or dimension of that air space. Many cracks of small dimension should have higher R values than one large crack, because of convective friction. It is also possible for the cracks not to pass all the way through the insulation, thereby reducing the short circuit effect. On the other hand, if the insulation slab pulls away from the inside and outside wall faces, circulation of air *around* the slab may cause heat loss even greater than predicted by the table.

What do other people think? The Swedish State Planning Organization assumed that the effect is exactly as predicted by Equation 6.1. In other words, that convection currents occurring in the shrinkage cracks of urea formaldehyde foam may reduce the effective insulating value of the foam

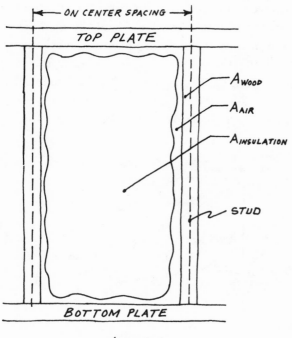

$$H_{TOTAL} = \frac{A_{TOTAL} \cdot \Delta T}{R_{EFF}}$$

$$H_{TOTAL} = \frac{A_{AIR} \cdot \Delta T}{R_{AIR}} + \frac{A_{WOOD} \cdot \Delta T}{R_{WOOD}} + \frac{A_{INSUL} \cdot \Delta T}{R_{NOM}}$$

$$\frac{1}{R_{EFF}} = \frac{A_{AIR}}{A_{TOTAL}} \cdot \frac{1}{R_{AIR}} + \frac{A_{WOOD}}{A_{TOTAL}} \cdot \frac{1}{R_{WOOD}} + \frac{A_{INSUL}}{A_{TOTAL}} \cdot \frac{1}{R_{NOM}}$$

56

Table 23. Nominal versus Effective R Values in Wall Framing

	fiberglass batt R=3.2/in.	cellulose, no settling, R=3.3/in.	cellulose, 6% settling, R=3.3/in.	urea formaldehyde, no shrink, R=4.8/in.	*urea formaldehyde, 3% shrink linear, R=4.8/in.	beadboard, R=3.9/in.	Styrofoam, R=5.25/in.	urethane, R=6.25/in.	solid softwood R=1.25/in.
				S4S 2 X 4 @ 16" o.c.					
$R_{nominal}$	11.2	11.6	11.6	15.8	15.8	13.7	18.4	21.9	4.4
$R_{effective}$	9.2	9.4	6.3	12.0	7.3	10.5	12.6	14.0	4.4
$R_{effective/inch}$	2.6	2.7	1.8	3.4	2.1*	3.0	3.6	4.0	1.25
				RGH 2 X 4 @ 24" o.c.					
$R_{nominal}$	12.8	13.2	13.2	19.2	19.2	15.6	21.0	25.0	5.0
$R_{effective}$	10.5	10.7	6.9	13.7	8.0	12.0	14.4	16.0	5.0
$R_{effective/inch}$	2.6	2.7	1.7	3.4	2.0	3.0	3.6	4.0	1.25
				S4S 2 X 6 @ 24" o.c.					
$R_{nominal}$	17.6	18.2	18.2	26.4	26.4	21.5	28.7	34.4	6.9
$R_{effective}$	15.0	15.4	8.4	20.1	9.5	17.6	21.5	23.7	6.9
$R_{effective/inch}$	2.7	2.8	1.5	3.7	1.7	3.2	3.9	4.3	1.25
				RGH 2 X 6 @ 24" o.c.					
$R_{nominal}$	19.2	19.8	19.8	28.8	28.8	23.4	31.5	37.5	7.5
$R_{effective}$	15.8	16.1	8.6	20.6	9.7	18.0	21.6	24.0	7.5
$R_{effective/inch}$	2.6	2.7	1.4	3.4	1.6	3.0	3.6	4.0	1.25

*Values based upon theoretical calculations using an air cavity R of 0.92 and 6% area shrinkage. The National Bureau of Standards reports $R_{effective/in.}$ = 2.6 with 3% linear shrinkage and S4S 2 X 4 @ 16" o.c. framing in a single test.

to one-half that of the uncracked foam. They recommend that the effective thermal resistance of foam in a 2" X 4", 16" on-center wall cavity be calculated on the basis of R 2.1/in., which agrees with Table 23.

On the other hand, the National Bureau of Standards feels that the effect may be somewhat less than calculated by the formula. They report that an actual test panel framed of 2"X4" studs 16" on-center yielded a measured R_{eff} of 9.2 and $R_{eff/in.}$ of 2.6 with an observed linear shrinkage of 3 percent. This compares to the theoretically calculated values in Table 23 of 7.3 and 2.1/in.

In summary I would like to point out that the effect of air spaces in insulation cavities is independent of the type of insulation. An uninsulated gap of 3 percent of a 16" stud space (only 1/2") loses the same amount of heat whether the insulation is solid foam, cellulose, or fiberglass. This is especially important in retrofitting, since the manufactured widths of fiberglass insulation most

often do not conform with the stud spacing. Air spaces are disasters. Good insulation can be rendered ineffective by careless installation.

Optimum Insulation, or Exactly How Much Insulation Pays for Itself?

Aside from the confusion surrounding vapor barriers and condensation, the question I am most often asked is "How much insulation should I install in my attic?" I dread vapor barrier questions because there are so few absolutes. In fact, after getting the full vapor barrier lecture most people look as if they wish they hadn't asked. But the insulation question is different. If you have just a few numbers, such as the number of degree days in your area, I can give you an exact answer.

I intend to give you the answer in all its glory. If you enjoy simple mathematics and logic, you're in for a treat. If you don't, and want only the results, I suggest you skip to Table 24.

DERIVATION

Once upon a time, people thought that the cost of a house was the number of dollars they paid for it. The cost of insulating a house would therefore be the amount of money paid the insulation contractor. In 1974 the Arabs educated us; we now know that the cost of owning a house includes not only the purchase price, but the cost of keeping it warm (and cool in the South). The long-term cost associated with insulation is the *life-cycle cost*, consisting of the initial cost of the insulation plus the cost of heat lost through the insulation over the life of the house. Illustration 57 shows the life-cycle cost of insulating and heating one square foot of the exterior surface of a house. The horizontal scale is thickness of insulation; the vertical scale is dollars per sq. ft. Curve A represents the cost of insulating 1 sq. ft. of exterior surface of the house. We assume that there is a minimum fixed cost, and thereafter an additional cost per inch of material installed. Curve A is therefore a straight line. Curve B represents the cost of the heat lost through the 1 sq. ft. surface over the lifetime of the insula-

tion. It starts at the cost of heat lost through the construction before the addition of insulation. The addition of but one inch of the common insulating materials will typically cut heat loss by a third. Curve B therefore drops very rapidly at first. However, the additional heat savings realized by increasing the insulation from, say, 20″ to 21″, is very small, since the total heat loss can never drop below zero. Curve B therefore gradually approaches zero at very large thicknesses of insulation.

The curve we are most interested in is C, the life-cycle cost. Curve C is found by adding curves A and B: the installation cost of 1″ of insulation plus the cost of heat through construction with 1″ of insulation; and so on, inch by inch. It turns out that curve C always has a minimum: i.e., there is always a certain thickness of insulation resulting in the lowest combined cost of insulating and heating the house over its life. We call this precise thickness of insulation the *optimum thickness*.

How is that precise point found? An obvious way is to do as I first suggested and calculate curves A and B inch by inch and add, but that's a lot of work! I don't generally have much faith in economists, but they do have one trick that impresses me. Economists use a technique that they call marginal analysis. Here's how it works. The marginal cost of doing something is the additional cost of doing it just a bit more. In our case, it is the additional cost of adding just one more inch of insulation. The marginal benefit, on the other hand, is the additional benefit realized by doing that last bit more—in this case, the additional lifetime fuel savings due to the last inch of insulation. Illustration 58 shows the marginal analysis for insulation. Curve A is once again the cost of insulating. This time curve B is the value of fuel *not* consumed due to insulating (fuel savings). It generally costs the same to increase the insulation thickness from 9″ to 10″ as to increase it from 1″ to 2″. Therefore, the marginal cost in this case has a constant value, as shown by curve C. The fuel saving realized by increasing the insulation thickness from 9″ to 10″ is a lot

57

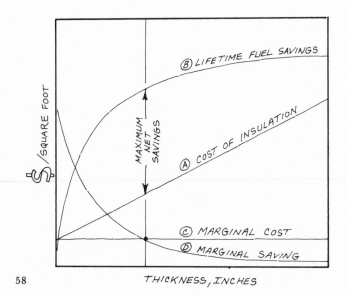

Equation 6.2

58

$$Cost = a_0 + a_1 D + a_2 D + a_3 D$$
$$where\ D = thickness\ in\ inches$$
$$a_0 = fixed\ cost$$
$$a_1 = cost\ per\ board\ foot\ (1'' \times 1\ sq.\ ft.)$$
$$of\ insulation$$
$$a_2 = cost\ of\ framing\ to\ create\ 1\ board$$
$$foot\ of\ space$$
$$a_3 = value\ of\ 1\ board\ foot\ of\ living\ space$$

The marginal cost (MC) of insulating is the additional cost of one more inch. Compute the cost of 5″ and 6″ insulation, using any values for *a* you wish, and you will see that:

Equation 6.3

$$MC = a_1 + a_2 + a_3$$

FUEL SAVINGS

We will find it easiest to attack fuel savings from the rear. Refer to Chapter 7 to refresh· your memory. We can modify the heat loss equation to express the cost of heat lost through one square foot of wall over the life of the house as

Equation 6.4

$$Fuel\ Cost = \frac{24 \times DD \times F \times PWF}{R_{eff/in} \times D \times 10^5}$$

$$where\ DD = degree\ days$$
$$F = cost\ per\ 10^5\ Btu\ of\ heat\ delivered\ to$$
$$the\ living\ space$$
$$R_{eff/in} = effective\ R\ value\ per\ inch\ as\ installed$$
$$D = inches\ of\ insulation$$
$$PWF = the\ present\ worth\ factor\ for\ the\ fuel$$
$$over\ the\ life\ of\ the\ house,\ reflecting$$
$$both\ lifetime\ and\ price\ increases$$
$$(see\ Chapter\ 1)$$

The marginal savings are just the negative of the marginal fuel cost. At this point, if you're not a student of the differential calculus, you'll have either to calculate the fuel costs at two different thicknesses (say 9″ and 10″) and subtract or to accept on faith that the marginal savings are given by

less than that realized by going from 1″ to 2″. Therefore, the marginal saving is given by the continually decreasing curve, D. The value of marginal analysis lies in the fact that the *optimum thickness* occurs at the precise point where *marginal cost equals marginal saving*. That this is so can be easily seen. At any thickness less than optimal, the marginal or incremental savings exceed the marginal cost. On the other hand, at any thickness greater than optimal, the cost of additional insulation exceeds the additional savings.

Since these curves can be expressed mathematically, we can mathematically define the optimum thickness by equating the expressions for marginal cost and marginal saving.

COST OF THE INSULATION

Except for the special cases of the empty attic and the empty floor joist cavity—spaces that exist whether we insulate or not—a strict cost accounting of insulating 1 sq. ft. of an exterior surface of a house must include: (1) the cost of the insulation, (2) the cost of special framing required to house the insulation, and (3) the value of space that otherwise could be used as living space. Expressed as an equation:

Equation 6.5

$$MS = \frac{24 \times DD \times F \times PWF}{R_{eff/in} \times D^2 \times 10^5}$$

According to marginal analysis, the optimum thickness, $D_{optimum}$, occurs at the precise point where MC=MS. Therefore

$$a_1 + a_2 + a_3 = \frac{24 \times DD \times F \times PWF}{R_{eff/in} \times D^2_{optimum} \times 10^5}$$

or

$$D^2_{optimum} = \frac{24 \times DD \times F \times PWF}{R_{eff/in} \times 10^5 \times (a_1 + a_2 + a_3)}$$

One small correction remains to be made. Note that we have calculated the fuel cost as if the R value of the construction were due only to the insulation. In fact, the uninsulated construction has a small R value, which we will call R_0. Therefore, the optimum thickness of insulation will be $R_0 \div R_{eff/in}$ inches less than given above.

Equation 6.6

$$D_{optimum} = \left(\frac{24 \times DD \times F \times PWF}{R_{eff/in} \times 10^5 \times (a_1 + a_2 + a_3)} \right)^{1/2} - \frac{R_0}{R_{eff/in}}$$

LIFE-CYCLE COST

The cost of insulating and then heating each square foot of house surface (LCC) is the sum of Equations 6.2 and 6.4.

Equation 6.7

$$LCC = a_0 + (a_1 + a_2 + a_3)D + \frac{24 \times DD \times F \times PWF}{(R_{eff/in} \times D + R_0) \times 10^5}$$

Results

The difficulty in determining the optimum thickness for a given situation lies not so much in the mathematics of Equation 6.6 (a grade-school child and a ten-dollar calculator are sufficient for that) but in assigning values to the variables. To save most readers the task of calculation, I list the resulting optimum thicknesses of insulations for the most common retrofit situations in Table 24. Use of the table and a simple factor tailor the answer to any fuel and any climate. I must point out, however, that the values in Table 24 result from particular assumptions. If you do not agree with my assumptions, you will of course get different answers. In that case, happy calculating!

Here are my assumptions:

Degree Days (DD): For the purpose of the table I make the nominal assumption of 10,000 degree days. The factor K below accounts for the difference between your number of degree days and 10,000.

Fuel Factor (F): Again, for the purpose of the table, I assume a nominal value of $1.00 for the cost of 10^5 Btu of delivered heat. The factor K changes that assumption. Due to the combination of high nominal DD and F, the optimum thicknesses in Table 24 appear to be unreasonably large, which of course they are!

Present Worth Factor (PWF): This is the first variable that you may question. I have used what I consider to be the rather conservative value of 34.8, on the basis of a thirty-year lifetime and an annual fuel price increase of general inflation plus 1 percent. Consult Table 1 for different values of PWF.

Table 24

optimum insulation thickness, assuming 10,000 DD and F = 1.0 for other DD and F values, multiply by K from Illustration 59		blown fiberglass $R=2.2$ $R_{eff/in.}=2.2$	fiberglass batt $R=3.2$ $R_{eff/in.}=2.7$	cellulose in attic $R=3.7$ $R_{eff/in.}=3.7$	cellulose in wall $R=3.3$ $R_{eff/in.}=2.8$	urea foam 0% shrinkage $R=4.8$ $R_{eff/in.}=3.7$	urea foam 3% shrinkage $R_{eff/in.}=2.6$ estimated	bead-board $R=3.9$ $R_{eff/in.}=3.2$	Styrofoam $R=5.25$ $R_{eff/in.}=3.9$	urethane $R=6.25$ $R_{eff/in.}=4.3$
Part of House	Labor by									
Open attic	Owner	36″	27″	20″						
	Contractor	36″	19″	20″						
Cathedral ceiling	Owner		21″	18″				14″	9″	7″
	Contractor		15″	15″				11″	8″	6″
Conventional stud wall (stud space not free)	Owner		12″		11″	8″	9″	9″	7″	
	Contractor		8″		8″	6″	7″	6″	5-1/2″	
Wall insulated outside framing	Owner		18″					12″	8″	6″
	Contractor		13″					9″	7″	5-1/2″
Floor, no perimeter wall	Owner		20″	16″				13″	8″	6″
	Contractor		14″	13″				10″	7″	6″
Floor over unheated basement or crawl space	Owner		11″					8″	3″	
	Contractor		8″					6″	2-1/2″	

Effective R Value Per Inch ($R_{eff/in}$): I have used the values from Table 23: $R_{nominal}$ where the insulation is unbroken by framing and $R_{eff/in}$ when installed between 24″ on-center framing.

Initial R Value (R_0): The R value before addition of insulation is assumed to be: open attic 3.0, cathedral ceiling 2.0, conventional wall 4.0, wall insulated outside framing 2.5, floor open to air 2.5, floor over unheated but enclosed basement or crawl space 10.0.

Insulation Cost per Board Foot (a_1): When insulation is to be installed in an owner-built home by the owner, I used the values listed in Table 20. To account for contracting costs I doubled the cost of fiberglass and added 5 cents per board foot to each of the rigid foams. Contracted costs only were used for the blown-in insulations, since it is not recommended that you do them yourself.

Cost of Framing (a_2): The cost of extra framing required to provide insulating space was calculated on the basis of 0.15 board feet of lumber per board foot of space for walls and floors, 0.11 for cathedral ceiling, and 0.0 for open attic. This factor was then multiplied by the cost of framing lumber—$0.27 per board foot for owner-built and $0.54, including labor, for contracted.

Cost of Living Space (a_3): a_3 has the value zero except for the case of the normal stud wall, where the addition of 1 board foot of wall insulation occupies 1/96 square foot of living space. In that case, a_3 is the per-square-foot cost of the house divided by 96. I have deducted the cost of plumbing fixtures, kitchen appliances, site services, and land in determining the value of a house to be: owner-built—$10/sq. ft., contracted—$20/sq. ft.

Using Table 24

To find the optimum thicknesses for your home you need only two numbers: the price you presently pay for fuel and the number of degree days for your location. In Illustration 59 find the price you pay for fuel along the bottom scale; draw a vertical line from that point; find the intersection of the vertical line with the curve for your number of degree days; from the intersection draw a horizontal line to the left and read the value of K from the scale. This value of K is the single factor by which all of the values of Table 24 are multiplied for your house.

Problem: You live in Augusta, Maine, and plan to heat with wood after retrofitting. The present cost of hardwood firewood in your area is $50 per cord, bought in 6-cord lots. From Illustration 50 you determine that your town has about 8,000 DD. How much insulation should you install in your attic?

Solution: Enter Illustration 59 at $50 per cord; run straight up to the curve labeled "8,000 DD"; run horizontally to the left; read K=0.49. Multiplying the values in Table 25 by 0.49, you find that you should install 13″ of fiberglass in the attic if you provide the labor yourself, 9″ if you pay a contractor. If you are having a contractor blow in cellulose, 10″ would be optimal.

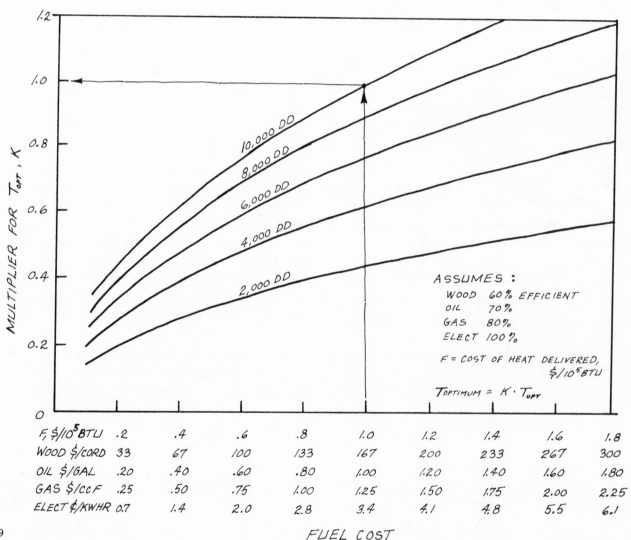

F, $/$10^5$BTU	.2	.4	.6	.8	1.0	1.2	1.4	1.6	1.8
WOOD $/CORD	33	67	100	133	167	200	233	267	300
OIL $/GAL	.20	.40	.60	.80	1.00	1.20	1.40	1.60	1.80
GAS $/CCF	.25	.50	.75	1.00	1.25	1.50	1.75	2.00	2.25
ELECT ¢/KWHR	0.7	1.4	2.0	2.8	3.4	4.1	4.8	5.5	6.1

FUEL COST

59

In the Southland, the summer cooling bill is often as great as the winter heating bill. Since heat flows in either direction through the commercial insulations equally well, it makes no difference to the calculation of optimum thickness or life-cycle cost whether we are heating, air conditioning, or both. To the winter heating degree days (Illustration 50) we simply add summer cooling degree days (Illustration 51). However, if we are using different fuels for the different operations we have to adjust the fuel factor (F). Note that in Equation 6.6 the factors F and DD occur as a pair. What we are looking for over the total year is the product:

$$DD_{total} \times F_{av} = DD_{heating} \times F_{heating} + DD_{cooling} \times F_{cooling}$$

Figure 58 is still valid provided we use DD_{total} and,

$$F_{av} = \frac{DD_{heating}}{DD_{total}} \times F_{heating} + \frac{DD_{cooling}}{DD_{total}} \times F_{cooling}$$

EXAMPLE

Problem: You have an old Cape outside Boston where there are 6,000 DD and have no plans to change from oil heat, for which you presently pay 50¢ per gallon. You plan to hire a carpenter to finish off the attic as a living space and desire a cathedral ceiling with the hand-hewn rafters exposed. What are the optimum levels of different insulations?

Solution: Enter Illustration 59 at 50¢ per gallon; rise vertically to the curve "6,000 DD"; run horizontally to K=0.55. Multiplying the contractor levels in Table 24 by 0.55 we find: fiberglass 8″, cellulose 8″, beadboard 6″, Styrofoam 4-1/2″, urethane 3″.

Which Insulation?

Table 24 and the factor K from Illustration 59 tell us the thickness of each insulation resulting in the greatest lifetime savings. But how do we determine which of the insulations to use? There are many criteria. The most interesting is usually *cost*. Equation 6.7 allows us to calculate the life-cycle cost at the optimum thickness of each insulation and thereby to choose between them.

Illustrations 60 through 65 compare the life-cycle costs in dollars per square foot resulting from the use of the optimum levels of each insulation for the specific assumptions of 8,000 DD and fuel costs of $50 per cord, 50¢ per gallon, and 2.75¢ per kilowatt hour. These values are for northern New England in 1978, but the *relative* comparison between insulation types applies to any region of the country. In the figures there are two columns over each insulation type representing the cases of owner-built (O) and contracted (C). The height of each column indicates the life-cycle cost (LCC) in dollars per square foot, each column being broken into three levels corresponding to wood heat (lowest cost), oil heat (medium cost), and electric heat (highest cost).

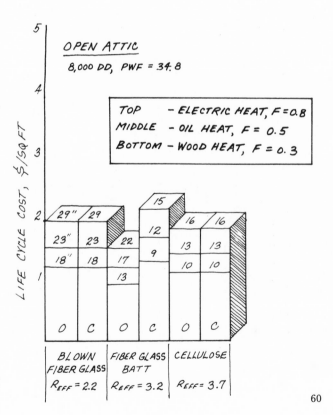

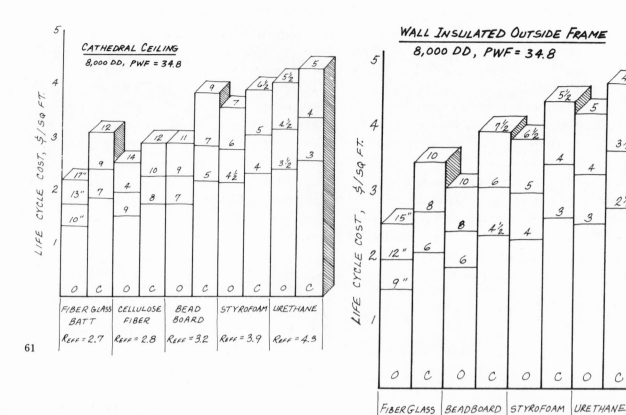

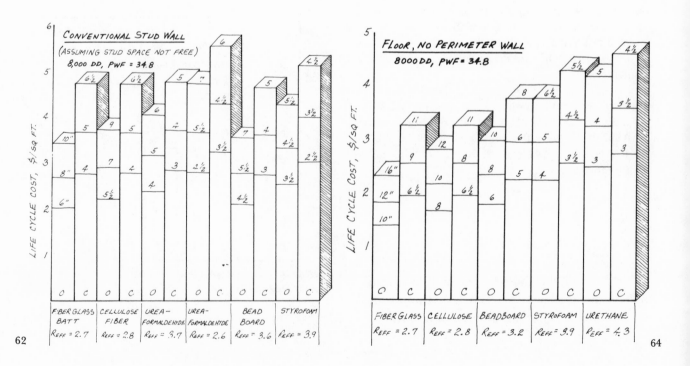

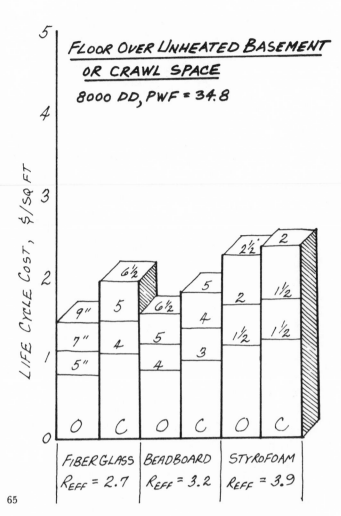

FLOOR OVER UNHEATED BASEMENT
OR CRAWL SPACE
8000 DD, PWF = 34.8

The numbers over each level are the optimum thickness in inches for which the life-cycle cost was computed.

I will summarize by making a few general observations:

(1) In every case except the conventional stud wall, the low-cost/low R fibrous insulating materials are more cost-effective than the high-cost foams.

(2) In the case of the conventional stud wall, the cost attributed to the loss of living space nearly balances the high cost of the foams, making it a toss-up among all of the materials considered. The one exception would be urea formaldehyde, assuming the low effective R associated with high shrinkage.

(3) The best of all possible worlds for readers in wooded rural areas appears to be a fiberglass-insulated, wood-heated, owner-built home; the worst of all a urethane-foam-insulated, all-electric, contracted home. For a modest 1,000-square-foot cathedral-ceilinged home in New England, the difference in life-cycle cost amounts to $3.00 per square foot, or $3,000 for the ceiling alone.

65

11.

Condensation and Vapor Barriers

Introduction

A large part of the condensation problem encountered in insulating buildings is simply the confusion surrounding the issue. In most people's minds water vapor, condensation, and heat are all linked together in one mysterious process as once were flies and horse manure. This is most unfortunate, not only because the matter is so essentially simple, but because the potential for damage to buildings is so large. If, at this point, your attention is flagging, put the book down. No other subject is as important to house construction or reconstruction; it deserves your utmost attention.

The Three States of Water

I hope I give no offense by referring you to Illustration 66. All natural substances occur in three states: solid, liquid, and gaseous. The solid state of water is *ice,* the liquid state *water,* and the gaseous state *water vapor.* You probably think you have seen water vapor, but you have not; no one has ever seen water vapor. What you

have seen is *condensed* water vapor in the form of tiny liquid water droplets. Of such stuff are made fog, clouds, and "steam." The reason we have never seen water vapor is the same reason we have never seen air. Water vapor is just a normal component of air, like oxygen, nitrogen, and carbon dioxide.

Air, Water Vapor, and Condensation

There is however one significant difference between water vapor and the other atmospheric gases: air will tolerate only so much water vapor. Beyond this maximum amount, excess water vapor will be forced out as condensed liquid. Illustration 67 shows how much water vapor air will hold. The left vertical scale is amount of water vapor per amount of air, both in pounds. The bottom horizontal scale is air temperature in degrees Fahrenheit. The saturation curve shows the amount of water vapor air will tolerate at any given temperature. The amount of water vapor in air is generally termed humidity. More impor-

SOLID   LIQUID   GASEOUS

66

tant for our purposes is *relative humidity,* defined as the actual amount of water vapor in the air compared to the amount possible at a given temperature. Point A in Illustration 67 represents air at 70° F and 50 percent relative humidity. The air represented by point A contains 50 percent as much water vapor as it could at 70° F.

If we were to cool the air and nothing else at point A, we would be simply moving it to the left. (We haven't added or removed any water vapor; we have only reduced its temperature.) As point A moves to the left, you can see that while the amount of water vapor remains constant, the relative humidity increases. Upon its reaching the saturation curve, something very significant happens. The region above the saturation curve is forbidden; it simply doesn't exist. In cooling the air further, the air necessarily follows the saturation curve down and toward the left, losing water vapor in the form of liquid condensation as it goes. The point at which saturation is first reached is called the dew point temperature.

The temperature versus humidity dependence is surprisingly strong. At 70° F and 50 percent relative humidity, the dew point is only 52° F. At 70° F and only 20 percent relative humidity the dew point is 28° F. This has great significance for those of us living in the northern half of the U.S. Below 20 percent relative humidity, we begin to experience nasal difficulty and put pots of water on the stove or fire up the humidifier. The average winter daily temperature in the northernmost regions is also below 28° F. The significance is that during the winter months, warm inside house air moving to the outside loses

some of its moisture by condensation on the way. If you live in an area having more than 6,000 degree days, your house has condensation. The question is what to do about it.

What's the Problem?

The problem is not condensation per se. The problem is dry rot. Dry rot is a nasty little fungus that makes its way through life by eating wood. Dry rot is a misnomer since the conditions for its activity are absence of light, wood to eat, moisture, and a temperature over 50° F. With these conditions in mind, let's examine the wall of your house. Illustration 68 shows the empty wall cavity of a typical old house. During the winter the temperature inside the house is around 70° F. Outside, the temperature is typically 20° F. Temperature falls as we traverse the wall cavity from inside to outside. (The rate at which it falls is proportional to the R factors of the various materials and air spaces, but that is of minor importance.) If the air at point A in Illustration 67 were to move from inside the house through the wall to the outside, its dew

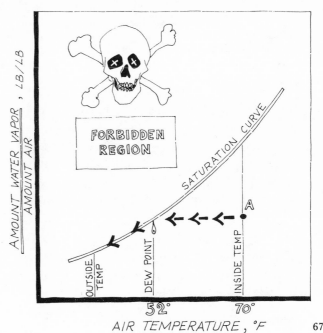

AIR TEMPERATURE, °F   67

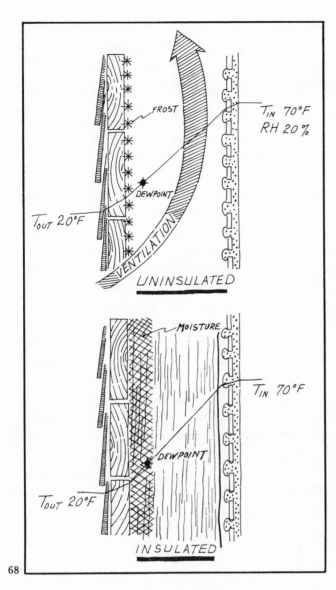

FROST

T_{IN} 70°F
RH 20%

DEWPOINT

T_{OUT} 20°F

VENTILATION

UNINSULATED

MOISTURE

T_{IN} 70°F

DEWPOINT

T_{OUT} 20°F

INSULATED

68

years old in apparently good condition? Again I refer you to the conditions necessary for dry rot. Dry rot is similar to most bacteria and fungi in requiring temperatures over 50°F for significant activity. You might eat hamburg which had been in the freezer for a month. But would you eat hamburg which had been on the kitchen counter for a month? The dry rot fungus is essentially in the freezer during the winter months. When summer arrives, with average daily temperatures in excess of 50°F, the frost has melted and evaporated—whisked away by the infiltrating air, which so readily finds its way into olds walls. In other words, the four conditions necessary for dry rot are never met simultaneously in the usual uninsulated wall.

But now comes the insulation man in his converted bread van with brochures promising annual fuel savings of 30, 50, and even 60 percent. Up go the ladders, whir go the drills, and into the previously empty wall cavities go various materials resembling either shaving cream or old mouse nests. What happens next winter? It is certainly easier and less expensive to maintain 70°F because we have inserted into the wall cavity a material resistant to heat flow. However, the presence of the insulation does little to stop the flow of water vapor through the walls. The dew point is still encountered inside the wall cavity. Instead of condensing on the sheathing boards, however, the water vapor is more likely to condense inside the insulation. While insulation doesn't act exactly like a sponge in pulling moisture out of the air, its finely spun or ground material presents enormous surface areas on which the vapor may condense. The insulation acts as a moisture storage medium within the walls and, more important, retards the air circulation necessary for drying. If enough wall-cavity moisture still remains by the time average daily wall-cavity temperatures reach 50°F, we have a problem; the hamburg is on the counter.

Is there any hope? Better than that—there's a solution. Refer back to Illustration 67. We have already seen that condensation occurs when warm air cools to its dew point temperature. Suppose

point would be encountered somewhere in the wall cavity. With an inside relative humidity higher than 50 percent, the dew point might even be achieved on the living-side surface of the wall, resulting in water running down the wall and perhaps even growth of mildew in a sunless room. More commonly, though, the relative humidity is between 20 and 30 percent and the condensation occurs on the inside of the outside sheathing boards. In the illustration, the condensation is shown as frost crystals, since water vapor at less than 32°F condenses as frost.

If this annual condensation is such a big deal, why do there exist houses a hundred or more instead that we start at 100 percent relative humidity, and raise the temperature. Start at any point on the saturation curve and increase the temperature (move horizontally to the right). Observe that the relative humidity drops. No matter how hard you try, you will never succeed in wringing water out of air as it warms up. The principle, then, is clear: *If we can guarantee that the air in a cavity originated from the outside rather than the inside, we will never have a condensation problem in that cavity.* Don't go any farther until you have assimilated this fact! Memorize it; write it inside your glasses; it shall be your guiding light.

How Does Water Vapor Get Where It Shouldn't Be?

There are three powerful forces at work continually forcing water vapor into house cavities: *diffusion, wind pressure,* and *stack effect.*

DIFFUSION

Gaseous diffusion has in the past been assigned all of the blame for winter condensation problems. Recent evidence indicates that it may actually play but a minor role compared to the other two forces, but it is always present as a significant force.

Join me in a little experiment I have cooked up. What pleases me most about this experiment is that it requires no equipment, no measurements, and above all no federal grants. All it requires is fantasy.

I have drilled a hole in the ceiling above a room. Look through the hole (Illustration 69A). Do you see all the people wearing white hats? Suddenly a small door opens and we see outside a great crowd of people wearing black hats. Except for the color of the tops of their hats, there appears to be no difference in the people.

Take a Break Time

Cover up the hole. We'll now take an hour-long break, during which time we shall lie back, have a glass of wine and a little cheese, and fantasize about what we will see when we next look through the hole.

Back to Work

Did you guess that what you'd see was Illustration 69B? Some black-hatted people have entered the room. The reason? Simply, why not?

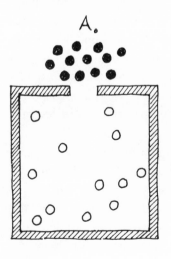

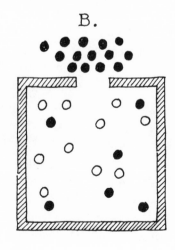

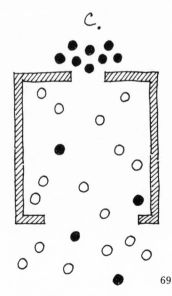

69

What's this? Suddenly a second door, five times larger than the first, opens at the other end of the room, and we see a great crowd of white-hatted people milling about outside. Quick! Cover up the hole and take another break.

Take a Break

What do you suppose we'll see if we look again in an hour? My guess is Illustration 69C. (I've performed this experiment many times before.) Some of the black hats wander out the larger door and are replaced by white hats wandering in.

I'm sure you have guessed by now that the black hats were water vapor molecules, the white hats ordinary air molecules, and the room a wall cavity. The point I'm illustrating is that we can almost guarantee a low concentration of water vapor in a wall cavity if the holes in the outer wall are much larger than the holes in the inner wall.

The process we have just observed is called diffusion. There is nothing mysterious about it; it is the most logical thing in the world. The tendency for water vapor molecules to move by random motion from a region of higher to a region of lower concentration has led to the concept of "vapor pressure." Although it is technically correct, I find that the use of this term misleads the average person into picturing water vapor squirting through holes in the wall. Water vapor molecules do not squirt: they drift—slowly, subtly, and unconsciously into less populated spaces.

WIND PRESSURE (Illustration 70)

Anyone who ever sat on the north side of an old farmhouse on a cold winter night with the wind howling from the north knows that wind blows through houses. The best that can often be said for an old farmhouse is that it cuts the wind speed somewhat. I used to live in such a house. The thermometer in the northeast corner of the

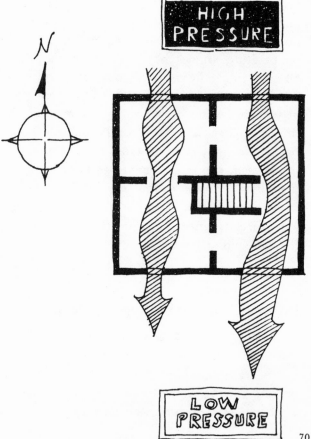

70

living room often read 50° F while the thermostat in the adjacent central hall read 70° F.

All houses leak air. The leakage is called infiltration. Heating the outside air as it continually enters and then leaves the living space accounts for a significant portion of your annual fuel bill. (See Chapter 9.) When the wind blows, a higher-than-normal air pressure is created against the windward wall. At the same time a lower-than-normal air pressure (vacuum) exists at the leeward wall. A very "tight" house may resist this pressure to the extent of exchanging its total air volume only once in several hours. A loose house may give up its air every ten minutes. But regardless of the degree of tightness, the fact remains that the air steadily moves from windward to leeward. This general drift of air can easily overwhelm the more subtle diffusion process discussed above.

71

Illustration 71 is a wind rose map of the United States for January showing the percentage of time the wind blows from the eight points of the compass. In most areas of the U.S., winter wind has a prevailing direction. In New England, where I live, the winter wind blows from the north, northwest, or northeast a full 75 percent of the time. This being the case, I know that air is generally moving from outside to inside through my north wall and from inside to outside through my south wall. I hate to make general statements for fear that people will use them as absolutes, but it does appear that in this case dry rot would be found more often in the south wall than the north. Discussions with local carpenters who work on old buildings tend to verify this fact.

THE STACK EFFECT (HOT AIR RISES)

The earliest balloons used not helium but hot air. A fire was built beneath the balloon, filling the bag with hot air; and up, up, and away! If it were not for the enormous weight of the average house we would also have to moor our houses, as in Illustration 72, during the winter. I have calculated the buoyant lifting force against the upstairs ceiling of a two-story, 25'×40' house with an inside-to-outside temperature difference of 80F°. It amounts to a remarkable 600 pounds, or 0.6 pound for every square foot of ceiling! Warm inside air struggles to escape upward through the ceiling. It also leaves via leaky upstairs windows, through recessed lighting, and around faulty chimney and vent pipe flashings. Any air that does succeed in escaping upward is replaced by air flowing in at the bottom, through doors, win-

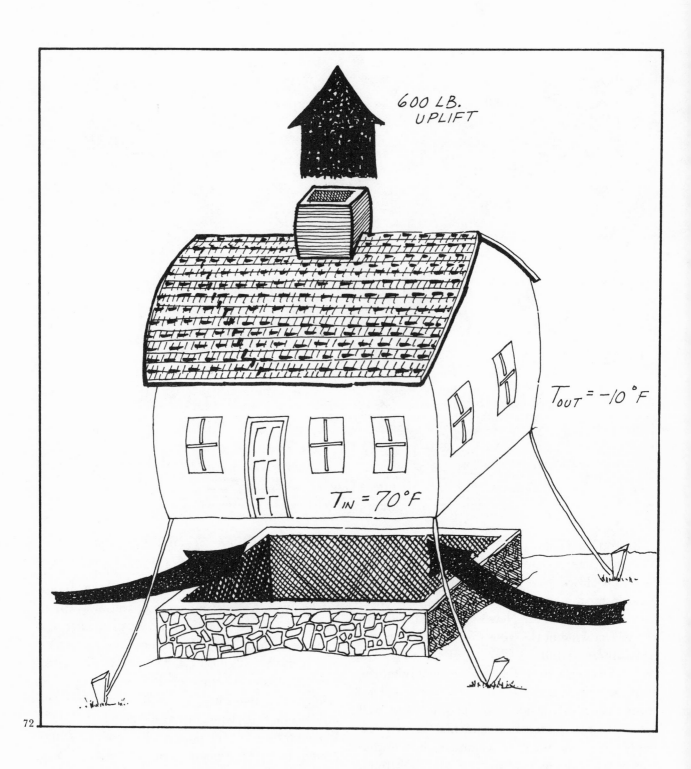

600 LB.
UPLIFT

$T_{OUT} = -10\,°F$

$T_{IN} = 70°F$

72

dows, electrical outlets, and foundation defects (usually the joint between the wood sill and the masonry foundation). Like wind pressure, the stack effect can easily overcome diffusion.

Water vapor is thus transported by all three of the above forces—the relative magnitudes of which vary with season, location, and construc- tion detail. Some of the forces act together, making serious condensation more likely; some work in opposite directions, making condensation less likely. For example, in the south wall diffu- sion and wind may push outward while the stack effect is sucking in. In the north wall, wind and stack effect unite against diffusion. In the attic all three forces work together, making the attic a prime candidate for condensation.

What Excess Moisture?

Telling a homeowner with dried-up nasal passages that his home has excess moisture is a bit like telling a beggar he has excess money. Houses in the northern United States, without benefit of humidifiers, generally run at between 20 percent and 30 percent relative humidity. In spite of the fact that the inside winter air dries and wrinkles our skin until it resembles a camel's knees, the air inside the house actually contains more water than the air outside. If air simply moved into a house and then out again, condensation would never occur, because no moisture had been added. In Illustration 67 point A representing the air would simply move from left to right and then back again to the starting point. Extra moisture in the air comes from a number of sources, as shown by Illustration 73. Obviously the fellow in the shower is adding tremendous quantities of water vapor to the air; he can hardly see the opposite wall through his own personal cloud of condensate. The spaghetti pot in the kitchen is boiling along without a lid and, if left unattended, will probably burn, having discharged its entire load of water into the air. The house plants strangely seem to require watering every day. Upstairs the laundry is drying as if it were hanging outdoors on a summer day. In fact, it has been estimated that the various activities of the average American family of 3-1/2 persons and a dog release 25 pounds of water into the house air each winter day. This figure does not include the use of a humidifier (around 10 pounds per day), venting a clothes dryer inside, or drying a cord of green wood by the stove (1,000 to 2,000 pounds of water total). It also ignores the sometimes tremendous evaporation of water from a damp basement.

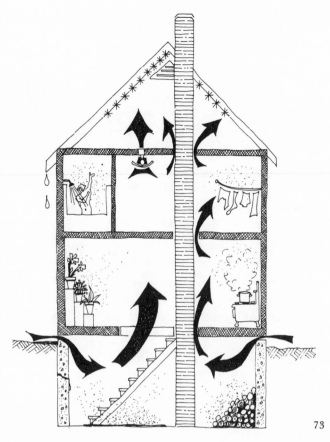

73

Woe Is Us– What Can Be Done?

There are three general sorts of things which we can do to reduce the condensation problem:
- produce less water vapor
- tighten the inside surfaces
- loosen (ventilate) the outside surfaces.

PRODUCE LESS WATER VAPOR

As shown in Illustration 73, there are a number of separate water vapor sources in the average house, which considered alone may seem insignificant but when taken in the aggregate amount to a very large amount of water. Addition of a humidifier or a wet basement may more than double the average figure. Reduction of most of the sources means simply using your head: cook with pot lids; dry laundry outside; open the bathroom windows a crack after bathing; reduce the amount of lush foliage in your horticultural inventory; and dry your firewood outdoors during the previous summer. Other reductions may require a little more effort. If you have a damp basement (bedrock, clay, or standing water is worst), your highest priority should be elimination of this source.

Unfortunately, the colder the outside and the greater the infiltration, the lower the inside relative humidity drops. A "tight" house retains its air longer. Thus, a given amount of added water vapor increases the relative humidity in a tight house more than in a drafty house. It is interesting to note a correlation between heat source and relative humidity. It has long been observed that houses heated with wood are generally dry and houses heated electrically are humid. The intuitive conclusion is that the heat of the wood flame dries the air more than the relatively cool electric heating element does. Strangely, this is not the reason. The truth of the matter is that only people with tight houses can afford electric heat. Folks with houses exchanging air every 10 minutes are more likely to heat with wood for economic reasons. If the house air is being replaced every 10 minutes it doesn't have a chance to increase its relative humidity!

Which brings us to the point of humidifiers and camels' knees. Humidifiers are required when the house air contains too little moisture. Since normal family activities already pump significant moisture into the air (25 pounds or 3 gallons of water per day), we well may ask where it's all going. The fact is, except in extreme cases, *use of a home humidifier is more a symptom than a cure.* It is a symptom of excessive air infiltration and excessive inside temperature. The cure is in reducing infiltration through a general tightening of the house and lowering the thermostat. Purposely adding moisture to the air moving through the walls is asking for trouble.

One of the most productive party conversations I ever had was with an eye, ear, nose, and throat specialist. Get this! Have you noticed that you get a runny nose when you go out on a cold day? Well, it turns out that the nose is nature's humidifier, adding water vapor to the air rushing into the lungs. If moisture were not added, the delicate throat and lung tissue would dry out and be damaged. Several years ago this doctor stopped recommending humidifiers to patients with winter respiratory problems and recommended instead sleeping under comforters in 50° F bedrooms (thus stimulating nature's air conditioner). His cure rate? — Over 90 percent.

TIGHTEN THE INSIDE SURFACE

There are two very strong reasons for tightening the inside surfaces of the house. The first is to guarantee that the air inside the wall, attic, or floor cavity originated primarily from the outside rather than the inside, thereby guaranteeing no condensation in the cavity. The second is the reduction of infiltration, thereby reducing the annual fuel bill. A membrane installed close to the warm side of the wall, ceiling, or floor with the purpose of preventing passage of water vapor is commonly called a "vapor barrier." We have seen that there are several mechanisms for the movement of water vapor, including wind pressure. Call it what you may — vapor barrier or wind barrier — installation of an unbroken membrane of low vapor permeability surrounding the living space is the best possible way to protect your house from damage while at the same time making it more comfortable.

Table 25 is a list of common building materials and their permeabilities. What we are searching for is: (1) an easily installed material of low permeability to form the warm side barrier and (2) materials of high permeability but long life for the exterior surface. As one runs down the list, it is obvious that those materials usually known as "vapor barriers" are indeed the best at their job. To my mind polyethylene is superior to aluminum foil in practice simply because it can be installed in room-sized sheets literally enclosing the room in a gigantic "Baggie." If you are installing aluminum foil (typically as 36″ wide

Table 25. Permeance of Building Material

type	material	permeance
Vapor barriers	1 mil aluminum foil	0.00
	6 mil polyethylene	0.06
Paint and wallpaper	2 coats aluminum paint	0.5
	1 coat of Glidden "Insulaid" latex vapor barrier paint	0.6
	vinyl wallpaper	1
	3 coats oil paint on wood	1
	2 coats oil paint on plaster	2
	3 coats latex paint on wood	10
	ordinary wallpaper	20
Foam insulations	1″ urethane	1
	1″ Styrofoam	1
	1″ bead-board	4
	4″ urea formaldehyde	9
Fibrous insulations	4″ mineral wool	30
	4″ cellulose	30
	4″ fiberglass	30
Masonry	4″ brick	1
	8″ concrete block	2
Papers	builders' foil	0.2
	15 lb. tar paper	18
	builders' sheathing paper	40
Other	1/2″ CDX plywood	0.5
	3/4″ board	3
	plaster	20
	gypsum drywall	50
	1/2″ insulating board	50

builders' foil or foil backing on fiberglass insulation), it is imperative that the overlapping edges be compressed between the framing and finish material as in a vise. It also appears that some current building practices are questionable. For example, it's pretty hard to beat 1/2″ CDX plywood as a vapor barrier, yet its use as exterior sheathing is a common practice. Even more dangerous is the installation of unperforated aluminum foil beneath vinyl or aluminum siding. And carefully installing a polyethylene vapor barrier and then subsequently cutting fifty 2″×4″ electrical receptacle holes in it is somewhat akin to buying a fiberglass boat and cutting holes in it.

Below, in order of decreasing effectiveness, are specific steps which may be taken to tighten the inside defense.

(1) When you are building an addition or gutting an existing building, a unique opportunity exists to install an unbroken barrier just beneath the wall finish material. Don't worry about staple or nail holes as long as they remain completely filled with the nail. Driving a nail into a boat doesn't make the boat leak; pulling it out does. Of course only an octopus could install a single polyethylene sheet covering both the walls and ceiling. The solution is lapping wall- and ceiling-sized pieces so that the overlapping joint is pressed tightly between the stud and drywall, or between ceiling joist and drywall. Rips in the membrane should be repaired with duct tape before covering.

Pounding nails through a new boat hull is one thing, but what would you do if some turkey cut fifty to seventy-five 2″×4″ holes in your brand-new boat? Electricians do this every time they wire a new house! Does this result in air infiltration? Try holding a match to a wall receptacle sometime. It has been estimated that the infiltration effect of the fifty to seventy-five electrical holes in the average house is equivalent to leaving an ordinary double-hung window open all winter!

The most effective solution to this problem is never penetrating the vapor barrier. This can be achieved by surface wiring with "wire mold" or equivalent wiring material. It can be made surprisingly inoffensive by installation as part of the baseboard and painting the same color.

An alternative solution is installation of the vapor barrier between studs or joists and strapping (Illustration 74). The cable is attached to the strapping and the electrical boxes installed in the space between the vapor barrier and the surface material. This requires loose installation of the vapor barrier to accommodate the depth of the box and protection of the electrical cable as it passes over studs or joists by 16-gauge metal strips. (Check with your local electrical inspector for details.)

(2) An equally effective vapor barrier can be installed in an older house without removing the existing plaster and lath at all. If the existing walls and ceilings are in less than perfect condition, yet you don't relish the idea of carting nine tons of plaster to the dump for every one ton you eat,

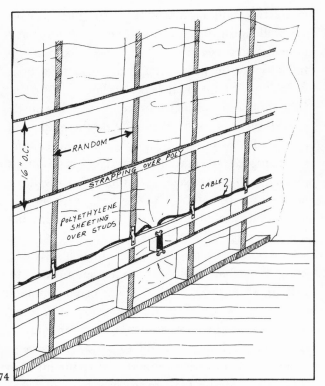

74

consider this alternative. Professional renovators sometimes simply staple polyethylene over the existing walls and ceilings and then apply 3/8″ drywall, using long drywall screws. Neat, clean, and cheap! The approximate cost: about 40 cents per square foot, including material, taping, and sanding. All that remains is painting or wallpapering the "new" house. What about the door and window trim? No problem! Trim usually measures 3/4″ in thickness. If the drywall is carefully installed, the trim will simply project 3/8″, and it looks surprisingly good. Caulk heavily around the window trim just before the drywall goes on, and you'll have eliminated a major source of infiltration.

Next we must deal with the electrical outlets and switches. If your wiring is inadequate, this is the time to upgrade. Holes knocked in the wall in order to fish wires won't require patching, so bash away! If the wiring is adequate, we need simply to bring the receptacles and switches forward 3/8″ to be flush with the wall again. First remove the cover plates; shim the receptacle forward 3/8″, using either a stack of washers or little predrilled pieces of 3/8″ plywood; install the

polyethylene sheet right over the receptacle or switch; after the wallboard is in place, sanded, and painted, install the cover plate. Only then carefully cut the polyethylene away from the face of the receptacle or switch handle.

(3) Vinyl wallpaper, properly installed, can be an effective vapor barrier. "Properly installed" means observing the same rules as with polyethylene. Carefully caulk around window and door trim before wallpapering. Remove electrical cover plates and apply the wallpaper right over the receptacles and switches, again carefully cutting away only what is necessary after replacing the cover plates. As an option, instead of papering over the receptacle, install sponge rubber gaskets, now available in most hardware stores, between the receptacle or switch and the cover plate (Illustration 75).

(4) If the wall and ceiling are in excellent condition, the least disruptive operation may be simply painting. Caulk around windows, doors, outlets and baseboard trim and then paint with two coats of a specially formulated latex vapor barrier primer paint such as Glidden's "Insul-Aid." Check the Yellow Pages for dealers. Again, gasket the electrical cover plate as in Illustration 75. You may be tempted to blow foam (available in aerosol cans) into electrical boxes in an attempt to stop infiltration. Don't do it! The primary purpose of the box is the prevention of electrical

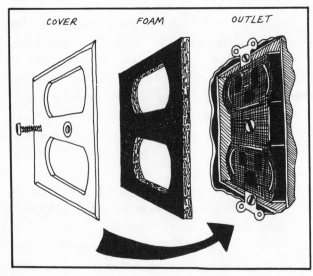

75

fires by isolating electrical short circuits from combustible materials. Therefore, use of a combustible plastic foam within the box is very dangerous!

In general, when thinking about infiltration, I find it very helpful to visualize the house as a boat. You are caulking your ark in anticipation of the flood waters. Will the house float? Using your imagination well, you can easily picture the water spurting from every receptacle, light fixture, and baseboard. Don't spare the caulk!

LOOSENING THE OUTSIDE

To "loosen the outside" means simply to make it easier for air to enter the wall cavity from the outside. The ideal exterior surface breathes water vapor while shedding water and stopping wind exactly like duck feathers. With this analogy, it is obvious that either cedar shingles or clapboards applied over 15 lb. sheathing paper or rosin paper and boards are excellent. The more modern practice of sheathing first with plywood may be better at stopping infiltration, but it is worse for condensation. The several layers of waterproof glue in the plywood form an excellent vapor barrier (see Table 25) on the wrong side of the insulation. Unless much care is taken in the installation of the interior vapor barrier, the structure may suffer premature damage.

Below are a number of points to consider regarding the exterior surface.

(1) If the house is old and has its original siding, the exterior surface is probably breathing well already. Tightening the inside defense will probably suffice to avoid damage.

(2) If your house suffers from peeling paint after repeated efforts to find a better paint or method of application, you've probably got an excess moisture problem. Because the wall has insufficient ventilation, the condensed moisture in the cavity has no choice but to force its way out under the paint, thereby building sufficient pressure to lift the paint physically from the surface. This is a serious situation, which, if left unattended, spells an early end to the structure.

If moisture is causing your paint to peel, ventilating plugs should be installed through the outside siding and sheathing. Two sorts of plugs are available. (a) Large screened or louvered plugs of 1″ to 4″ diameter are available at most lumberyards. Holes are drilled and the proper plug is inserted at the top and bottom of each stud space flush with the exterior surface. (b) Less obvious are 3/8″ diameter plastic plugs inserted at a steep angle at the bottom edge of clapboards or other lapped siding. These are normally invisible but, being so tiny, require a great number to achieve the same effect. Along the same idea are hollow ventilating nails, which are simply driven in rather than inserted in drilled holes.

(3) In order to blow insulation into existing walls from the outside, insulation contractors usually remove several strips of siding and drill 2″ holes in the sheathing boards for insertion of the hose. It is a common practice to plug the holes with cork or wood plugs before replacing the siding. From a ventilation standpoint it would be better either not to plug the hole (for foam) or to apply a small piece of screen over the hole (for loose fill). Tiny shims under the replaced siding would further increase the effectiveness of these vent holes.

(4) When they are installing aluminum and vinyl sidings, I have seen a few contractors first cover the existing siding with unperforated aluminum builders' foil. The foil dramatically reduces air infiltration in an old house, thereby reducing the heating bill, increasing comfort, and impressing the homeowner with its "insulating qualities." As you can now see, this practice is extremely dangerous. Actually, the *insulating* value of the siding is equivalent to about 1/2″ of the common wall cavity insulations. The same increase in comfort could be achieved by enclosing the entire house in a giant garbage bag! I have no technical quarrel with vinyl or aluminum siding properly applied, but the use of unperforated foil building paper and the application of such siding as "cure" for peeling paint is improper, deceptive, and dangerous.

(5) Since we are trying to stop infiltration of

cold air as well as migration of water vapor, tightening the inside is of higher priority than loosening the outside. In fact, the outside wall should only be purposely ventilated in case of peeling paint or other evidence of a severe condensation problem.

The Attic

The same condensation problem exists in roofs as in walls. The general solutions are the same as well: produce less water vapor, tighten the inside surface, loosen the outside. But since the roof geometry is different from that of the wall, the specific solutions often look different.

Because all three water vapor mechanisms work together in transporting water to the attic, the attic is a prime candidate for condensation. Of the three mechanisms, the most powerful is the stack effect. When a strong stack effect exists, most of the incoming replacement air originates in the cellar. Therefore, when a serious condensation problem exists, a damp cellar is the first place to look for excess water vapor production. It has been suggested that heating a wet cellar is a solution. Not so. Heating the cellar air will not only increase the uptake of water but also provide additional buoyancy, pushing the air into the attic faster than ever. The cellar may become dryer, but look for the missing water in the attic.

Tightening the inside surface involves the same procedures as in the case of the wall. In new construction a polyethylene vapor barrier is installed on the warm side of the insulation just before the dry wall. In old house work, the ceiling may be ripped down and replaced; a new layer of 3/8″ Sheetrock applied over a poly sheet and the old ceiling; or the ceiling simply painted with two coats of latex vapor barrier paint. The only electrical devices to deal with are lighting fixtures. It is a simple matter to tape poly or duct tape over the ceiling box, allowing only the fixture nipple to penetrate. If the ceiling is accessible from above,

installation of a vapor barrier is even simpler. Strips of polyethylene are fitted carefully over the ceiling and between the joists before placing the insulation in the joist space.

I stress the tightening of the ceiling less than of the wall because the attic is usually much easier to ventilate. With the exception of tile and cedar shingles, most roofing materials are excellent vapor barriers. Asphalt shingles, asphalt roll roofing, and asphalt built-up roofing are as tight as poly. However, as shown in Illustrations 76A to 76F, there is nearly always a way to ventilate a roof effectively.

The recommended ventilation of attics and roofs is stated as a ratio: Total Vent Area (inlet plus outlet) divided by Area of Ceiling. With no effective vapor barrier installed the ratio should be 1/150; with a vapor barrier 1/300. Inlet and outlet areas should be roughly equal.

As in ventilating excess heat from a house, merely having openings doesn't guarantee air motion. The inlets and outlets should be placed either: (a) low in the soffits and high in the ridge or peak (stack effect) or (b) at opposite ends of the attic (cross-ventilation). Soffit vents are either of the round plug or continuous strip variety. You can make your own by simply sawing a strip out of the soffit. However, screening with 1/4″ mesh hardware cloth is a wise precaution against varmints such as flying squirrels and birds in the attic. Gable end vents are louvered and come in triangular as well as rectangular frames. Rooftop vents are either mushroom vents, for use at discrete points, or continuous-ridge ventilators.

Although this chapter is about condensation, there is a second important reason for ventilating the roof. Without ventilation, attic temperatures can easily build up to 150° F during a clear summer day. This, of course, results in unnecessary heat gain through the ceiling. Heat build-up in the roof can be not only uncomfortable, but also destructive to the house. When insulation physically touches the underside of a roof, there is no way for heat to escape downward. The combination of a black roof and insulation that

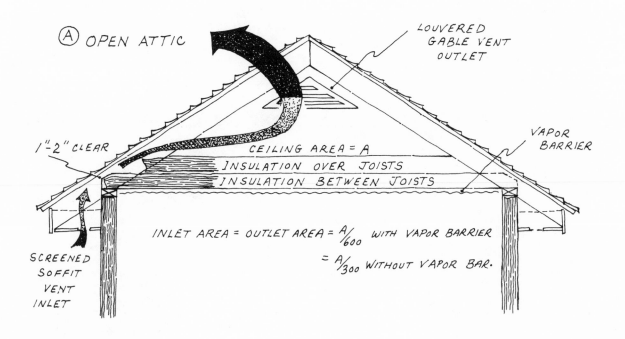

Ⓐ OPEN ATTIC

LOUVERED
GABLE VENT
OUTLET

VAPOR
BARRIER

1"-2" CLEAR

CEILING AREA = A
INSULATION OVER JOISTS
INSULATION BETWEEN JOISTS

INLET AREA = OUTLET AREA = $A/600$ WITH VAPOR BARRIER

= $A/300$ WITHOUT VAPOR BAR.

SCREENED
SOFFIT
VENT
INLET

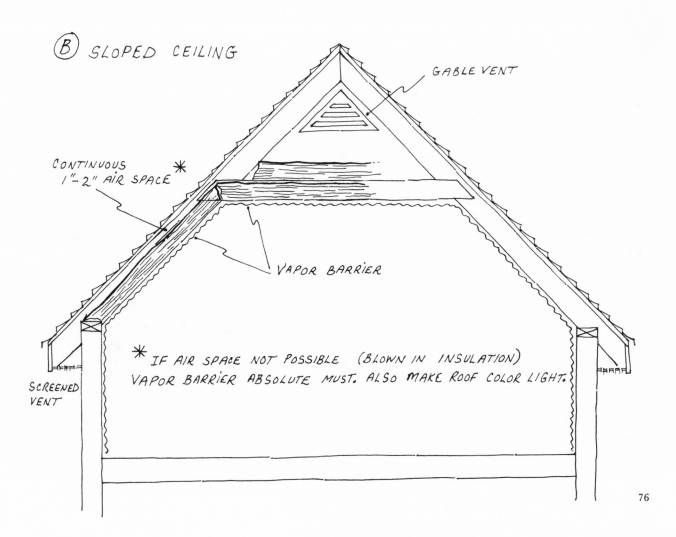

Ⓑ SLOPED CEILING

GABLE VENT

CONTINUOUS
1"-2" AIR SPACE ✳

VAPOR BARRIER

✳ IF AIR SPACE NOT POSSIBLE (BLOWN IN INSULATION)
VAPOR BARRIER ABSOLUTE MUST. ALSO MAKE ROOF COLOR LIGHT.

SCREENED
VENT

76

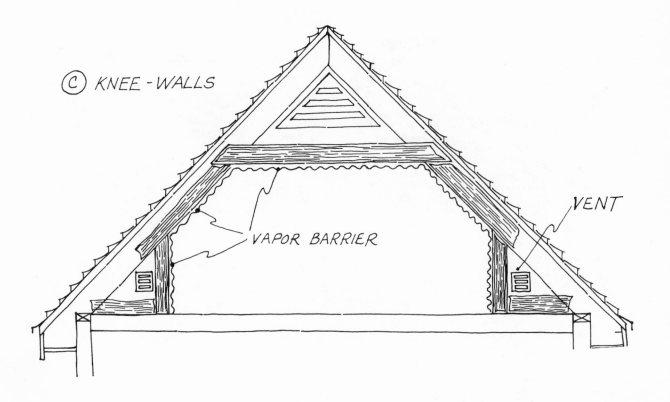

© KNEE-WALLS

VAPOR BARRIER

VENT

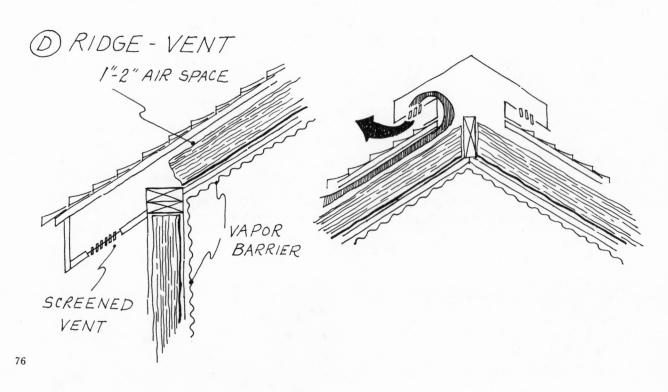

Ⓓ RIDGE-VENT

1"-2" AIR SPACE

VAPOR BARRIER

SCREENED VENT

76

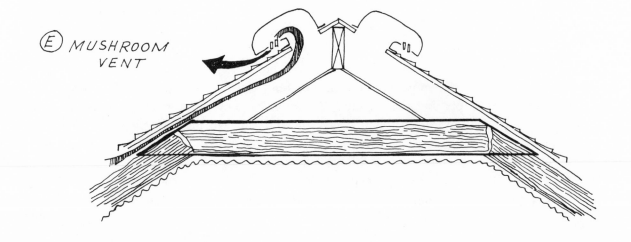

E MUSHROOM VENT

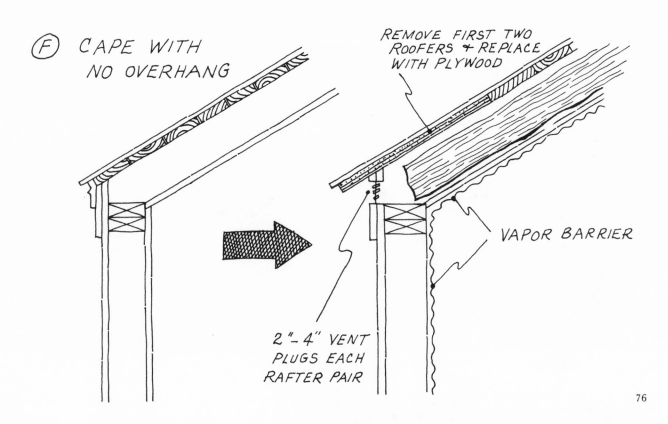

F CAPE WITH NO OVERHANG

REMOVE FIRST TWO ROOFERS + REPLACE WITH PLYWOOD

VAPOR BARRIER

2"- 4" VENT PLUGS EACH RAFTER PAIR

76

touches the underside of the roof boards can result in temperatures in excess of 200° F within the boards. Over a number of years all of the volatiles in the wood may be driven off by the heat, causing the board to resemble half-cooked charcoal. Roofing contractors find that in such a situation the roof often looks as if it had been in a fire. The wood is considerably weakened and requires replacement. When insulation is blown into the roof space, there is no way to keep the blown-in insulation from touching the underside of the roof and blocking the ventilation. I wouldn't use the blown-in insulation here but would remove the sloping portion of the ceiling and install fiberglass blanket 1 or 2 inches less thick than the rafter. If you do use blown-in insulation, at least change the color of the roof to white.

The Floor

The floor presents less of a problem than the other surfaces because the strong stack effect generally results in a net upward and inward motion. However, I have seen cases where flagrant violation of the vapor barrier principles has caused trouble. In one case the floor consisted merely of two layers of pine boards without even builders' paper between. As an afterthought, to hold unfaced fiberglass insulation up between the joists and to stop the winter winds from blowing through the cracks between the boards, a continuous polyethylene sheet was stapled beneath the joists. By April several gallons of water had accumulated in each joist space. The floor structure was acting as a giant still!

In new construction a 1/2" or 5/8" CDX or under layment plywood subfloor is an effective vapor barrier. If you are relying on the plywood as a vapor barrier, block the joints or caulk with nonhardening material. If insulating the floor of an existing house, either staple poly strips up between the joists or use foil-faced fiberglass blanket or batt with the foil up toward the warm side. Reverse flange insulation facilitates the installation provided the joist spacing is either 16" or 24" on-center. Many materials may be used to hold the insulation up against the force of gravity, but whatever you use, make sure it breathes better than the floor above. If you have a floor infiltration problem, solve it on the warm side of the insulation.

12.

Finally, How to Really Insulate

It's one thing to talk about insulation R factors; it's another thing to do it. Anyone who has ever attempted to insulate a house built prior to 1900 has experienced the supreme level of frustration. Aside from the blown-ins, commercial insulations, along with all other building materials, are presently made assuming the house to have been built on the 16″, 24″, 48″ module. If you ever come across an old house built along this logic, you can be sure it was mere accident. Sometimes I think old-time carpenters' rules must have had stud markings at 27″. Not only did they use irregular framing; they didn't stand in awe of the 90° angle. The house I presently live in was built not as a rectangle, but as a parallelogram with its sides parallel to street and side lot lines!

All of which is to say we're going to have to exercise a lot of ingenuity in getting our house properly insulated. The rest of this chapter consists of the best solutions of which I am aware for a myriad of situations.

There are 18 million totally uninsulated homes in this country. An equal number have only token amounts of insulation. These homes will be either insulated or abandoned. If you come up with a good solution in doing yours, please let me know, so that we can share your good work in the next edition.

Principles

As we have seen in previous chapters, there are certain principles that must be followed in insulating properly and successfully.

I. THE INSULATION MUST FILL THE SPACE EXACTLY.

II. IN AREAS HAVING MORE THAN 6,000 DEGREE DAYS, A VAPOR BARRIER MUST EXIST ON THE WARM SIDE OF ANY INSULATION THAT IS PERMEABLE.

III. VENTILATION SHOULD BE PROVIDED BETWEEN THE COLD SIDE OF THE INSULATION AND THE EXTERIOR SURFACE OF THE HOUSE.

IV. IF THE INSULATION IS OF A TYPE DAMAGED BY WATER, IT MUST BE PROTECTED AGAINST RUNNING WATER CAUSED BY DRIVING RAINS AND ICE DAMS.

Each of the below solutions obeys these four principles. Since the physical variations must

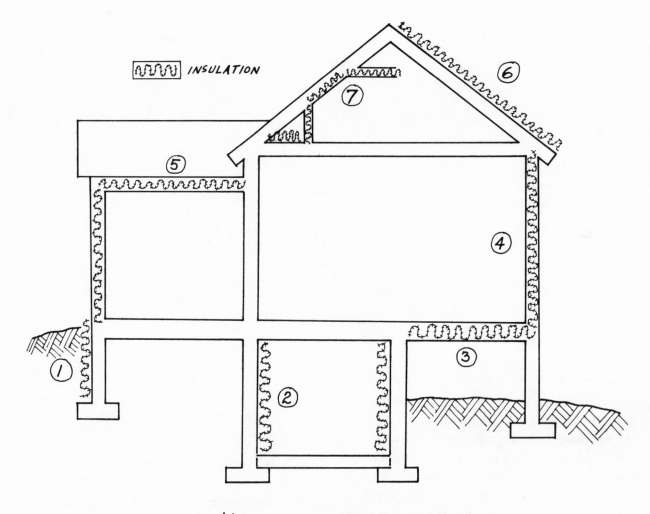

INSULATION

KEY: 1. OUTSIDE FOUNDATION WALLS
2. INSIDE BASEMENT WALLS
3. UNDER FLOORS
4. EXTERIOR WALLS
5. CEILINGS
6. CATHEDRAL CEILINGS
7. ATTIC KNEE WALLS AND SLOPES

77

number in the thousands, it is impossible to anticipate every situation. Use these solutions as a guide; judge your final product by the principles.

Illustration 77 shows the insulation areas that will be addressed. It also shows the order in which we will proceed, from the ground up.

I. Outside Foundation Walls (Illustration 78)

It is presently felt that the best place to insulate a foundation wall is actually outside the wall. The reasons are twofold: (1) By enclosing the

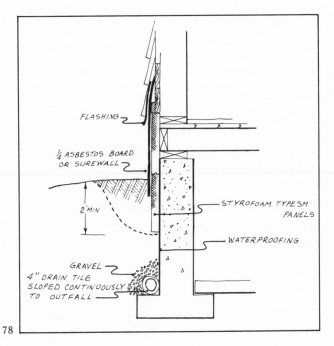

FLASHING

¼ ASBESTOS BOARD
OR SUREWALL

2' MIN

STYROFOAM TYPE SM
PANELS

WATERPROOFING

GRAVEL
4" DRAIN TILE
SLOPED CONTINUOUSLY
TO OUTFALL

78

top of the footing all around the foundation. Clean the concrete wall with a stiff brush and a garden hose; let the concrete dry; do your water-proofing; stick type SM Styrofoam or urethane panels to the wall, using liberal amounts of Dow #11 foam mastic or Goodrich PL200; backfill immediately to apply pressure and prevent damage to the foam panels.

The Styrofoam or urethane must be protected from sunlight and physical damage. Cover the exposed foam either with panels of 1/4″ asbestos board or CP-10 Vi-Cryl, a vinyl-acrylic latex from Childers Products Company. Finally, re-move the first few courses of siding, install aluminum flashing under the siding and over the foam, and replace the siding. The foam will be less noticeable if the bottom courses of siding are shimmed out, using a horizontal nailer.

II. Inside Basement Walls

Two basic distinctions may be made between basements: those that serve as living space and those that don't.

The best interior solution for basement walls containing a heated living space is simply to

concrete wall inside the insulation, we have in-corporated a huge thermal mass into the house. Thermal mass is the weight of a material times its specific heat and is a measure of the energy required either to raise or lower its temperature. By making the concrete a part of the furnish-ings, as it were, we guarantee that the temper-ature of the basement will be relatively immune to sudden or large temperature variations. Any-one who has suffered from frozen pipes can see the value. (2) It is nearly impossible to keep water out of the basement in a soil with a high water table. Basement walls also tend to sweat in the summer. This water is best seen and not hidden behind and within interior basement wall insulation.

The solution shown in Illustration 78 is partic-ularly appropriate where you presently have a wet basement. Wet basements are cured not from the inside by some "miracle paint" (it would be a miracle if they worked!), but from the outside by installation of a drain tile at the footing to lower the water table locally, or some form of im-permeable coating applied liberally to the wall, or both.

Since you now have two good reasons to do so, call the backhoe man ("Excavating Contractor" in the Yellow Pages). Have him excavate to the

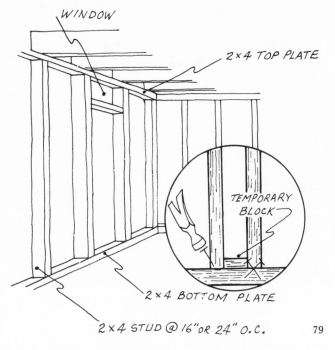

WINDOW

2 x 4 TOP PLATE

TEMPORARY BLOCK

2 x 4 BOTTOM PLATE

2 x 4 STUD @ 16″ OR 24″ O.C.   79

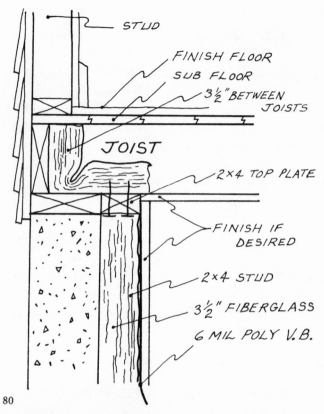

STUD

FINISH FLOOR

SUB FLOOR

3½" BETWEEN JOISTS

JOIST

2×4 TOP PLATE

FINISH IF DESIRED

2×4 STUD

3½" FIBERGLASS

6 MIL POLY V.B.

80

assume they don't exist and frame up a wood stud wall (Illustrations 79 and 80). Experienced carpenters will find it easy to lay out and assemble the wall on the floor and then raise it into place. The height of the wall is critical, as you will find the concrete floor and the joists above very unyielding. Make the wall just a tad shorter than your tape measure indicates. You can always shim the plates with shingles. If you're not experienced, install first the top and bottom plates

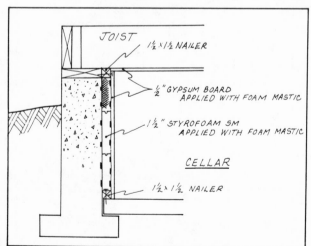

JOIST

½ × ½ NAILER

½" GYPSUM BOARD APPLIED WITH FOAM MASTIC

1½" STYROFOAM SM APPLIED WITH FOAM MASTIC

CELLAR

½ × ½ NAILER

81

and then nail the studs in place. The 14-1/2" or 22-1/2" long block shown in the inset will make it easier to toenail the studs, top and bottom, without playing croquet with your foot. Nail the bottom plate to the floor over a heavy bead of caulk, using a power-actuated stud driver, available at tool-rental stores. If the basement is damp, use pressure-treated wood for the bottom plate.

A polyethylene vapor barrier should be installed on the warm side of the wall from top to bottom plate. The space between the floor joists above the sill can be insulated with a fiberglass batt with facing or a solid piece of foam wedged tightly into place.

A second option that works well provided the basement wall is smooth, clean, and dry is to stick Styrofoam panels to the concrete and then 5/8" fire-rated gypsum drywall to the foam, as shown in Illustration 81. First install nailers, top and bottom, of the same thickness as the foam to be installed. Next apply Dow #11 foam mastic to the panels and press into place. Before proceeding with the drywall, wait a day to make sure the foam is very secure. If the mastic bond didn't "take," install vertical 1" × 6" strapping over the foam 24" on-center, nailing at the top and bottom nailers and at center points, using concrete nails. Next install sheets of gypsum drywall by either sticking them to the foam, using the foam mastic, or by screwing them to the strapping, using drywall screws. It doesn't hurt to use a vapor barrier between the drywall and the strapping if you're using screws.

If the cellar serves only as storage space or if you don't wish to make the large investment of turning the basement into living space, install just the insulation (Illustrations 82 and 83). It seems never to occur to people that insulation can be used alone; that studs are not a catalyst that brings out insulating qualities. In fact, as we've seen in Chapter 10, framing actually compromises insulating value. When there is little chance of physical damage, simply hang 24" wide fiberglass blanket from sill to floor, just like a gigantic down comforter. Staple the adjacent flanges together. Some publications have suggested that

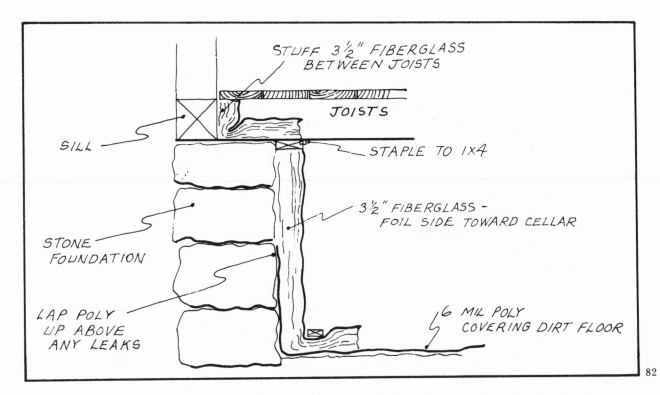

STUFF 3½" FIBERGLASS
BETWEEN JOISTS

JOISTS

SILL

STAPLE TO 1X4

STONE
FOUNDATION

3½" FIBERGLASS –
FOIL SIDE TOWARD CELLAR

LAP POLY
UP ABOVE
ANY LEAKS

6 MIL POLY
COVERING DIRT FLOOR

82

the fiberglass blankets need extend only two feet below ground level. This may prove false economy, as cold air generated between the blanket and wall will fall out at the bottom just as coins will fall out of your pocket when you stand on your head. Not only that, but the cost of fiber-glass blanket alone is so low that it always pays to go all the way. A board laid on the blanket at the bottom will seal the cold air pocket. The stapling of the flanges is also critical to prevent convection. Fold the flange on itself before stapling just as you would in wrapping meat for the freezer.

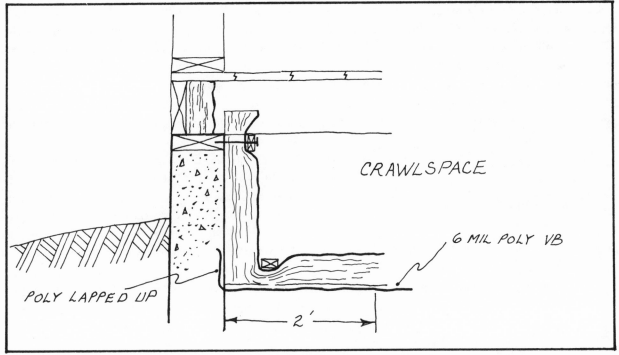

CRAWLSPACE

6 MIL POLY VB

POLY LAPPED UP

2'

83

Fiberglass blanket will recover from a few brief encounters with water, but a sustained encounter will destroy its insulation value. If your basement wall or floor is ever wet, lay a 6 mil polyethylene sheet over the floor and lap it up the sidewalls to above the highest point of water incursion.

Warning. There is a possible danger in insulating the basement walls. In the particular case of a full concrete basement in a poorly drained soil in an extreme northern area (more than 8,000 degree days), heating the basement has, in the past, prevented the ground adjacent to the foundation from freezing. (Have you ever wondered why the flowers bloom first next to your foundation?) If the poorly drained soil were to freeze to the local frost depth (4'-6'), it could conceivably push the foundation wall in. If this is your situation you have three choices: (1) Excavate around the foundation; install drain tiles sloped continuously to an outfall; backfill with gravel, sand, and finally clay; and grade away from the foundation. In other words, do what should have been done in the first place. (2) Since frost penetrates distance and not necessarily depth, we can fool the frost. Excavate about a foot, apply foam panels to the outside basement wall from sill to about one foot below grade; turn 90° and lay more foam panels horizontally to a distance of four feet out from the wall, making a giant foam "L"; backfill over the foam. To reach the foundation wall, the frost now has to travel a total distance of five feet. (3) Continue to heat the ground. Enjoy the flowers; they're the most expensive you'll ever get!

III. Under the First Floor

If you are inclined to treat the basement more as a root cellar than the local poolroom and Laundromat, why heat it at all? At a depth of eight feet, the ground temperature never varies more than a few degrees from the average annual temperature. Even where I live in Maine, that temperature is a little above freezing. With a floor at this temperature and the ceiling above at the living-space temperature, the temperature of the basement is likely to run close to the ground temperature.

In my area the ground temperature (ask a local well driller for the "ground" or "well-water temperature") is 44°F. The floor above the basement runs at about 60°F and is insulated with 3-1/2" of fiberglass. The above-ground exposure of the basement walls averages 12". Last winter my basement was the focus of considerable attention, since I had first thrown out the furnace and then entrusted several hundred pounds of Maine's finest potatoes to its keeping. All through December and the early part of January the temperature of the basement remained at a steady 45°F. Suddenly we had a record-setting seven days in which the daytime temperature never exceeded 10°F and the nighttime low hovered around –10°F. With mounting anxiety I recorded the basement temperatures. Each day the temperature crept lower—but at only 1F° per day! On the last cold day the basement set its own record, +39°F. The following week it retraced its steps, recovering to 44°F within several weeks.

The old-timers knew this; they knew a lot we have still to learn. Some one of these days I'm going to check into the library of a "backward" town and get myself a proper education. But I digress. The old-timers didn't even require a house; they built root cellars deep into the south slopes of hills, or placed vegetables in more shallow pits and covered them with insulating hay and leaves. But the one thing they never did in cold country was expose their basement walls more than a modest 12" or so. The modern practice of building on a slope and exposing eight feet of basement wall and a sliding glass door constitutes indecent exposure! That basement wall loses heat as rapidly as glass. In my area, a basement such as that would freeze without benefit of the heat loss from the furnace.

Since a properly designed basement, soundly constructed and sealed against infiltration, runs just slightly below the average annual temperature, the floor above is not losing heat to the

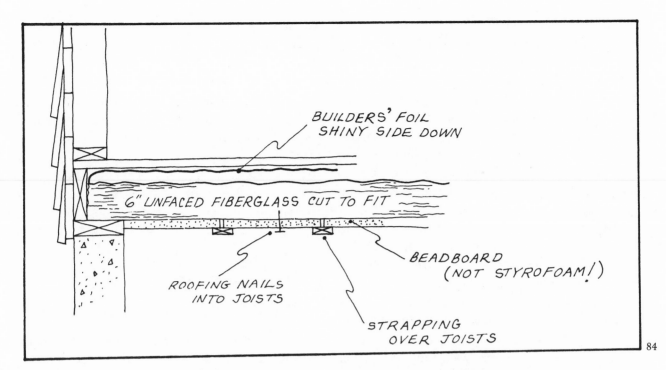

BUILDERS' FOIL
SHINY SIDE DOWN

6" UNFACED FIBERGLASS CUT TO FIT

ROOFING NAILS
INTO JOISTS

BEADBOARD
(NOT STYROFOAM!)

STRAPPING
OVER JOISTS

84

winter outside temperature but to the annual average temperature. Effectively the floor loses heat as if it were exposed to about one-half the normal number of degree days. If we are using degree days to calculate heat loss, the same result is obtained by doubling the actual R value of the floor. Since the actual R value of a normal uninsulated floor is about 5, it is assumed in calculations to be 10. Whenever we insulate the floor above a basement, we can apply the same rule. The optimum amounts of insulation above tight basements are therefore smaller than for roofs or floors exposed to outside air.

Illustrations 84 and 85 show two ways of deal-

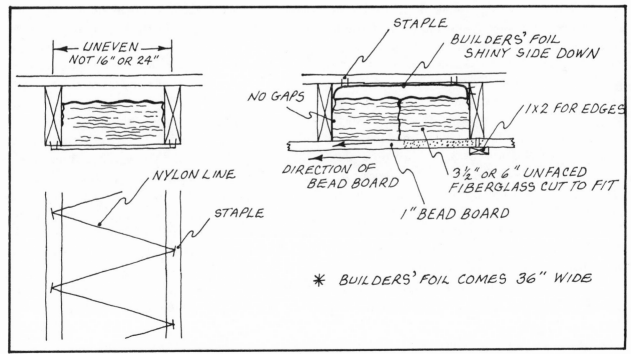

UNEVEN
NOT 16" OR 24"

STAPLE

BUILDERS' FOIL
SHINY SIDE DOWN

NO GAPS

1X2 FOR EDGES

NYLON LINE

STAPLE

DIRECTION OF
BEAD BOARD

1" BEAD BOARD

3½" OR 6" UNFACED
FIBERGLASS CUT TO FIT

✳ BUILDERS' FOIL COMES 36" WIDE

85

ing with the first floor. The choice of materials here is even smaller than in the attic. Gravity rules out loose-fill materials, leaving fiberglass blanket and batt and the rigid foams. Once again we are likely to encounter strange joist spacings. We are also sure to encounter cross-bridging, wiring, plumbing, and flooring nails! In fact, this is likely to prove as difficult a project as herding a pack of Cub Scouts through an art museum. So get some moral support, good lighting, a sturdy step stool, goggles, a dust mask, and a radio.

The first thing to notice is that the vapor barrier, if required, goes up, not down as your intuition indicates. If your joist spacing is 16″ or 24″ on-center, reverse-flange fiberglass batts will make the job easier. These have the vapor barrier up but the flange down, as if someone had your problem in mind. Simply staple the flanges to the underside of the joists as if they were wall studs. Remember when you encounter cross-bridging and plumbing, the first rule of insulating: THE INSULATION MUST FIT EXACTLY. If it does not, you've largely negated your efforts by inviting air leaks and convection currents. Break the insulation when an obstacle is encountered. Creatively snip the fiberglass along the same plane as the obstruction and slide the fiberglass over and under the obstruction like a glove; resume on the other side. Don't worry too much about the vapor barrier in insulating above a basement. A tight basement generally remains warm enough to prevent condensation in the insulation.

Uneven or weird joist spacing (the usual case) calls for a different strategy. This time staple builders' foil (aluminum foil bonded to kraft paper and available in rolls 36″×250′) up against the subfloor between the joists. This serves three purposes: it is a vapor barrier; it cuts down the infiltration between the floor boards; it adds R factor by creating a low-emissivity air space. Once again, don't worry excessively about the vapor barrier function. Holes made by the flooring nails are not significant. It is much more important to fasten the foil tightly against the boards.

Our only remaining problems are to fit the in-sulation exactly and overcome the force of gravity. Measure each joist space carefully; deduct the width of the full batts you are using; carefully cut the remaining width plus 1/2″ from a full batt, using a board to compress the batt and at the same time serve as a straightedge while you cut with a sharp knife. To hold the insulation in place, staple nylon line or fine wire in a zigzag pattern between the joists as you go, fitting the batts carefully, ever so carefully! Finally, remember that patience is a virtue.

IV. Floors Exposed to Outside Air

If the foundation of a building admits sufficient outside air, there will be little difference between the heat loss from the floor and the heat loss from the roof. In such a case the floor is simply a roof that never gets rained on. The statement that heat rises is true but not absolute. *Hot air* rises and thus carries heat with it. But in other ways, heat always travels from warmer to cooler, whether in the roof, wall, or floor. In insulating we must observe three significant differences between exposed and not-exposed floors. (1) Since the exposed floor is subject to the same sustained temperature differences as the roof, we do have to worry about condensation and vapor barriers. (2) With roughly the same temperature differences as the roof, the optimum amounts of insulation will be roughly the same—in other words, large. (3) Moving air can penetrate loose-fill insulation and steal heat by convection.

Illustrations 84 and 85 show how to insulate exposed floors. If the floorboards have large gaps through which cold air rises into the living space, now is the time to stuff the gaps from the underside of the subflooring with scrap fiberglass. You may find it easiest to cut strips from a roll of fiberglass "sill sealer," which measures only 1″ × 6″. Next, staple builders' foil tightly against the floor. This serves as a vapor barrier and further reduces infiltration. Next, install unfaced fiberglass batts the full depth of the joist space. While a dead air space above a smaller batt would theoretically provide insulation value, the probability of a true dead air space with a floor exposed to wind is very small. Last, to protect the underside of the fiberglass from the wind and critters of all manner, nail up sheets of 1″ beadboard, using long roofing nails and strapping. The beadboard is cheap, adds to the insulating value, protects the fiberglass, and breathes well enough to not constitute a vapor barrier in all but extreme cases. If next spring you observe the beadboard to have trapped moisture, vent it with a 1″ spade bit.

V. Exterior Walls

Exterior walls are unique in occupying space that otherwise might be used for living. Therefore, unless that space is already committed to an existing plaster wall in good condition, we should consider the value of the space in choosing our optimum insulation.

If the interior wall surface is presently in good condition, we naturally desire to insulate the wall cavity with minimal disruption. The obvious way to do this is by blowing in insulation from the outside. Considering the current unresolved status of urea formaldehyde shrinkage I feel that the usual choice will be cellulose. Protect yourself by insisting on

a reputable contractor (get references)
a class I or II fire-rated material treated with non-corrosive chemicals
an installed sidewall density of 3.5 lb./cu. ft. for a single story and 4.25 lb./cu. ft. for a two-story wall without blocking
a contract that guarantees free follow-up work if an infrared survey detects missed areas or settling within a year of installation.

If you are in an area with more than 6,000 degree days, the burden is on you either to maintain your house at a relative humidity less than 30 percent through the winter or to create an effective vapor barrier on the inside surface by

installing vinyl wallpaper, or
painting all inside surfaces with two coats of special latex vapor barrier paint
and caulking all wall breaks (trim and electrical fixtures).

If the wall surface is in less than perfect condition but you still don't relish the devastation of gutting the wall, an effective vapor barrier can be created as discussed in Chapter 11 by stapling clear 4 or 6 mil polyethylene over all surfaces, including the electrical outlets. Before installing the polyethylene, shim the electrical fixtures forward 3/8″. Finally, install 3/8″ drywall, using drywall screws. When you're done you have a vapor barrier, a brand new surface waiting for paint or wallpaper, and trim that simply projects 3/8″ instead of the usual 3/4″ (more elegant, to my mind!).

INSULATING BY GUTTING
(A BIT OF AN ASIDE)

What separates the true, hard-core retrofitter from the ordinary run of homeowner is *gutting*. The mere sound of the word strikes terror into the hearts of most gentlefolks. A term better suited to the activity will never be found. There are, believe it or not, people who get off on gutting; I confess to being one.

Gutters are all around you, generally unrecognized by society only because of a lack of outlet for their creativity. It is very important that gutting be done by those suited to it. There is nothing so demoralizing as having a fake on the job. The productivity of four good gutters can be easily halved by the mere presence of a faintheart or complainer.

How does one recognize a gutter? Aside from the obvious but rare case of the person who puts his fist through a door every time he's pissed off, I've found several indicators. Generally the gutter can be recognized by his or her slight build, expressive eyes, and unnaturally mild behavior. Large size, hairiness, offensive talk, and a swaggering walk are all bad signs.

I came to this discovery quite accidentally. One summer I was teaching housebuilding to a class of prospective owner-builders. At the same time, I was retrofitting my present house. I invited the class to the site for an afternoon of gutting. Six showed up: a lovely couple in their seventies, who disappeared into the basement with propane torch and hacksaw (they apparently got off on dismembering plumbing), a jocular trio of large, hairy, boisterous males in their twenties, who spent the afternoon alternating between drinking beer, telling off-color jokes, and throwing acoustic tiles at each other, and a rather meek-looking fellow in blue gabardine pants. The latter disappeared into the upper story carrying a wrecking bar, sledgehammer, six-pack of beer, and a radio. All afternoon the sound of an opera was punctuated by great "booms," shaking the house to its foundation and temporarily distracting the jocks from their locker-room banter. Toward the end of the afternoon an eerie silence settled. Fearing the worst, I climbed the stairs. There, standing knee-deep in a sea of plaster, wood lath, and acoustic tile, and caked with cobwebs and black soot, stood the happiest man I had ever seen.

Over the next few days, he singlehandedly proceeded to demolish the remaining spaces as well. After the rubbish had been trucked to the dump and the disorder turned to order by an industrial vacuum cleaner, he disappeared, never to be heard from again.

There are several reasons to gut. The obvious reason is walls and ceilings that need replacing. It is a great deal more disruptive and requires additional time to remove the existing walls and ceilings rather than simply adding another layer, but if you remove walls or decide to move them to other locations, it probably requires no more total time to get right down to the frame. The second reason is to work on the frame. Dry rot, shifting of the foundation, and racking are all structural problems that should be rectified before attempting any other building improvements. Money spent on cosmetics without first curing structural problems will be largely wasted.

AFTER GUTTING

After gutting there is but a small chance that you will find the wall studs to be either 16″ or 24″

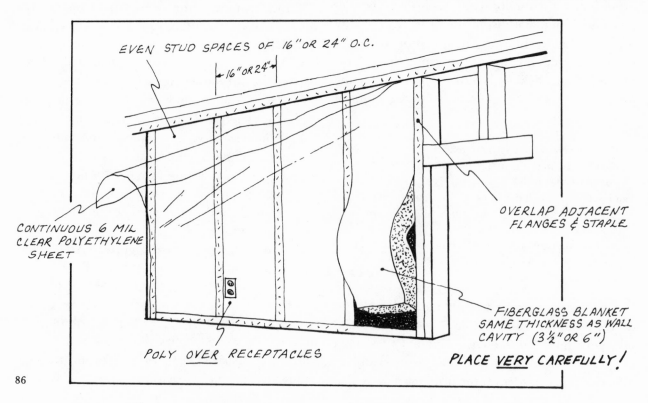

EVEN STUD SPACES OF 16″ OR 24″ O.C.

16″ OR 24″

CONTINUOUS 6 MIL CLEAR POLYETHYLENE SHEET

OVERLAP ADJACENT FLANGES & STAPLE

POLY OVER RECEPTACLES

FIBERGLASS BLANKET SAME THICKNESS AS WALL CAVITY (3½″ OR 6″)

PLACE VERY CAREFULLY!

86

on-center. If you do, insulating the old building will prove no more difficult than insulating a new one. First, decide upon the thickness of wall which is optimal for your climate and fuel. A thicker wall can be achieved simply by nailing strips of wood to the face of each stud. Then fit kraft or foil-faced fiberglass blanket or batt into the stud cavity and staple the flanges to the narrow face of the studs as in Illustration 86. Overlap the flanges so that they will be pressed between the stud and wallboard. Because polyethylene is so inexpensive and so effective, I strongly recommend that you next install a continuous 6 mil sheet over all insulated surfaces. If a break is necessary, make sure the pieces overlap over a stud or joist.

Wiring presents a difficult choice. Conventional wiring runs through the studs and breaks through the vapor barrier at each receptacle. If you choose this route, install the vapor barrier right over the receptacles as discussed above.

I feel so strongly about infiltration, however, that I am personally unwilling to break what also functions as a wind barrier. If you don't mind surface wiring, run "wire mold" conduit along the top of the baseboards and paint it the same color. If not, run horizontal strapping at 16″ or 24″ on-center around the room over the polyethylene. Staple the cable and cover with a 16-gauge piece of protective sheet metal at each stud crossing. Fasten the drywall or boards to the strapping and the electrical boxes to the drywall, using the special flanges developed for that purpose. Check with your local electrical inspector to verify his acceptance of this technique; it involves an interpretation of the code.

With a nonstandard stud spacing, the problem differs only in two respects: how best to fill the space with insulation, and how to apply drywall easily. If the stud space is less than 23″, I would cut unfaced fiberglass batts, using a board to compress the insulation and at the same time serve as a straightedge. For widths greater than 23″, consider slabs of beadboard, available in widths up to 48″. As shown in Illustration 87, use final full-width pieces to hold in the first layers,

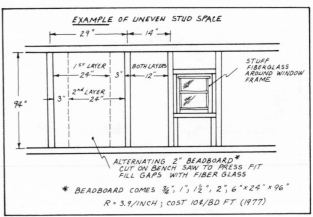

EXAMPLE OF UNEVEN STUD SPACE

STUFF FIBERGLASS AROUND WINDOW FRAME

ALTERNATING 2″ BEADBOARD* CUT ON BENCH SAW TO PRESS FIT FILL GAPS WITH FIBER GLASS

* BEADBOARD COMES ¾″, 1″, 1½″, 2″, 6″×24″×96″
R = 3.9/INCH ; COST 10¢/BD FT (1977)

87

consisting of scraps. Rip the foam on a table saw or radial saw and stuff irregularities or mistakes with fiberglass. You'll find that beadboard is somewhat compressible, so cut it about 1/4″ oversize and force it into place, using a board to distribute the blows of a hammer.

BARN AND COTTAGE WALLS

Suppose you have an older structure that never reached the finished wall stage. The boards and framing of such buildings are often quite attractive in a rustic sort of way. Not only would it be an aesthetic loss to install fiberglass and drywall, but an economic loss in terms of living space. In fact, a strict economic analysis shows it to be cheaper in terms of life-cycle cost to insulate on the outside of such buildings. Illustration 88 shows how to add 3-1/2″ of rigid foam to an unfinished cottage without in any way changing its inside appearance. Other thicknesses can be accommodated by simply changing the dimensions of the framing. R factors can be traded for dollars by substituting beadboard for Styrofoam. Check prior to the work with the local building inspector. He may insist on 5/8″ Sheetrock between the foam and the interior.

MASONRY HOUSES

A brick or stone house is always the most difficult to insulate. Usually, but not always, a 1″ to 2″ air space exists between two layers of brick,

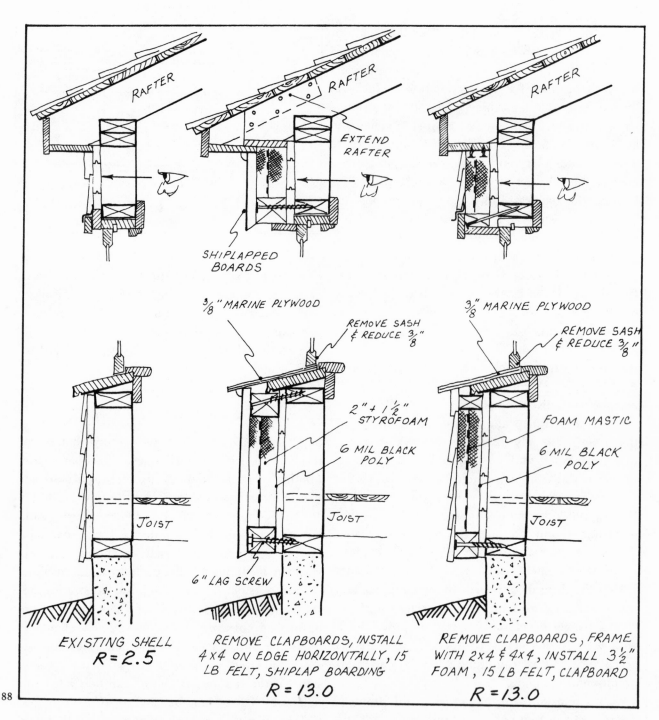

RAFTER

RAFTER

EXTEND
RAFTER

RAFTER

SHIPLAPPED
BOARDS

3/8" MARINE PLYWOOD

REMOVE SASH
& REDUCE 3/8"

3/8" MARINE PLYWOOD

REMOVE SASH
& REDUCE 3/8"

2" + 1 1/2"
STYROFOAM

FOAM MASTIC

6 MIL BLACK
POLY

6 MIL BLACK
POLY

JOIST

JOIST

JOIST

6" LAG SCREW

EXISTING SHELL
R = 2.5

REMOVE CLAPBOARDS, INSTALL
4 X 4 ON EDGE HORIZONTALLY, 15
LB FELT, SHIPLAP BOARDING
R = 13.0

REMOVE CLAPBOARDS, FRAME
WITH 2 X 4 & 4 X 4, INSTALL 3 1/2"
FOAM, 15 LB FELT, CLAPBOARD
R = 13.0

88

as shown in Illustration 89. This can be verified in the attic, through an interior or exterior electrical fixture or, as a last resort, by drilling through one of the exterior mortar joints with a masonry drill and probing.

Rigid Styrofoam panels or sprayed urethane could be applied to the outside of the building and then covered with wood siding or expanded metal lath and stucco. A commercial version of the foam and stucco combination is called Drivit. Although it is done, either operation is likely to change the appearance of a building in a way unacceptable to most brick house dwellers.

The second option is to remove selected bricks and spray in urea formaldehyde. This is a very expensive operation, which should be analyzed on the basis of life-cycle cost. It usually pays back but is far down the list of priorities. The effect of

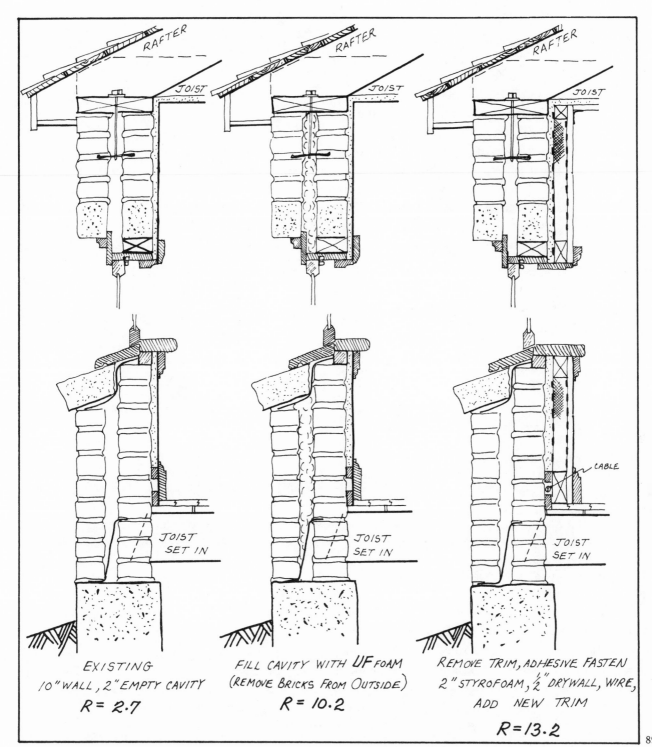

EXISTING
10" WALL, 2" EMPTY CAVITY
R = 2.7

FILL CAVITY WITH *UF* FOAM
(REMOVE BRICKS FROM OUTSIDE)
R = 10.2

REMOVE TRIM, ADHESIVE FASTEN
2" STYROFOAM, ½" DRYWALL, WIRE,
ADD NEW TRIM
R = 13.2

89

urea formaldehyde shrinkage is less serious here than in the frame wall because of the thinner cavity. If the wall cavity is open in the attic, the third solution is to pour loose-fill vermiculite down into the cavity. Cellulose should not be used, since wind-driven rainwater is a common occurrence in brick walls.

The fourth and most effective option is the application of foam to the interior. As shown in Illustration 89, the window, door, ceiling, and baseboard trims are all carefully removed and saved. Wood nailers of the same thickness as the foam are installed in place of the just-removed trim. Precisely cut Styrofoam or beadboard panels are fastened to the walls between the nailers, using Dow #11 foam mastic. Drywall is then applied over the foam, using mastic for the foam areas and drywall screws for the nailers. Use drywall with aluminum foil backing if available. Finally, replace the trim previously saved. New wood will have to be used at least around the windows.

The baseboard area offers ample opportunity for electrical wiring. As usual, show your electrical inspector a sketch of what you plan to do and agree upon the wiring materials and methods to be used. He may even have good suggestions. He's seen more wiring than anyone else around!

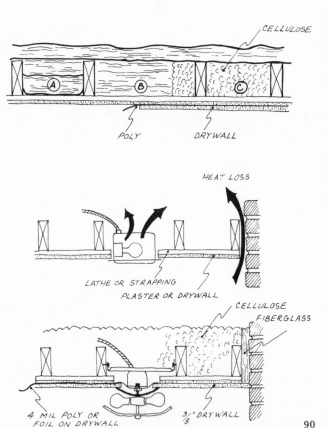

VI. Ceilings (Illustration 90)

Of all the areas of the house, the attic ceiling is the easiest to handle and the least expensive to insulate and offers the greatest return on your investment.

First determine whether you wish to do the work yourself. If not, call a cellulose contractor. Get in writing bids that include

laying down strips of polyethylene between the joists if a vapor barrier doesn't already exist
baffling the soffit vents if required
installation of the optimum thickness of cellulose
installation of gable vents if required
a statement of how many bags of cellulose will be used.

If you don't contract the job out, your first job is to measure the joist depth and spacing. If the joists are conventionally spaced, simply install a single unfaced blanket or combination of blankets equal to the joist depth over polyethylene strips. As always, place the blankets as if you were tucking the baby in for the night. Don't compress the batts; don't leave air gaps; place the blankets in such a way that they exactly fill the space at their stated thickness. Fill any gaps, such as at joist splices, with loose-fill fiberglass, cellulose, Zonolite (foam pellets), or vermiculite. Finally, unroll a top layer of unfaced fiberglass blanket at a right angle to the joists to bring the total thickness up to the optimum. Why not use foil or kraft-paper-faced blanket or batt? Because you want absolutely no air space between the ceiling material below and the bottom of the fiberglass and the joists and the sides of the batts. The convective heat loss upward through such channels can be great. The facing and flanges on faced fiberglass are stiff and make precise fitting nearly impossible.

If the joist spacing is nonstandard, again lay strips of polyethylene or builders' foil between the joists and place unfaced blanket or batt between the joists. If the batt is wider than the joist spacing, cut the batt 1/2" wider than the joist space, using a knife and board; if the batt is narrower, push it all the way to one side and carefully fill the gap with loose-fill material. Top off to the optimum depth, using unfaced blanket in the opposite direction.

I have no objection to your renting a blowing

machine and installing your own cellulose in the attic. My previous objection concerned the walls. I predict, however, that you'll be working for rather low hourly wages.

What if the attic is floored over? Three options exist:

(1) Rip up the boards and make furniture of them. Wide pine boards from the attic are particularly prized by cabinetmakers because of their color and dryness, so be extremely careful not to split them in removal. It's quite conceivable that the wide pine boards could pay for your insulation.

(2) Have cellulose blown under the boards. If so, remove at least a few boards, since ventilation is extremely important without an effective vapor barrier beneath.

(3) Lay a vapor barrier as a continuous poly sheet over the existing floor and lay or blow insulation in a continuous blanket over that. Make sure, however, that the edges are well sealed and insulated, as there will be a layer of warm air just beneath the floor searching for an exit. Imagine sleeping in a cold room with your only "blanket" a foam surfboard. Failure to seal the edges will make your floor-top insulation blanket about as effective!

Two obstructions commonly occurring in attics are the recessed ceiling fixture and the chimney. All light fixtures must be ventilated; a recessed light fixture must necessarily be vented into the attic. We thereby vent directly to the outdoors up to 100 watts of electric heat, which otherwise could be used to heat the house directly. To simply cover the fixture with insulation would result in overheating of the fixture and a possible fire. It is illegal to insulate within three inches of a recessed fixture. The best solution is removal of the recessed fixture as shown in Illustration 90. It is also illegal to place combustible material within 2″ of a masonry chimney. If we don't insulate the 2″ gap all around the chimney, however, we invite substantial convective losses. Regardless of the type of insulation used to cover the major part of the ceiling, insulate around the

chimney with unfaced fiberglass, stuffing fiberglass in the cracks between the drywall or plaster and the masonry. Openings around vent pipes should be similarly stuffed.

In an older house, you can often look down into interior wall cavities from the attic above. These uncapped wall cavities result in tremendous convective heat losses into the attic. Stuff fiberglass batt deeply into the exposed cavities to stop this convection.

VII. Cathedral Ceilings

Cathedral ceilings present the greatest challenge of all the surfaces of a house. All of the extremes seem to coalesce here into one giant insoluble mess. Hot air rises and the heat loss potential is therefore greatest of all upward; the sun shines from nearly overhead in the summer, and so summer heat gain is also maximized here. Limited space exists between the rafters and creating more costs money; the waterproof roofing surface is a vapor barrier on the wrong side.

If we resist the initial impulse to panic, however, the problem can be seen to be soluble. The key is to stand back and look at the cathedral ceiling as merely an attic with an extremely low headroom. Starting at the interior surface we need, in order: (1) a vapor barrier to prevent warm, moist inside air from reaching the dew point temperature, (2) insulation to retard heat loss and gain, (3) ventilation air to carry off whatever moisture does rise and cool the underside of the roofing, (4) a long-lasting waterproof exterior surface.

Requirement 3, ventilation, deserves elaboration. In the winter, without a perfect vapor barrier—or worse, with no vapor barrier at all—moisture originating as far away as the basement will travel upward by the stack effect and condense either against the roof boards or in the insulation. If it happens in the fibrous or loose-fill insulation, the R factor may be degraded, leading to increased heat loss. Ventilation air allows the condensed moisture to evaporate and dissipate before building up. A second common winter occurrence is the ice dam. Snow on the roof constitutes a very effective insulation. As a rule of thumb, 11″ of dry fresh snow is equivalent to 3-1/2″ of fiberglass insulation. Since with snow on the roof the roof surface is sandwiched between two layers of insulation, its temperature will be somewhere between the indoor and outdoor temperatures. Often this temperature is slightly above freezing, leading to a slow melting of the snow from beneath. The melted snow runs down the roof until it reaches an area of roof whose underside is exposed to outdoor air and which is therefore below freezing. There the water freezes and builds into an "ice dam" trapping liquid water in an upslope pond. We first become aware of the ice dam when the pond backs up beyond the overlap of the roofing material, cascading water down onto our ceilings, down the walls and window frames. A continuous flow of cold outside ventilating air under the roofing boards would keep the entire roof surface at the same temperature and therefore prevent the formation of ice dams. The third reason for the ventilating air space is the overheating of the roofing boards in the summer mentioned before.

Illustration 91 shows six effective variations on a cathedral roof for existing buildings. Illustration 91A is for a not-so-old house having conventional rafter spacing. Use foil-faced blanket or batt of thickness 1″ to 2″ less than the rafter depth and cover with a poly vapor barrier and drywall ceiling. The funny-looking apparatus at the peak of the roof is a ridge ventilator, a very easily installed and hardly noticeable fabricated strip of aluminum, which allows ventilation air to escape from the length of the roof. The air inlets at the bottom are soffit vents, either continuous or round plugs. Allow 1 square foot of inlet for every 600 square feet of roof area.

Illustration 91B shows a roof framed of hand-hewn beams and horizontal purlins. Since the purlins run horizontally, ventilation inside the roofing boards is impossible, so we simply strip off the roofing shingles, nail on 1″ or 1-1/2″ nailers every 24″ on-center, and board or plywood over to form a new roof surface. Use either fiberglass or foam to insulate between the purlins.

Illustration 91C shows deep rafters and no purlins. I have elected here to guarantee an air space by first installing 1″ to 2″ strips up against the roof boards. Rigid foam panels, easily cut on the table or radial saw, provide a high R factor. Use up scrap pieces sandwiched between full pieces top and bottom. Installation of the foam and drywall is made easy by the 16″ or 24″ on-center strapping.

In Illustration 91D I have achieved a greater insulating depth and solved the nonstandard rafter spacing problem at the same time by nailing up 2×3 or 2×4 studs, 24″ on-center at right angles to the rafters. Pre-drill the studs before nailing up for an easy job.

In Illustration 91E, the rafters, purlins, and roof boards are all so attractive that I have decided to pay a higher life-cycle cost and insulate outside the present roof. The customary way to do this has been to lay down the foam and nail the roofing all the way through the foam into the roofing boards, using ultralong roofing nails. With optimum levels of foam insulation now reaching over 3 inches this becomes ridiculous! Not only that, but on very cold days, moisture will condense on the tips of the nails and either drip on my head or stain the roof boards. Illustration 91F shows a better, although more expensive, solution. Toe nail 2″×6″ or 2″×8″ rafters into every purlin. If the new roof surface is to be plywood, place the new rafters 24″ or 48″ on-center. If tongue-and-groove roofers are used, save a lot of cutting by spacing the rafters the width of the foam panels apart, either 24″ or 48″. If a 48″ spacing is used, additional support for the roof boards or plywood can be gained from a strip of wood nailed lightly to the foam in the center of the span. It is best to remove the original roofing surface and install a black polyethylene vapor barrier before

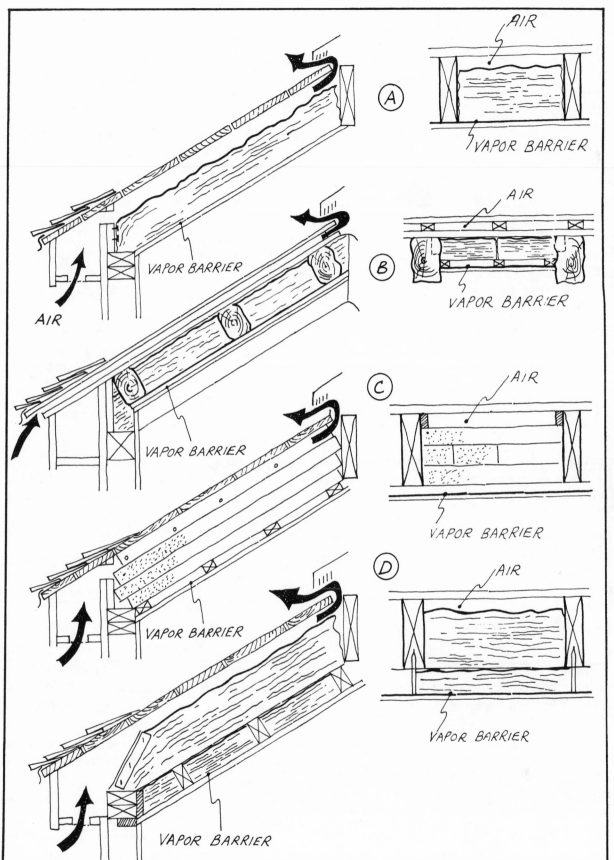

A

AIR

VAPOR BARRIER

B

AIR

VAPOR BARRIER

AIR

VAPOR BARRIER

AIR

VAPOR BARRIER

C

AIR

VAPOR BARRIER

D

AIR

VAPOR BARRIER

91

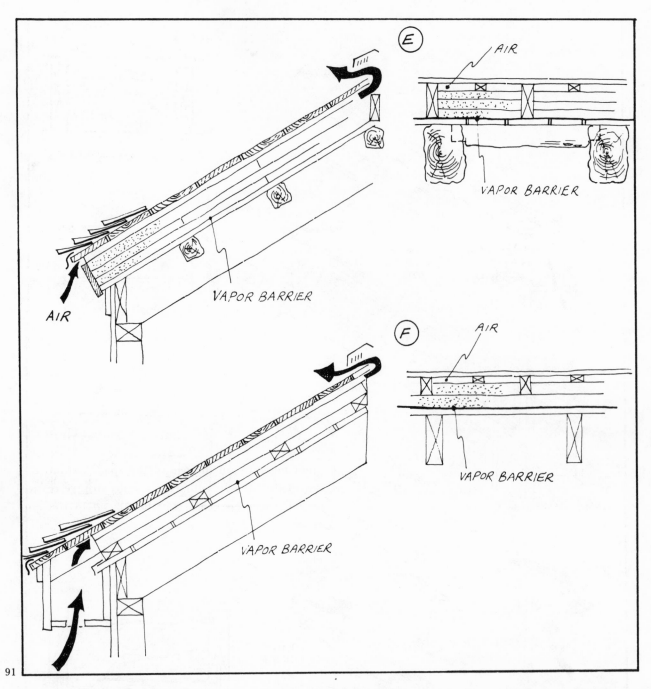

the new rafters. If the polyethylene will show from below, lay down brown kraft paper first.

Attic Knee Walls and Rafter Slopes (Illustration 92)

I dread questions about knee walls. When a questioner has knee walls on his mind, he has it on his face as well. The signs are familiar: furtive glances from side to side and a quivering lower lip. After I've just talked about proper ventilation of the roof, this person approaches, looking exactly like a child about to ask for a cookie after just having stolen six.

"I have this ceiling," says he. "The wife and I have just redone the room . . ."

Knee walls and rafter slopes are a problem because the presence of the knee wall almost guar-

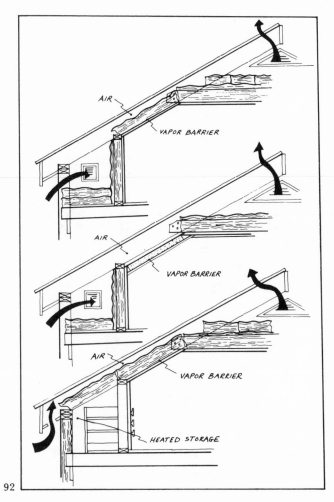

92

antees that the rafter slope has been finished in plaster or drywall. And the portion of roof unoccupied by that sloping ceiling is so damned small! Unfortunately, the principles of insulation have not changed for that small section of roof. I will not give you permission to insulate that slope without a ventilating air space.

There are two basic choices for insulating the slope. The easier, to my mind, is biting the bullet, tearing down the offending ceiling, insulating by any of the methods in Illustrations 91A through 91D, installing a vapor barrier, and finishing with drywall.

If you insist, glue Styrofoam panels to the (I hope) sound existing ceiling and then fasten 5/8″ Sheetrock to the foam, using Dow #11 mastic.

The other question addressed in Illustration 92 is the location of ventilation inlets and outlets. If the ceiling doesn't extend to the peak, the best ventilation is achieved with a louvered vent at each gable end. If the building has only one exposed end because of intersecting with a second building, either a ridge vent or a rooftop mushroom vent would be better. The location of the inlet depends on the use of the space behind the knee wall. If it is utilized for cold storage or not at all, louvered vents may be placed in the end walls. If the space is heated (the illustration shows built-in drawers), the rafters are insulated and the inlet is placed in the soffit.

13.

Windows, Doors, Shades, and Shutters

Introduction

Despite all the active solar hoopla put forth by the federal government and the solar industry, there remains today a basic solar fact of life: *there is no more efficient solar collector than the everyday south-facing window.* One doesn't have to think too long to discover why this fact is not generally promoted. There is simply no money to be made in the idea. You will learn in this chapter just how much solar heat is gained by your windows and simple things you can do to increase their performance.

Why Is the Ordinary Window Such an Efficient Collector?

Most solar enthusiasts have the impression that a solar collecting device must: (1) face due south, (2) be tilted at an angle from the horizontal equal to the latitude plus 15°, (3) be painted black. In fact, none of these is true. Aside from local weather anomalies, the amount of solar energy received varies with the orientation relative to

south as the cosine of the angle. At due south the angle is zero, the cosine of 0 is 1.00, and the received radiation is maximum. At 30° either east or west of south, the angle is 30°, the cosine of 30° is 0.87, and the received radiation is thus 87 percent of the maximum.

A similar relationship exists in the vertical, compounded by reflection from the ground. In order for a fixed collector to maximize the collection of radiation from the sky over the winter heating season, the collector should theoretically by inclined from the horizontal by the local latitude plus 15°. Allowing for a ground reflectance of only 20 percent, the collection over the range of latitude angle minus 15° to latitude plus 45° is within 10 percent of the maximum, however. In northern areas the ground may be covered with snow from roughly December 1 to April 1, increasing the ground reflectance to over 50 percent. Ground-reflected radiation is received more strongly on a south-facing vertical surface. In fact, at latitudes above 40° N, the total amount of radiation received by a south vertical surface during the major part of the heating season may be greater than the amount received by a collector at the "ideal" angle. We see, therefore, that the roof collector has no angular advantage over the ordinary south-facing window.

Now for efficiency. The cover glass for the collector is essentially the same as the glass in your window, transmitting about 86 percent of the direct normal incident radiation and 80 percent of the total day-long radiation. A low-iron glass transmitting an additional 5 percent may be used, but you could use this type in your window also. The difference between the collector and the window lies primarily in what happens to the radiation after it passes through the glass. The collector sits atop your roof, insulated from the living space, waiting to rise in temperature to roughly 120° F. At lower collector temperatures, the heat may not be worth collecting. The temperature has to be significantly higher than that of the living space in order for the house heating system to utilize it. Moreover, the temperature of the collector must be higher than the existing temperature of the storage system, or the heat in storage will be pumped backward to the outdoors. On partly cloudy days a lot of radiation is wasted periodically heating the collector as the sun darts behind the clouds. Thus, the collector fails to collect a significant percentage of the incident radiation. The ordinary window, however, collects all of the transmitted radiation. It just sits there, passively accepting whatever radiation is beamed at it.

Another way of looking at the difference is to compare the heat gains and heat losses of the two systems. During the day the two systems receive identical amounts of heat *gain.* Heat *loss,* as we learned in Chapter 3, is a function of the difference in temperature between the inside and the outside, $\Delta T = T_{in} - T_{out}$. The window has a typical daytime ΔT of 70° F – 30° F or 40F°. The collector has a ΔT of 120° F – 30° F or 90F°. The rate of conductive heat loss back to the atmosphere is thus seen to be at least twice as great in the collector. During the night hours the collector loss to the atmosphere is not important, since it is thermally disconnected from the house. The nighttime loss from the window continues and it

is thus a serious matter. We will learn in this chapter how to reduce the nighttime loss from the window and thus boost its solar efficiency. If we define the 24-hour solar collection efficiency as:

$$Efficiency = \left(\frac{heat\ gain - heat\ loss}{radiation\ falling\ on\ surface\ per\ 24\ hour} \right)$$

we get for Boston, Mass.:

solar collector:	40%
single-glazed window:	30%
double-glazed window:	50%
single-glazed window plus night shutter:	54%
double-glazed window plus night shutter:	63%

Table 26 lists the net heat gains and losses of both ordinary and shuttered windows facing eight points of the compass in six different cities. The numbers refer to equivalent gallons of oil per square foot of window per heating season either gained or lost by the window.

The average window has an area of about 10 square feet, so we can interpret Table 26 as heat gained or lost per window by multiplying all of the figures by 10.

For example, for Boston, Massachusetts, we can make the following observations: (1) A single-glazed window with no storm window facing north loses about 12 gallons of oil per year; adding a storm window cuts the loss to 6 gallons; adding an insulating shutter to the window without a storm window reduces the loss to 4 gallons; adding both storm window and shutter reduces the loss to only 1 gallon. (2) A single-glazed window facing due south has a net gain (solar gain minus conductive loss) of 7 gallons per year; the net gain is increased to 12 gallons with a storm window; a single-glazed window plus shutter gains 15 gallons; a double-glazed window plus shutter gains 16 gallons. (3) The same sort of performance gain turns east- and west-facing windows from losers to gainers.

Table 26. Net Heat Gain (+) or Loss (–) in Therms per Square Foot of Unshaded Window during the Heating Season (Note: 1 therm = 1 gallon of fuel oil or 100 cu. ft. gas)

| | | | | orientation of window | | | | |
location and type	N	NE	E	SE	S	SW	W	NW
Albuquerque, N.M.								
Single-glazed	−0.6	−0.4	0.6	1.6	2.0	1.6	0.6	−0.4
Double-glazed	−0.3	0.1	0.9	1.8	2.2	1.8	0.9	0.1
Single-glazed plus shutter	0.0	0.2	1.2	2.2	2.6	2.2	1.2	0.2
Double-glazed plus shutter	0.1	0.3	1.2	2.1	2.5	2.1	1.2	0.3
Atlanta, Ga.								
Single-glazed	−0.4	−0.2	0.4	1.0	1.2	1.0	0.4	−0.2
Double-glazed	−0.2	0.1	0.6	1.2	1.4	1.2	0.6	0.1
Single-glazed plus shutter	0.0	0.2	0.8	1.4	1.6	1.4	0.8	0.2
Double-glazed plus shutter	0.1	0.2	0.8	1.3	1.6	1.3	0.8	0.2
Boston, Mass.								
Single-glazed	−1.2	−1.0	−0.4	0.3	0.7	0.3	−0.4	−1.0
Double-glazed	−0.6	−0.4	0.2	0.8	1.2	0.8	0.2	−0.4
Single-glazed plus shutter	−0.4	−0.3	0.4	1.1	1.5	1.1	0.4	−0.3
Double-glazed plus shutter	−0.1	0.0	0.5	1.2	1.6	1.2	0.5	0.0
Chicago, Ill.								
Single-glazed	−1.3	−1.2	−0.6	0.1	0.5	0.1	−0.6	−1.2
Double-glazed	−0.6	−0.5	0.1	0.7	1.1	0.7	0.1	−0.5
Single-glazed plus shutter	−0.4	−0.3	0.3	1.0	1.4	1.0	0.3	−0.3
Double-glazed plus shutter	−0.2	−0.1	0.5	1.1	1.5	1.1	0.5	−0.1
Kansas City, Kan.								
Single-glazed	−1.0	−0.8	−0.2	0.5	0.9	0.5	−0.2	−0.8
Double-glazed	−0.5	−0.3	0.3	0.9	1.3	0.9	0.3	−0.3
Single-glazed plus shutter	−0.3	−0.2	0.4	1.1	1.5	1.1	0.4	−0.2
Double-glazed plus shutter	−0.1	0.0	0.6	1.2	1.6	1.2	0.6	0.0
Washington, D.C.								
Single-glazed	−0.8	−0.7	−0.1	0.5	0.9	0.5	−0.1	−0.7
Double-glazed	−0.4	−0.2	0.3	0.9	1.2	0.9	0.3	−0.2
Single-glazed plus shutter	−0.2	−0.1	0.5	1.1	1.5	1.1	0.5	−0.1
Double-glazed plus shutter	−0.1	0.1	0.6	1.2	1.5	1.2	0.6	0.1

In case you are interested, you already know how to calculate the net gains and losses for your town: the *solar gains* are calculated using Illustration 53 and Table 19; the annual *conductive heat losses* are found using Equation 5.2; *net gain* is the solar gain minus the conductive loss.

Insulating Shades and Shutters

The thermal resistance, R, of windows, shades, and shutters can be calculated using the method and tables of Chapter 7. Table 27 shows the calculation and resulting R values of single and

Table 27.

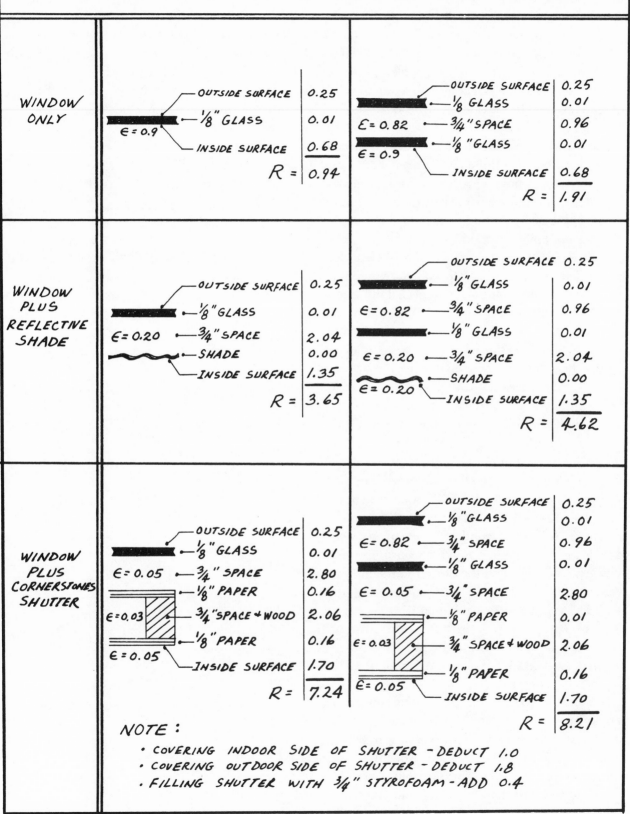

R FACTORS OF WINDOWS, SHADES, AND SHUTTERS

WINDOW ONLY

OUTSIDE SURFACE — 0.25
1/8" GLASS — 0.01
E = 0.9
INSIDE SURFACE — 0.68
R = 0.94

OUTSIDE SURFACE — 0.25
1/8 GLASS — 0.01
E = 0.82   3/4" SPACE — 0.96
1/8 "GLASS — 0.01
E = 0.9
INSIDE SURFACE — 0.68
R = 1.91

WINDOW PLUS REFLECTIVE SHADE

OUTSIDE SURFACE — 0.25
1/8" GLASS — 0.01
E = 0.20   3/4" SPACE — 2.04
SHADE — 0.00
INSIDE SURFACE — 1.35
R = 3.65

OUTSIDE SURFACE — 0.25
1/8" GLASS — 0.01
E = 0.82   3/4" SPACE — 0.96
1/8" GLASS — 0.01
E = 0.20   3/4" SPACE — 2.04
SHADE — 0.00
E = 0.20   INSIDE SURFACE — 1.35
R = 4.62

WINDOW PLUS CORNERSTONES SHUTTER

OUTSIDE SURFACE — 0.25
1/8" GLASS — 0.01
E = 0.05   3/4" SPACE — 2.80
1/8" PAPER — 0.16
E = 0.03   3/4" SPACE & WOOD — 2.06
1/8" PAPER — 0.16
E = 0.05   INSIDE SURFACE — 1.70
R = 7.24

OUTSIDE SURFACE — 0.25
1/8" GLASS — 0.01
E = 0.82   3/4" SPACE — 0.96
1/8" GLASS — 0.01
E = 0.05   3/4" SPACE — 2.80
1/8" PAPER — 0.01
E = 0.03   3/4" SPACE & WOOD — 2.06
1/8" PAPER — 0.16
E = 0.05   INSIDE SURFACE — 1.70
R = 8.21

NOTE:
- COVERING INDOOR SIDE OF SHUTTER — DEDUCT 1.0
- COVERING OUTDOOR SIDE OF SHUTTER — DEDUCT 1.8
- FILLING SHUTTER WITH 3/4" STYROFOAM — ADD 0.4

double glazing and of the shades and shutters I will show you how to make. The R values of both the shade and shutter are due primarily to the creation of low-emissivity dead air spaces. The shade, consisting of a metalized plastic film of emissivity 0.20, creates one air space between itself and the window; the shutter, made of 2 layers of 1/8″ thick cardboard faced with aluminum foil of emissivity 0.05, creates two dead air spaces, of emissivity 0.05 and 0.03.

The creation of *truly* dead air spaces is *critical* for two reasons: (1) If the insulating device is well sealed to the window at the two sides and the bottom, it forms a giant pocket. Cold air formed in the space is dense and fills the pocket from the bottom up. Since the cold air is heavy, it is stable and little convection occurs. If the pocket were not sealed at the bottom, the cold air would rush out, only to be continually replaced by warm room air flowing in at the top. With the proper dimensions, it is conceivable that an unsealed "insulating" shade or shutter would result in a convective heat loss as great as that of the window alone. (2) To the extent that the insulating device does insulate, the surface temperature of the window glass will be lowered. For example, if the overnight outdoor temperature were 10° F and the inside temperature 60° F, the temperature of the inside surface of a double-glazed window with shutter would be only 42° F. Without the shutter the temperature at the glass will be only 18° F. Moisture will now condense out of whatever air flows through the air space onto the glass surface. Upon opening the shutter in the morning we will be greeted by either a small greeting from Jack Frost (properly sealed insulator) or a quarter-inch of ice (poorly sealed). The light frost will evaporate in place. The ice will melt and run down onto the window sill, wall, and floor and ultimately cause damage.

In spite of these warnings, effective insulating shades and shutters are easy to make and pay back typically in two to five years. I have used both types in my house. Of the two, I prefer the shutters for the following reasons: (1) The shutters will last longer, being constructed of a 1/8″ thick high-density cardboard used in the construction industry as a building sheathing. (2) Forming two dead air spaces, the shutter R value is approximately twice that of the shade. (3) The shutter, when covered with a decorative fabric, costs no more than good curtains or draperies and replaces them. (4) The shutter is easily sealed at the top and can be used to insulate against summer heat gain as well as winter heat loss.

How to Make Insulating Shades (Illustrations 93A, B, and C)

Step 1. Buy insulating curtain material 6″ or more wider than your windows. One example of such material is Astrolon or "Space Blanket," manufactured by the King-Seeley Corp., Woburn, Mass. If

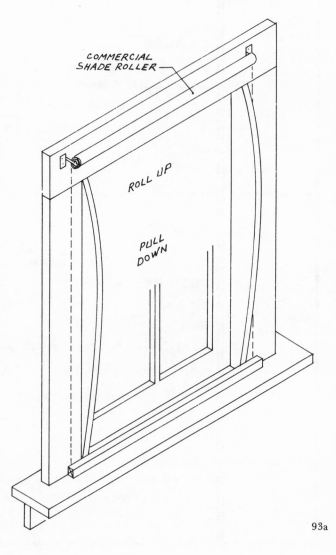

COMMERCIAL SHADE ROLLER

ROLL UP

PULL DOWN

93a

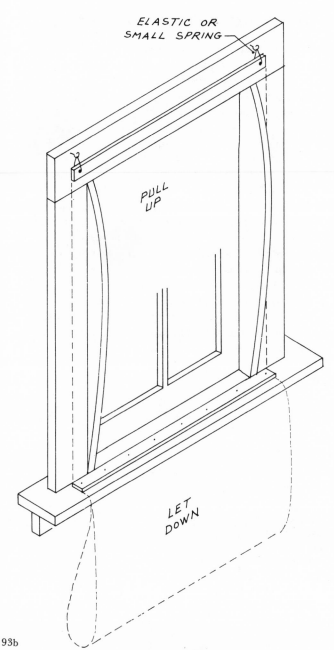

ELASTIC OR
SMALL SPRING

PULL
UP

LET
DOWN

93b

curved position. The function of the curve is to seal the sides when the shade is stretched taut.

Step 3. Cut the insulating fabric 6″ wider and several inches longer than the window inside dimension; hem or otherwise reinforce the edges.

Step 4. If the shade is to be mounted at the top and pulled down, staple the fabric to a commercial spring-loaded roller and install at the top. Staple the bottom of the curtain to a 3/4″ × 3/4″ stick. The way in which the bottom stick seals to the window sill is critical. A number of options exist: a heavy weight, Velcro strips, kitchen cabinet catches, magnets recessed into the windowsill and a metal bottom strip, etcetera.

Step 5. If the shade is to be raised from the bottom (the preferred method, functionally), staple the fabric to a 3/4″ × 3/4″ strip of wood and screw the strip down to the windowsill. Then staple the top of the fabric to a second strip of wood so that the

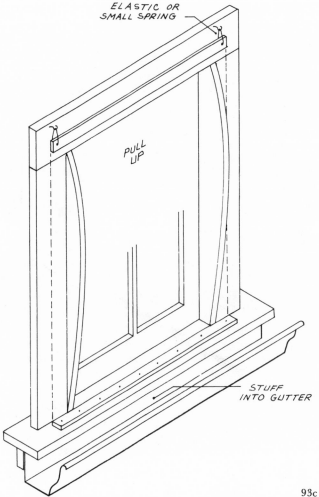

ELASTIC OR
SMALL SPRING

PULL
UP

STUFF
INTO GUTTER

93c

you can't find a suitable material in your local fabric store, it can be purchased mail-order from L. L. Bean, Freeport, Me., in the form of a hemmed blanket.

Step 2. Cut thin boards the same height as the window inside dimension, with a curved outer edge as shown in Illustration 93. The curved edge should project approximately 1″ beyond the window trim and should have a rounded edge so that the fabric will not be torn. The curve can be formed either by cutting the curve with a jigsaw or soaking a 1/2″ × 1″ strip of pine overnight and nailing it in the shade just reaches the bottom of the top window trim. Install screw hooks at the top of the window trim and use either strong rubber bands or small springs to fasten up the top of the shade. The springs or elastics will provide the tension to pull the fabric tight along the convex sidepieces. Note that the reinforced fabric edges must extend at least an inch outside the curved sidepieces.

Step 6. If the shade is raised from the bottom, consider installing a short length of commercial enameled aluminum rain gutter, painted the same color as your window, under the windowsill. The shade can be neatly stuffed into the gutter during the day.

Of course, commercial variations on this shade exist now, but why buy them when you can make them for a quarter of the cost? The insulating fabric can also be sewn loosely to a more decorative fabric without hurting its thermal performance.

How to Make Shutters (Illustration 94)

Step 1. Measure the height (H) and width (W) from inside to inside of the present window trim.

Step 2. Cut, with a utility knife and straightedge, four pieces of Thermoply from the $4' \times 8'$ sheet so that when two are placed side by side they measure $(H-3/8'') \times (W-3/8'')$. Thermoply is a commercial building product manufactured by Simplex Industries of Adrien, Mich. Do not call or write me inquiring about local dealers, since I do not have a list of such. Simply tell your local lumberyard about the product and the manufacturer's name and address.

Step 3. Cut eight lengths of $3/4'' \times 1-1/2''$ pine to form two rectangles of the same dimensions as the Thermoply. The width of the pine is not critical, but $1-1/2''$ is recommended.

Step 4. Fasten Thermoply to both sides of the pine frames, using Elmer's White Household Glue and a staple gun. The staples serve to hold the Thermoply and wood together while the glue dries; they may be removed later.

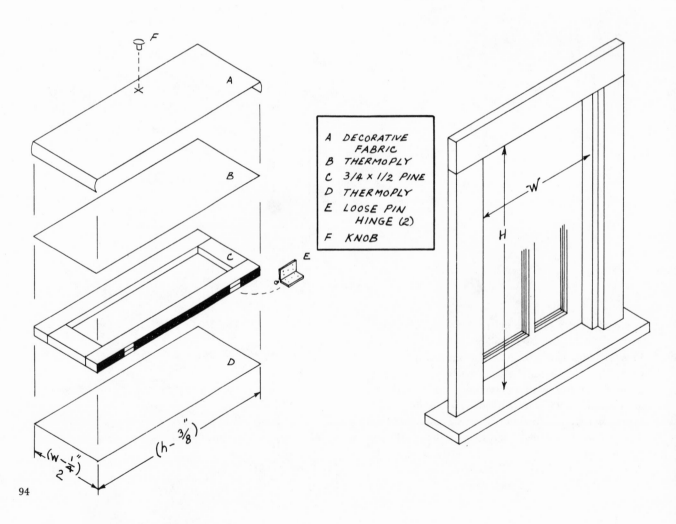

A DECORATIVE FABRIC
B THERMOPLY
C 3/4 x 1/2 PINE
D THERMOPLY
E LOOSE PIN HINGE (2)
F KNOB

94

Step 5. Fasten two sets of 3/4″×1-1/2″ loose-pin hinges to the pine edges 6″ from the top and bottom of each shutter. Do *not* mortise (set into the wood) the hinges. If the window is more than 60″ high, use three hinges on each shutter. Using 3/4″ wide hinges may result in the shutters' not folding flat against the wall. If this is a problem, wider hinges can be used so that the shutter pivots about a point farther into the room.

Step 6. Staple the fabric of your choice around the edge of each shutter, cutting away from the hinges. This is the most difficult part.

Step 7. Staple a weatherstrip (old-fashioned felt works well) along the hinge edge of each shutter but not over the hinges.

Step 8. Place a scrap piece of Thermoply under each shutter while holding it in place and mark the location of the hinges against the window trim.

Step 9. Open the shutter and fasten the hinges to the window trim.

Step 10. The shutter pair should now prove slightly too wide for the space, so that when they are closed simultaneously, moderate force is required to pop them into the closed position. If too loose, staple a felt weatherstrip to one or both of the mating edges. The shutter should stay closed; if not, install a cabinet "bullet catch."

Step 11. Nail a 3/4″×1″ strip of pine to the window-sill at the bottom so that the shutters close tightly against it. The shutter sides and bottom now form a tight cold-air pocket. If the window is leaky, do the same at the top to form a seal against infiltration.

Step 12. As a final touch, add a pair of knobs so that your "wall" can be turned back into a window at sunrise!

If you have trouble finding all of the component parts, the shutter is marketed as a complete do-it-yourself kit, including white/foil faced stock and special wide hinges, as the Sunsaver® by the Homesworth Corp., Brunswick, Maine.

GOOD LUCK AND HAVE A WARMER WINTER!

14.

Weatherstripping and Caulking

Introduction

Few homeowners realize the contribution of infiltration to their fuel bill. The physical movement of cold air into a house (infiltration) and the equal and opposite movement of warmed air out of a house (exfiltration) account for between 20 and 50 percent of the typical annual fuel bill. Why are we so unaware of it? Probably because it's a hard item to sell. Radio, television, newspapers, and the Yellow Pages all promote attic and wall insulation and storm windows and doors. These are concepts easily grasped. A man comes and blows a foot of insulation into the attic; there it is for all to see. Another man installs triple-track baked-enamel storm windows all around the house. "Look, Jane. See my storm windows. They are saving heat." Infiltration, on the other hand, is hard to visualize. The solution is not a blanket of this or that insulation. Nor is it a physical object that we can buy. It is rather an attention to detail. It is considering every building joint, every door, every window, every flashing a potential leak—and then caulking that leak.

Grab a ruler right now and start looking hard at your windows and doors. How wide is the crack between the window and the trim, between the top and bottom sashes, between the door and its frame? The total length of crack between the sill plate and foundation, at the four building corners, and around the doors and windows of a *small* 1,000-square-foot house amounts to the length of a city block, or about 400 feet! If this crack width averaged only 1/16 of an inch, the total area (area=length×width) open to the great outdoors would be 2 square feet! The total area of opening represented by the 50 or more electrical wall outlets is another several square feet. As I said above, the effect of all the cracks and holes in the exterior wall of a house is equivalent to leaving a double-hung window open all winter! Only a fool would do that, wouldn't he?

Where Does Infiltration Occur?

In a home with poor quality, nonweatherstripped windows, the major part of the infiltration may be through and around the windows. In an old farmhouse, the major infiltration may come in through holes in the stone foundation and exit via the fireplace. In the average house, however, a

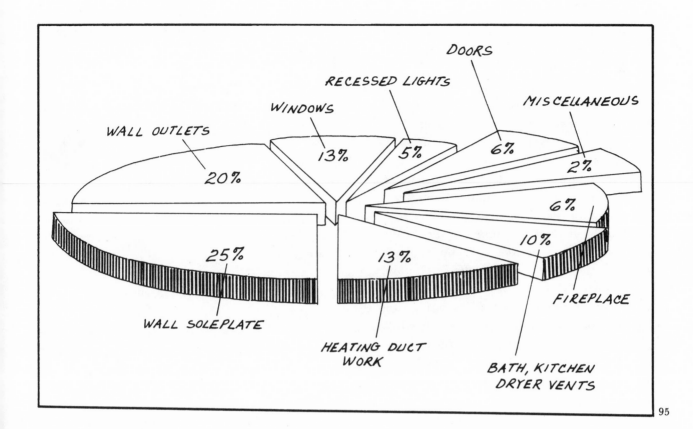

WALL OUTLETS 20%

WINDOWS 13%

RECESSED LIGHTS 5%

DOORS 6%

MISCELLANEOUS 2%

6%

10%

25%

13%

WALL SOLEPLATE

HEATING DUCT WORK

BATH, KITCHEN DRYER VENTS

FIREPLACE

95

large number of seemingly insignificant sources add up to a large fuel bill. Part of the problem noted above is the very diversity of sources.

Illustration 95 shows the results of an infiltration test on an average new home. I think you will find these results as surprising as I did. Most of us are aware of window and door infiltration, but the test showed that the infiltration heat losses between the foundation and wall and through the wall electrical outlets were each larger than the combined door and window losses! As much heat was lost through attic and cellar heating ductwork as around the windows, and nearly as much air was lost to the attic through recessed light fixtures as around the doors!

There are two ways to stop infiltration. If the air is leaking around a movable object, we *weatherstrip;* if the leak is through a fixed joint, we *caulk.*

Can a House Be Too Tight?

I don't recall ever expounding on the merits of supertight house construction without someone in the audience raising one of three objections: (1) "My fireplace won't draw now unless I open a window." (2) "I built a house like that and it was so tight water ran down the windows all winter." (3) "A house like that will stink!"

I have to confess that my answers usually leave the objectors less than satisfied. The way in which the objections are stated, however, makes me suspect that no answers would prove satisfactory. Be that as it may, I will answer the objections; you can choose between the merits of my answers and the alternative—a higher fuel bill.

(1) Why, pray tell, is this person using a fireplace in the first place? Anyone interested in fuel economy would button up the fireplace (0–15

percent efficient) and insert an airtight stove (50–65 percent efficient), which would have no trouble obtaining sufficient air. Fireplaces can be used at the beginning and the end of the heating season with no serious fuel bill impact, and for those who insist on seeing the flame there are combination openable stoves and airtight stoves with glass doors.

(2) If moisture condenses on double-glazed windows all winter, the relative humidity of the house is too high. The natural relative humidity of outside air after warming to the inside temperature averages between 20 and 30 percent in most northern areas and results in window condensation only on the very coldest nights of the year. Higher relative humidities result from the addition of water vapor to the air, either by damp basements or human activities such as bathing, cooking, drying laundry, and growing plants. All of these sources of moisture can be controlled if we so desire.

(3) Once again, a stinking house is related to human activity (or the lack of it). It has been proven through the ages that bathing and laundering clothes (particularly bedding) will go a long way in relieving "housetosis." Anyone who can't conform to the present minimum ventilation requirement of 10 cubic feet of air per minute per person has a personal hygiene problem either bodily or mentally. Kitchen and bathroom odors can be eliminated before they spread, by the brief operation of exhaust fans without major impact on the fuel bill.

An Infiltration Goal

The recognized minimum ventilation specification for respiration and odor control is presently 10 cubic feet of air per minute (CFM) per person. Recent studies have shown that this figure is excessive, provided minimal remedial measures are applied to odor control (in layman's terms— taking baths). For the moment, however, let's accept that figure and calculate its meaning.

The average family consists of 3-1/2 persons plus a 1/2 person equivalent in cats, dogs, or whatever other critters satisfy the family's collective urge to return to the jungle. Therefore, the ventilation requirement for the average family is:

$$4\ persons \times 10\ \frac{CFM}{person} \times \frac{60\ minutes}{hour}$$
$$= 2{,}400\ \frac{cubic\ feet\ of\ air}{hour}$$

This average family resides in an average house having 1,500 square feet of floor area and a ceiling height of 8 feet. The total air volume of the house is therefore

$$1{,}500\ sq.\ ft. \times 8\ ft. = 12{,}000\ cu.\ ft.$$

The minimum ventilation requirement is thus seen to be satisfied by a total house volume

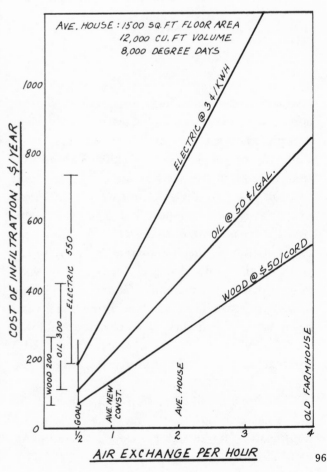

air exchange rate of 1/5 air exchange per hour. I can guarantee you that unless you live in a submarine, your house exchanges air faster than that!

The often-stated goal in new-house construction is 1/2 air exchange per hour. Field tests have shown, however, that the average new house exceeds 1 exchange per hour. The majority of houses, regardless of age, have a rating of between 1 and 2 exchanges per hour. And, of course, with the old farmhouse the figure is much higher.

In Illustration 96 I have plotted the fuel cost in dollars per year due to infiltration for the average 1,500 square foot house in an 8,000 degree day climate, using three different fuels. The annual savings that would result from tightening the house are easily calculated from the graph. In decreasing the air exchange rate from 2 per hour to 1/2 per hour, the annual fuel savings amount to: wood heat, $200; oil heat, $300; and electric heat, $550! In reducing the infiltration further, however, we encounter the law of diminishing returns. The additional savings derived from dropping from 1/2 to 1/3 exchange per hour are only $17, $25, and $46. If we tighten the house no further than 1/2 exchange per hour, we will be spared using the five-day deodorant, so let's adopt 1/2 air exchange per hour as our retrofit goal. Keep in mind when we get to the window and door leakage tables that 1/2 air exchange per hour in a 12,000 cu. ft. house is 100 CFM: 100 CFM out of the house plus 100 CFM into the house, for a total leakage of 200 CFM.

Weatherstripping (Sealing the Moving Parts)

Doors and, to a lesser extent, windows are parts of the house membrane which ordinarily move. Basic window and door designs have not changed much over the years; weatherstripping materials have. Fortunately it is a relatively simple task

Table 28. Air Leakage of Doors

type of door	weatherstrip	leakage at 15–20 mph (in cfm)
Wood, solid core	brass	10
Wood, solid core	plastic	20
Wood, solid core plus aluminum storm	plastic	17
Wood, hollow core	brass	9
Wood, french	brass	11
Steel, insulated	magnetic	15

From National Bureau of Standards, "Acoustical and Thermal Performance of Exterior Residential Walls, Doors, and Windows."

to retrofit old windows and doors with new weatherstripping.

Let's first consider the different types of doors. Table 28 lists measured amounts of infiltration between various doors and their frames at a wind velocity of approximately 15 mph. All of these doors were new and properly fitted. Since none of the infiltration is through the body of the door itself, we can make the following gross observations: (1) A properly weatherstripped exterior door should leak no more than 10 CFM. (2) Adding a storm door to a well-weatherstripped door does little to decrease infiltration. (3) Of the three types of weatherstrip used, the spring metal (brass here) type proved consistently more effective. This latter observation is good news, since the metal type of weatherstrip is widely available, easy to install on existing doors, and long-lasting.

Table 29 lists the results of an identical infiltration test on common window types. My conclusions are: (1) There is nothing better than a fixed (unopenable) window in the winter. (2) Single-hung (one-half movable only) is next best. (3) The new plastic-sheathed wood windows are better than either aluminum or the old-fashioned wood types. Since these results were obtained on brand-new windows, you can see that holding the total infiltration of 10 or more retrofitted double-hung windows under 200 CFM will require unusual tactics.

First of all, ask yourself how many windows you need. In Chapter 13 we found that windows

Table 29. Air Leakage of Windows

type of window	size	leakage at 15–20 mph (in cfm)
Single-hung, aluminum	3' X 4'	5.6
Double-hung, wood	3' X 5'	24.6
Double-hung, wood/plastic	3' X 5'	5.0
Awning, wood/plastic	3' X 4'	10.4
Casement, aluminum	3' X 4'	26.0
Casement, wood/plastic	4' X 5'	9.3
Sliding glass door, wood/ plastic	6' X 7'	15.6
Fixed, wood/plastic	3' X 5'	2.2
Sliding, aluminum	3' X 4'	16.3
Jalousie, aluminum	3' X 4'	82.6

From National Bureau of Standards, "Acoustical and Thermal Performance of Exterior Residential Walls, Doors, and Windows."

facing north are total losers during the heating season. Many of us are out of the house during the winter daylight hours, eliminating the lighting requirement; and during the winter months we certainly don't need cross-ventilation. All of the north- and some of the east- and west-facing windows are therefore candidates for elimination, or at least seasonal blocking off.

Second, how often do you move the upper sashes of your double-hung windows? If you can't think of a better reason to keep this feature than spring cleaning, one-half of your infiltration problem can be solved immediately by simply removing the upper sash, caulking it, pressing it back in place, and screwing it fast to the stops!

Third, the spring metal type of weatherstrip found to perform so well in the case of doors can be used equally effectively on movable windows. Since a single sash of a normal double-hung window has only one-half the crack length of a door, we should be able to reduce its infiltration to 5 CFM or less.

How to Weatherstrip

There are lots of different weatherstripping materials on the market. The felts and sponge rubbers are effective for one season in a house

with children and critters. The vinyls have an inherently longer life but are highly visible and tend to be destroyed by painting. I'm not going to waste your time or mine, but will get straight to the installation of the best weatherstrip on the market, the spring metal strip.

The metal strips are available in straight lengths or rolls, V-shaped or single, and aluminum, copper, bronze, or stainless steel finishes. Aluminum is by far the cheapest and is quite satisfactory. Try to buy it by the 100-foot roll. Buying it by the length or kit wastes material and costs twice as much.

WINDOWS

Illustration 97 shows where the spring metal is applied on a double-hung window. The top sash is caulked permanently in place; strips are installed in each of the side channels formed between the parting strip and the stop; another strip is nailed to the bottom of the bottom sash; the final strip is nailed to the bottom of the top sash on the face that mates with the bottom sash when closed.

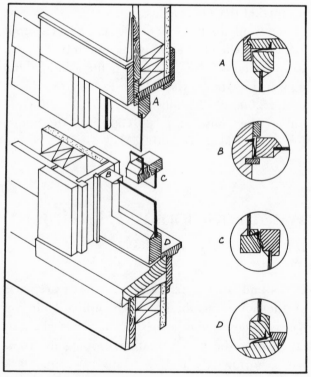

97

Step 1. Carefully remove the inside window stop, bottom sash, parting strip, and top sash.

Step 2. If your windows still have sash weights, cut the cords, remove the pulley plates, and permanently tape over the holes, using duct tape. You won't need sash weights any longer.

Step 3. Make whatever repairs are required to the sashes, such as painting and reglazing.

Step 4. Lay a generous bead of caulk around the top and sides of the outside stop; press the top sash into place against the caulk; nail a block of wood under the sash to support its weight; replace the parting strip.

Step 5. Cut two strips of metal weatherstrip several inches longer than the height of the bottom sash; position the strips in the side channels with the opening of the V toward the outdoors; nail, tack, staple, or stick with adhesive the strip in place, making sure that the strip doesn't bind against the parting strip.

Step 6. After fastening securely, flare the weatherstrip outward, using your fingers or a wide screwdriver.

Step 7. Push the sash into place. The pressure of the weatherstrip should be adequate to hold the window up when opened. If not, flare the strip more or use a small stick to prop the window open when needed.

Step 8. Measure and cut the weatherstrips for the top and bottom at an angle so that all four weatherstrips fit like a mitred picture frame when closed.

Step 9. Remove the sash; install top and bottom weatherstrips; replace the sash.

Step 10. Replace the inside stop.

Note: If the weatherstrip at the mating edge of top and bottom sashes is unsatisfactory, use a stick-on felt, sponge rubber, or vinyl strip. The same type of metal weatherstrip can be used on awning and casement windows.

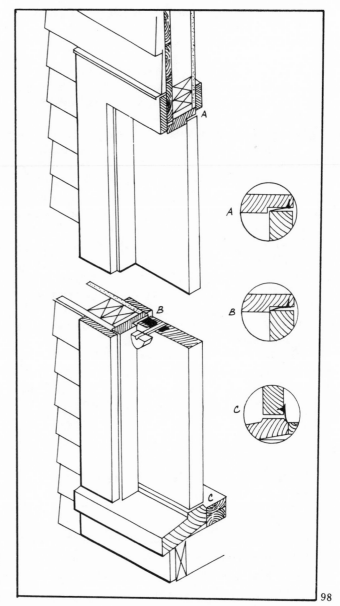

98

DOORS (ILLUSTRATION 98)

Spring metal weatherstripping works equally well on exterior doors. However, since we walk on the threshold, we will have to use a different type of weatherstrip on the bottom of the door.

Exterior doors are amazingly rugged considering the abuse they receive. Your doors probably won't require replacing, but they very well might use a bit of trimming and work on the hinges.

Door hinges are subjected to extraordinary loads. Often the screws have worked loose and enlarged the screw holes so that the door sags. Rather than move the hinges to new wood (which requires mortising the hinges) the screw hole can usually be salvaged by stuffing with toothpicks or other wood splinters dipped in waterproof glue.

After the hinges are secure, check the fit of the door. The weatherstrip will require a minimum of 1/8" clearance at the top and sides. Since the weatherstrip is very stiff, it cannot follow a rapidly varying clearance. If the edges of the door are very rough, plane them lightly to restore a straight edge.

Step 1. Measure and cut the side pieces, B. Holding the side pieces in place, mark the location of the hinges and the striker plate; cut away these small pieces.

Step 2. Holding each piece with the V-opening away from the open door and with enough clearance not to bind, install each piece with a nail at each end.

Step 3. Check for proper operation. Next, nail the center of each piece and then add the rest of the nails. Use only the nails supplied with the weatherstripping or recommended by the manufacturer. Drive the nails flush, using a nail set or similar tool, being very careful not to dent the weatherstrip sealing face.

Step 4. Mitre the top piece, A, so that it fits against the side pieces exactly. Install the top piece, using the same procedure.

Step 5. Flare the edge of the weatherstrip out, using your fingers.

Step 6. Install a doorsweep weatherstrip at the bottom of the opening side of the door (Illustration 98C). Purchase the type with elongated screw holes so that it can easily be adjusted during the season.

Caulking (Sealing the Fixed Joints)

Many people have the impression that caulking the joints of a house is largely a waste of time. They have arrived at this conclusion after seeing their labors fail as the caulk dries, shrivels, breaks away, and finally falls out. This problem is due largely to the mistaken assumption that there are "fixed joints" in a house. I call them fixed joints here only in distinction to the joints that are de-

signed to move. The house is actually a dynamic assemblage of joints moving in response to wind gusts, frost heaves, door slams, and expansion and contraction due to changes of temperature and humidity. The relative motion is greatest in two areas: where dissimilar materials (such as masonry and wood) meet, and where wood parts of differing direction of grain, such as trim and siding, meet.

Sometimes a clue to just how much relative motion occurs at a given place can be obtained by checking the displacement of paint fissures. When last painted, the paint film was continuous; subsequently the joint has moved. The displacement of the two edges of a crack is an indication of the severity of the problem. I consider any displacement of $1/16''$ or more a serious problem requiring a caulk especially designed for moving joints. This does not include the cracks between shingles and clapboards, as they are necessary.

Table 30 lists the caulks and their characteristics. It is tempting to make generalities as to durability and ease of application. I refer you however to consumer publications such as *Consumer Reports* for up-to-date ratings of specific products. Generalities as to chemical formulation, brand name, and price as an indication of quality are impossible among the dozens of products.

A few general statements can be made:

(1) A moving joint is one displaying motion of $1/16''$ or more.

(2) Gaps wider than $1/4''$ should be first stuffed with oakum caulk (available at plumbing supply or hardware stores) and then covered with the best grade of moving joint caulk.

Table 30. Caulking Compounds

type	for moving joints?	paintable?	relative cost	cleanup fluid
Butyl rubber	no	yes	low	paint thinner
Latex	no	must	low	water
Oil	no	yes	low	paint thinner
Neoprene rubber	yes	yes	medium	toluene
Polysulfide	yes	no	high	toluene
Polyurethane	yes	yes	high	paint thinner
Silicone	yes	no	high	paint thinner

(3) Cleaning and priming (if called for by the manufacturer's instructions) are extremely important.

(4) Don't use silicone caulk if you plan to change the color of your house subsequently, because it won't accept paint.

HOW TO CAULK

Step 1. Buy caulk by the case if you plan to do the whole house. One tube will make a 1/4" bead 25 feet long. Find out in advance what the dealer will refund for unused tubes.

Step 2. Make repairs to areas to be caulked. Don't consider caulking a substitute for replacing badly deteriorated wood. Nail loose boards soundly.

Step 3. Clean joints thoroughly; use a paint scraper and wire brush to remove accumulations of old caulk and paint. Wash with detergent; rinse with clean water; let dry; prime according to the directions on the tube.

Step 4. Wait for warm weather. Few caulks can be used successfully below 60° F. If the caulk is too stiff, wrap the caulking gun in a heating pad. Store caulk inside before use. If the caulk is too runny, cool it in the refrigerator.

Step 5. Cut the nozzle at the proper size and angle to give a bead that overlaps both sides of the joint.

Step 6. After running a continuous bead the length of the joint, smooth the caulk with your finger or as directed.

Step 7. Clean up immediately. Some caulks, such as silicone, are impossible to remove completely after curing.

Really Big Cracks

Really big cracks cannot be sealed with caulk. Such cracks usually indicate a structural problem that should be rectified. The most common super-crack, however, is either in the foundation wall or between the foundation and the wood sill. Foundation wall cracks should be repaired by repointing with mortar. Trowel-on Surewall and Blockbond mixes make the repair of concrete block walls fairly simple.

The joint between the foundation and sill is especially troublesome in older houses. Polycel One, a urethane foam in an aerosol can, provides the perfect solution. If they are accessible, application from the inside is simplest; if not, the bottom layers of siding and sheathing should be removed to expose the sill to view. The urethane spray can be applied to any crack that is a source of infiltration. Do not expose it to fire or sunlight, however. It is a flammable urethane foam and it deteriorates in sunlight.

One piece of final advice: do it the right way the first time. Properly done, it should remain tight for twenty years.

Cutting Down on
That Store-bought Fuel

15.

Solar Retrofit

Introduction

Retrofitting a house for solar energy presents two problems: *aesthetics* and *economics*. A large part of the designer's function in new solar architecture is the harmonious incorporation of solar hardware into the overall design. Active solar hardware consists of: (1) a large surface area of collector necessarily mounted on an unshaded south roof or wall, (2) an extensive system of heat transfer plumbing or ductwork, and (3) a heat storage medium of either several thousand gallons of water or up to a thousand cubic feet of gravel. Since hardware of this magnitude is impossible to camouflage, solar architects have dropped back to the "form follows function" dictum. Active solar houses are designed around the solar system, and most of them use the external collector as the visual focus.

So where does that leave the handsome Queen Anne House facing and shadowed by two towering maples? Even the vociferous solar industry has given up on that one!

The second difficulty is economic. An optimal active solar system designed so that part of the collector cost is charged to the roof, designed to minimize plumbing, and incorporating storage into the foundation is today barely competitive with electric heat. No doubt it will, mass-produced, compete with oil heat in the near future. But it is difficult to see how it will ever compete with wood heat in the wooded eastern and northwestern parts of the country.

I'm a solar supporter of the first order, feeling that nonpolluting solar energy is the only rational energy choice for space heating in large areas of the United States. Because of this, I warn you about jumping into retrofitting your present house with collectors and storage. If too many homeowners find after installing solar hardware that their neighbors with nuclear-generated electric heat are economically better off, we will have been dosed with what solar inventor Steve Baer calls "solar pesticide." The entire solar movement, including the harmonious and economical passive solar approach, will have been nipped in the bud by overzealous solar hype.

Collectors and storage for space heating, no. But there *are* two very aesthetic and economical retrofit options beyond the simple addition of south-facing windows open to you: *solar domestic water heaters* and *passive solar greenhouse-collectors*.

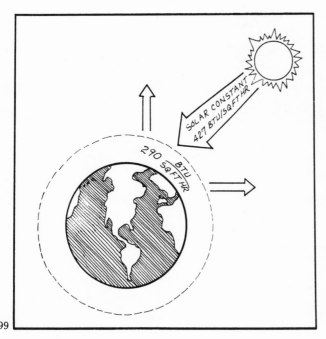

99

Solar Geometry

In order to build anything solar successfully, we must first understand solar: *what* is solar energy, *where* does it come from, *when* do we get it, *how* much do we get?

Illustration 99 shows the amount of solar radiation received by one square foot of the earth's surface on a clear day. The radiation is generated by a nuclear reaction in the sun and emitted by the 10,000°F surface of the sun, some 93,000,000 miles from the earth. (As solar proponent William von Arx says, the proper distance for a nuclear reactor!) The sun is so distant that it approximates a point source of radiation. Its radiation therefore follows the inverse square law of physics, the intensity of the radiation decreasing with the square of the distance from the source. The earth–sun distance varies about 3 percent as the earth follows its very slightly elliptical annual orbit. The intensity of radiation therefore varies slightly through the year. The average intensity of radiation received at the cloudless top of the earth's atmosphere is called the *solar constant,* 428 Btu/sq. ft. hr.

In traversing the earth's atmosphere in a direction normal to the earth's surface, about 1/3 of the radiation is absorbed, reflected, and scattered even under cloudless conditions. The maximum intensity received at sea level, under cloudless conditions, with the sun directly overhead, is about 325 Btu/sq. ft. hr.

We refer to the pile of air standing in a vertical column over each square foot of the earth's surface as 1 atmosphere. The weight of this column is an incredible 14.7 pounds per square inch, or 2,100 pounds per square foot. Small wonder that some of the radiation is lost in passing through. In traversing the atmosphere at an angle other than normal to the earth's surface, the solar ray has to pass through more than 1 atmosphere. Illustration 100 shows that the mass of air traversed is one atmosphere divided by the sine of the sun's altitude. At an altitude of 60° above the horizon, the path length is 1.16 atmosphere; at 30°, 2.0 atmospheres; at 14.5°, 4.0 atmospheres; and at 0° (on the horizon), a whole lot of atmospheres! If 1/3 of the radiation is lost in traversing 1 atmosphere, then it is easy to see that even the noon ray in winter in the northern U.S. has lost some of its punch. The losses near the horizon are so great that we can view the rising and setting sun unshaded. Of importance to us is the general rule that solar radiation received before 9 A.M. and after 3 P.M. is not very important to midwinter solar heating.

The warming effect of the sun's radiation is proportional to its intensity as received on a surface. In Illustration 101A we see radiation coming in at an angle of 30° from the horizontal. Call the intensity of this radiation I_0. It is easy to see from the units of intensity, Btu/sq. ft. hr., that the same amount of radiation falling on a larger surface results in a smaller intensity. If I_0 is the intensity received on a surface normal to the direction of the radiation, then the radiation on a surface at angle α from the direction of radiation is $I_0 \sin \alpha$. In 101B and 101C we see that the intensity on surfaces sloped down 10° to the south and 10° to the north are $0.64\ I_0$ and $0.34\ I_0$. This phenomenon explains the observed fact that the

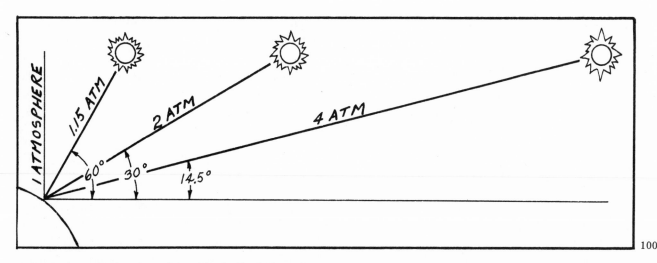

biological arrival of spring (as judged by the growth of plants close to the ground) is up to six weeks earlier on a southern slope than on a northern slope.

In discussing windows, shades, and shutters, I earlier made the observation that it has not been established that the tilted collector is always superior to the south vertical wall as a radiation collector. Illustration 102 demonstrates the logic behind this statement. If we make the simplifying assumption that the ground is a specular reflector (reflects like a mirror), then it becomes easy to calculate the relative radiation received by the tilted collector and the south vertical wall. Bare ground is far from being specular, but the resulting error is small, since the percentage reflected is small anyway. Snow-covered ground or ice-covered water bodies are close to being specular.

In the illustration the direct incident ray, D, has intensity I_0. The reflected ray, R, has intensity I_0 times the reflectivity of the ground, either 0.20 for bare ground or 0.60 for average snow. Using the angular relationship of Illustration 101 we can calculate the received intensity on the surface due to direct ray, reflected ray, and the sum of the two. The table shows that for a sun altitude of 30° the tilted collector receives more total radiation as long as the ground is bare, but the vertical wall receives more when the snow covers the ground. Without arguing over a few percentage points, I simply conclude that it makes little difference whether a collector is tilted or vertical in the northern snow belt. This, of course, is wonderful news for retro-

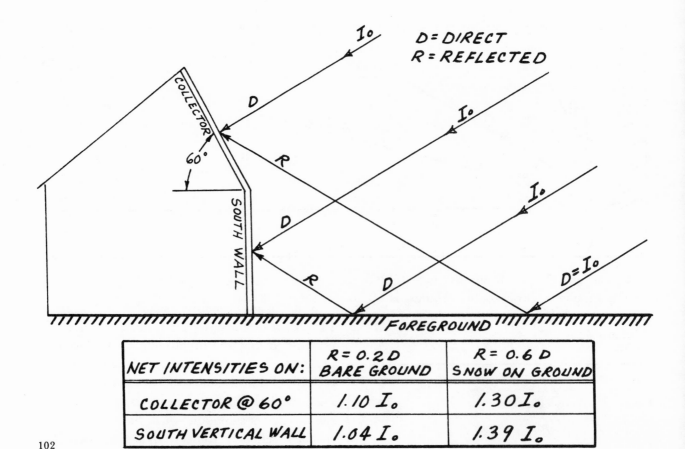

NET INTENSITIES ON:	R = 0.2 D BARE GROUND	R = 0.6 D SNOW ON GROUND
COLLECTOR @ 60°	$1.10\ I_0$	$1.30\ I_0$
SOUTH VERTICAL WALL	$1.04\ I_0$	$1.39\ I_0$

102

fitters who don't have a great deal of choice in roof angles.

Solar Weather

The variability of received radiation as a function of latitude, time of year, and local sky conditions is often referred to as solar weather. Anyone considering installing solar equipment of any sort should consider the local conditions in calculating the economic return on investment. The amount of radiation received on a clear day, while of academic interest, is of little value in solar economic calculations. The most valuable information available to us is the average amount of radiation received in Btu per sq. ft.$^{-1}$ per day^{-1} on horizontal, vertical, and tilted south-facing surfaces at specific sites. This information is available to an accuracy of about ± 10

percent for about 120 cities in the United States and Canada. This data is listed in Table 31 for forty cities.

The Solar Greenhouse = Collector

One of my objections to the solar collector sitting atop the roof is that it serves no function beyond generating heat. If we were simply to increase the depth of the collector from several inches to ten feet we could climb in and enjoy the warmth of the sun! Looked upon this way, the passive solar house is nothing more than a live-in solar collector.

The amount of radiation received by a passive solar house with complete south wall glazing is, however, far too great to be utilized immediately. Unless some provision has been made to utilize or store the excess heat, the house must be vented on clear days. This, of course, is as wasteful as opening a window with the furnace running. There are two general solutions to this problem in passive design. In the first, materials of sufficient mass and surface area are incorporated into the house structure to soak up the excess heat like a sponge. The absorbed heat is later returned by the structure during cold, dark periods. The second approach is to attach a heat-collecting structure to an ordinary structure as an appendage. The excess heat from the solar appendage is then fed to the larger, non-solar structure in order to lower the latter's fuel bill. Passive solar designers have discovered that the attached greenhouse, suitably modified, is the ideal solar appendage. It can be added to any structure having a decent solar exposure and can thus be added to our bag of retrofit tricks.

Below is described an extremely simple and inexpensive structure easily added to virtually any structure by a competent carpenter. The same basic structure can be internally set up in any of three different heating modes:

symbiotic, where the excess heat is blown immediately and directly into the adjacent living space
drum wall, where excess radiation is absorbed by a stack of dark-painted barrels of water, resulting in a reasonable daily greenhouse temperature range
hybrid gravel storage, when the excess heat is stored and retrieved from a subfloor gravel bed, using a blower.

you can be sure that a plant exists somewhere that will find here its Bali Hai.

TEMPERATURE

Plants will generally tolerate, if not thrive in, temperatures from 32° F up to about 90° F. Some plants do best in the 40s; some do best in the 70s; most do well between 50° and 70°. Moving plants into a "solar" greenhouse, with its relatively uncontrolled temperatures, is similar to spring transplanting; allow a few days for "hardening up," both to the temperature and the radiation.

HUMIDITY AND WATER

Since different species can be found thriving in rain forest and desert, it is obvious that plants can be found that will tolerate relative humidities of anywhere from 10 percent to 100 percent. Commercial greenhouses in the northern U.S. have difficulty maintaining winter relative humidities in excess of 50 percent because of condensation on the cold glazing. Although this shuttered greenhouse is capable of sustaining higher humidities, don't test it. High humidity–high temperature greenhouse air, when vented into the living space, will rise in relative humidity as its temperature falls. The result will be excessive condensation on windows (in extreme cases, even on the walls) and, ugh, mildew! For this reason the symbiotic system, with its large air

Plant Needs

A good architect designs to the needs of his clients. It is not unreasonable, therefore, to consider the needs and desires of the plants that will occupy the structure; to do otherwise may result in a collector as sterile as the one on the roof. Illustration 103 shows the physiological needs of plants. Fortunately plants have evolved suited to an extremely wide range of variables. If you build as shown and take note at least of the basic needs

103

Table 31. Solar Availability

		Jan.	Feb.	Mar.	Apr.	May
Albuquerque, N.M. lat. 35.03°						
Average temperature		33.8	39.2	44.6	53.6	62.6
Degree days		930	703	595	288	81
Slope	0°	1,134	1,436	1,885	2,319	2,533
	30°	1,872	2,041	2,295	2,411	2,346
	60°	2,169	2,179	2,189	1,990	1,724
	90°	1,950	1,815	1,599	1,182	868
Ames, Ia. lat. 42.02°						
Average temperature		19.4	24.8	32.0	48.2	59.0
Degree days		1,370	1,137	915	438	180
Slope	0°	640	931	1,204	1,484	1,767
	30°	1,105	1,375	1,486	1,575	1,704
	60°	1,320	1,516	1,459	1,366	1,354
	90°	1,230	1,320	1,134	918	818
Apalachicola, Fla. lat. 29.45°						
Average temperature		53.6	55.4	59.0	66.2	73.4
Degree days		347	260	180	33	0
Slope	0°	1,078	1,340	1,623	2,025	2,242
	30°	1,549	1,722	1,830	2,007	2,010
	60°	1,678	1,733	1,656	1,592	1,426
	90°	1,435	1,374	1,152	903	692
Atlanta, Ga. lat. 33.39°						
Average temperature		42.8	44.6	51.8	60.8	68.0
Degree days		636	518	428	147	25
Slope	0°	839	1,045	1,388	1,782	1,970
	30°	1,232	1,359	1,594	1,805	1,814
	60°	1,360	1,389	1,475	1,478	1,349
	90°	1,189	1,130	1,068	899	725
Bismarck, N.D. lat. 46.47°						
Average temperature		8.6	12.2	26.6	42.8	53.6
Degree days		1,708	1,442	1,203	645	329
Slope	0°	581	924	1,292	1,653	2,029
	30°	1,160	1,519	1,714	1,829	2,008
	60°	1,467	1,765	1,760	1,639	1,635
	90°	1,421	1,599	1,422	1,138	1,011
Boise, Id. lat. 43.34°						
Average temperature		30.2	33.8	41.0	48.2	57.2
Degree days		1,113	854	722	438	245
Slope	0°	522	858	1,248	1,789	2,161
	30°	888	1,279	1,575	1,945	2,106
	60°	1,058	1,421	1,568	1,708	1,674
	90°	989	1,247	1,233	1,148	991

(Btu per Sq. Ft. per Day Falling on Surface)

June	July	Aug.	Sept.	Oct.	Nov.	Dec.
71.6	77.0	73.4	68.0	55.4	42.8	33.8
0	0	0	12	229	642	868
2,721	2,540	2,342	2,084	1,646	1,244	1,034
2,390	2,289	2,312	2,387	2,251	1,994	1,780
1,651	1,635	1,817	2,155	2,334	2,274	2,106
754	795	1,011	1,455	1,878	2,011	1,927
68.0	73.4	71.6	62.6	51.8	35.6	24.8
30	0	6	96	363	828	1,225
1,992	1,973	1,693	1,351	1,008	688	526
1,841	1,859	1,728	1,571	1,398	1,129	933
1,400	1,438	1,442	1,469	1,485	1,318	1,131
800	834	918	1,076	1,250	1,207	1,068
78.8	80.6	80.6	78.8	69.8	60.8	55.4
0	0	0	0	16	153	319
2,176	1,992	1,866	1,693	1,539	1,226	972
1,870	1,752	1,771	1,809	1,916	1,736	1,432
1,272	1,231	1,351	1,558	1,876	1,859	1,577
606	615	740	1,007	1,434	1,566	1,371
75.2	77.0	77.0	71.6	62.6	51.8	44.6
0	0	0	18	124	417	648
2,040	1,981	1,848	1,517	1,288	975	740
1,801	1,782	1,795	1,656	1,638	1,415	1,113
1,281	1,294	1,410	1,461	1,638	1,545	1,247
659	680	811	990	1,292	1,332	1,107
62.6	69.8	68.0	57.2	44.6	30.2	15.8
117	34	28	222	577	1,083	1,463
2,161	2,253	1,907	1,406	1,005	592	456
2,039	2,173	2,016	1,722	1,521	1,083	943
1,591	1,723	1,734	1,672	1,696	1,327	1,210
938	1,023	1,139	1,272	1,484	1,258	1,188
64.4	73.4	71.6	62.6	51.8	39.2	32.0
81	0	0	132	415	792	1,017
2,353	2,463	2,095	1,679	1,156	666	452
2,184	2,336	2,180	2,036	1,690	1,128	805
1,657	1,800	1,834	1,947	1,844	1,336	980
923	1,008	1,156	1,440	1,578	1,237	931

Table 31. Continued

		Jan.	Feb.	Mar.	Apr.	May
Boston, Mass. lat. 42.22°						
Average temperature		30.2	30.2	35.6	46.4	57.2
Degree days		1,083	972	846	513	208
Slope	0°	511	729	1,078	1,340	1,738
	30°	830	1,021	1,313	1,414	1,677
	60°	970	1,101	1,281	1,226	1,335
	90°	895	950	996	831	810
Boulder, Colo. lat. 40.00°						
Average temperature		32.0	33.8	37.4	48.2	57.2
Degree days		992	826	809	482	236
Slope	0°	740	988	1,478	1,695	1,695
	30°	1,247	1,418	1,836	1,791	1,618
	60°	1,471	1,538	1,797	1,535	1,272
	90°	1,355	1,318	1,375	1,003	759
Caribou, Me. lat. 46.52°						
Average temperature		10.4	14.0	24.8	35.6	48.2
Degree days		1,690	1,470	1,308	858	468
Slope	0°	504	846	1,351	1,473	1,745
	30°	963	1,362	1,808	1,613	1,721
	60°	1,201	1,570	1,865	1,441	1,406
	90°	1,156	1,417	1,510	1,006	887
Charleston, S.C. lat. 32.54°						
Average temperature		50.0	50.0	57.2	64.4	71.6
Degree days		487	389	291	54	0
Slope	0°	931	1,115	1,443	1,896	2,025
	30°	1,376	1,449	1,652	1,915	1,855
	60°	1,519	1,477	1,522	1,557	1,366
	90°	1,325	1,196	1,093	929	721
Chicago, Ill. lat. 41.59°						
Average temperature		24.8	28.4	35.6	48.2	59.0
Degree days		1,265	1,086	939	534	260
Slope	0°	353	541	836	1,220	1,563
	30°	492	693	970	1,273	1,502
	60°	538	715	924	1,098	1,196
	90°	479	602	712	746	734
Cleveland, Ohio lat. 41.24°						
Average temperature		28.4	28.4	35.6	46.4	57.2
Degree days		1,159	1,047	918	552	260
Slope	0°	456	662	1,148	1,388	1,925
	30°	690	889	1,395	1,459	1,851
	60°	783	938	1,357	1,258	1,458
	90°	710	798	1,047	844	861

June	July	Aug.	Sept.	Oct.	Nov.	Dec.
66.2	71.6	69.8	62.6	53.6	42.8	32.0
36	0	9	60	316	603	983
1,837	1,826	1,565	1,255	876	533	438
1,701	1,722	1,593	1,449	1,184	818	736
1,303	1,340	1,331	1,352	1,244	931	875
759	791	857	993	1,044	842	820
66.2	73.4	71.6	62.6	53.6	41.0	35.6
88	6	0	139	367	690	905
1,935	1,917	1,618	1,518	1,142	819	670
1,772	1,787	1,628	1,755	1,567	1,326	1,188
1,332	1,366	1,342	1,625	1,650	1,535	1,434
750	780	843	1,168	1,371	1,392	1,344
59.0	64.4	60.8	53.6	42.8	32.0	17.6
183	78	115	336	682	1,044	1,535
1,767	1,874	1,657	1,226	773	405	390
1,668	1,804	1,736	1,474	1,103	654	765
1,315	1,441	1,492	1,419	1,199	766	966
803	882	991	1,080	1,038	711	942
77.0	80.6	78.8	75.2	66.2	57.2	50.0
0	0	0	0	59	282	471
2,062	1,925	1,826	1,502	1,263	1,049	795
1,811	1,726	1,765	1,628	1,583	1,520	1,194
1,277	1,249	1,379	1,428	1,570	1,656	1,335
647	656	787	960	1,229	1,423	1,181
69.8	73.4	73.4	64.4	53.6	39.2	30.2
72	0	12	117	381	807	1,166
1,688	1,743	1,485	1,153	763	442	280
1,561	1,639	1,503	1,311	990	626	384
1,198	1,274	1,252	1,212	1,020	687	417
707	754	806	887	846	610	373
66.2	71.6	69.8	64.4	53.6	41.0	32.0
66	9	25	105	384	738	1,088
2,058	2,029	1,815	1,384	968	519	423
1,894	1,903	1,849	1,602	1,313	767	677
1,429	1,462	1,534	1,491	1,379	857	789
803	836	962	1,085	1,151	767	729

Table 31. Continued

		Jan.	*Feb.*	*Mar.*	*Apr.*	*May*
Dallas, Tex. lat. 32.51°						
Average temperature		44.6	48.2	55.4	66.2	78.4
Degree days		608	437	314	71	0
Slope	0°	851	1,131	1,452	1,673	1,920
	30°	1,231	1,473	1,663	1,681	1,761
	60°	1,347	1,503	1,533	1,371	1,303
	90°	1,170	1,217	1,099	834	698
Davis, Cal. lat. 38.33°						
Average temperature		44.6	48.2	51.8	57.2	62.6
Degree days		583	414	332	178	72
Slope	0°	581	942	1,480	1,944	2,342
	30°	873	1,299	1,803	2,047	2,216
	60°	981	1,379	1,740	1,735	1,689
	90°	879	1,163	1,313	1,101	921
Dodge City, Kas. lat. 37.46°						
Average temperature		30.2	33.8	41.0	53.6	62.6
Degree days		1,051	840	719	354	124
Slope	0°	953	1,204	1,590	1,988	2,073
	30°	1,598	1,718	1,938	2,083	1,952
	60°	1,872	1,848	1,866	1,755	1,491
	90°	1,706	1,562	1,396	1,100	831
Fairbanks, Ak. lat. 64.49°						
Average temperature		−11.2	−2.2	8.6	30.8	46.4
Degree days		2,359	1,901	1,739	1,068	555
Slope	0°	70	279	858	1,417	1,756
	30°	504	791	1,600	1,840	1,883
	60°	809	1,110	1,962	1,884	1,715
	90°	901	1,152	1,849	1,527	1,255
Great Falls, Mont. lat. 47.29°						
Average temperature		21.2	26.6	32.0	42.8	51.8
Degree days		1,349	1,154	1,063	642	384
Slope	0°	508	843	1,333	1,579	1,929
	30°	1,007	1,384	1,801	1,751	1,916
	60°	1,273	1,610	1,869	1,576	1,570
	90°	1,236	1,463	1,523	1,104	985
Greensboro, N.C. lat. 36.05°						
Average temperature		37.4	39.2	46.4	57.2	66.2
Degree days		784	672	552	234	47
Slope	0°	754	1,001	1,303	1,727	1,962
	30°	1,147	1,344	1,524	1,777	1,834
	60°	1,291	1,403	1,435	1,483	1,391
	90°	1,149	1,164	1,062	931	773

June	July	Aug.	Sept.	Oct.	Nov.	Dec.
80.6	84.2	84.2	77.0	66.2	55.4	46.4
0	0	0	0	55	284	521
2,193	2,167	1,983	1,688	1,338	962	814
1,920	1,934	1,918	1,846	1,692	1,368	1,230
1,342	1,380	1,492	1,623	1,684	1,478	1,377
663	694	836	1,083	1,319	1,265	1,219
69.8	73.4	71.6	69.8	62.6	51.8	44.6
0	0	0	0	56	321	546
2,585	2,540	2,249	1,833	1,281	795	544
2,326	2,337	2,269	2,133	1,748	1,225	859
1,675	1,721	1,835	1,967	1,828	1,386	991
839	885	1,078	1,384	1,503	1,236	905
73.4	78.8	77.0	68.0	55.4	41.0	32.0
9	0	0	33	251	666	939
2,426	2,393	2,146	1,815	1,399	1,031	854
2,177	2,193	2,148	2,090	1,917	1,661	1,492
1,569	1,614	1,728	1,913	2,003	1,908	1,783
798	839	1,014	1,335	1,639	1,709	1,652
57.2	59.0	53.6	42.8	26.6	3.2	-7.6
222	171	332	642	1,203	1,833	2,254
1,940	1,635	1,336	677	316	99	22
1,939	1,674	1,555	956	679	469	252
1,692	1,483	1,495	1,041	887	721	416
1,190	1,064	1,154	905	883	787	471
60.8	68.0	68.0	57.2	48.2	33.8	28.4
186	28	53	258	543	921	1,169
2,176	2,338	1,947	1,487	964	567	412
2,061	2,266	2,074	1,855	1,473	1,056	859
1,617	1,804	1,794	1,820	1,652	1,304	1,107
960	1,074	1,187	1,395	1,453	1,244	1,091
73.4	77.0	75.2	69.8	57.2	46.4	39.2
0	0	0	33	192	513	778
2,069	1,992	1,749	1,517	1,211	894	684
1,853	1,818	1,724	1,692	1,580	1,345	1,080
1,344	1,347	1,382	1,522	1,610	1,499	1,240
710	729	827	1,056	1,296	1,318	1,122

Table 31. Continued

		Jan.	Feb.	Mar.	Apr.	May
Indianapolis, Ind. lat. 39.44°						
Average temperature		28.4	32.0	39.2	51.8	60.8
Degree days		1,113	949	809	432	177
Slope	0°	541	788	1,148	1,447	1,808
	30°	819	1,065	1,368	1,507	1,721
	60°	927	1,124	1,311	1,286	1,343
	90°	835	950	998	848	788
Ithaca, N.Y. lat. 42.27°						
Average temperature		23.0	24.8	32.0	44.6	53.6
Degree days		1,271	1,140	1,004	570	248
Slope	0°	449	747	1,038	1,281	1,727
	30°	699	1,054	1,257	1,347	1,667
	60°	803	1,141	1,224	1,168	1,327
	90°	735	985	951	794	807
Key West, Fla. lat. 24.33°						
Average temperature		69.8	69.8	73.4	77.0	80.6
Degree days		16	25	5	0	0
Slope	0°	1,205	1,511	1,806	2,108	2,134
	30°	1,624	1,859	1,969	2,021	1,855
	60°	1,693	1,808	1,720	1,535	1,262
	90°	1,394	1,376	1,132	800	582
Laramie, Wyo. lat. 41.18°						
Average temperature		21.2	24.8	28.4	37.4	46.4
Degree days		1,212	1,042	1,026	702	428
Slope	0°	824	1,097	1,561	1,833	2,018
	30°	1,489	1,652	1,986	1,964	1,940
	60°	1,805	1,833	1,972	1,699	1,524
	90°	1,689	1,595	1,526	1,116	892
Las Vegas, Nev. lat. 36.05°						
Average temperature		42.8	48.2	53.6	62.6	73.4
Degree days		688	487	335	111	6
Slope	0°	1,027	1,421	1,859	2,290	2,585
	30°	1,691	2,055	2,287	2,398	2,410
	60°	1,962	2,214	2,198	1,996	1,783
	90°	1,772	1,861	1,622	1,205	904
Little Rock, Ark. lat. 34.44°						
Average temperature		41.0	44.6	51.8	60.8	69.8
Degree days		756	577	434	126	9
Slope	0°	729	964	1,318	1,675	1,944
	30°	1,058	1,254	1,520	1,704	1,801
	60°	1,164	1,285	1,414	1,407	1,351
	90°	1,020	1,051	1,033	872	738

June	July	Aug.	Sept.	Oct.	Nov.	Dec.
71.6	75.2	73.4	66.2	55.4	41.0	32.0
39	0	0	90	316	723	1,051
2,014	1,995	1,789	1,491	1,078	648	478
1,837	1,855	1,801	1,711	1,450	974	750
1,371	1,408	1,477	1,576	1,511	1,092	864
759	792	911	1,128	1,247	974	791
64.4	68.0	66.2	59.0	50.0	39.2	28.4
45	6	28	132	415	744	1,153
1,984	1,970	1,693	1,310	913	460	364
1,836	1,858	1,731	1,522	1,245	673	573
1,400	1,440	1,447	1,424	1,315	751	664
802	838	923	1,046	1,105	673	614
82.4	84.2	84.2	84.2	78.8	73.4	69.8
0	0	0	0	0	0	18
2,001	1,968	1,846	1,640	1,452	1,223	1,076
1,674	1,679	1,700	1,686	1,698	1,599	1,477
1,098	1,127	1,248	1,399	1,591	1,634	1,560
525	538	641	861	1,164	1,320	1,307
55.4	62.6	60.8	53.6	42.8	32.0	24.8
150	28	37	219	543	909	1,085
2,308	2,183	1,936	1,546	1,174	835	673
2,119	2,047	1,978	1,812	1,653	1,409	1,247
1,583	1,564	1,639	1,694	1,765	1,659	1,531
863	879	1,019	1,230	1,483	1,522	1,452
82.4	87.8	86.0	78.8	66.2	51.8	44.6
0	0	0	0	78	387	617
2,747	2,489	2,308	2,051	1,579	1,170	957
2,428	2,259	2,294	2,369	2,175	1,889	1,657
1,692	1,634	1,820	2,155	2,268	2,164	1,968
784	817	1,031	1,473	1,839	1,926	1,811
77.0	80.6	78.8	73.4	62.6	51.8	42.8
0	0	0	9	127	465	716
2,069	2,054	1,900	1,627	1,274	898	688
1,836	1,857	1,858	1,802	1,639	1,306	1,043
1,315	1,355	1,469	1,606	1,653	1,431	1,174
681	712	851	1,094	1,314	1,241	1,048

Table 31. Continued

	Jan.	Feb.	Mar.	Apr.	May
Madison, Wisc. lat. 43.08°					
Average temperature	17.6	21.2	32.0	44.6	55.4
Degree days	1,473	1,274	1,113	618	310
Slope 0°	564	812	1,232	1,455	1,745
30°	973	1,189	1,546	1,553	1,692
60°	1,165	1,309	1,534	1,356	1,353
90°	1,090	1,143	1,203	921	827
Medford, Ore. lat. 42.23°					
Average temperature	37.4	41.0	44.6	50.0	57.2
Degree days	918	697	642	432	242
Slope 0°	434	780	1,222	1,782	2,168
30°	667	1,112	1,516	1,920	2,099
60°	763	1,208	1,493	1,672	1,656
90°	696	1,045	1,162	1,112	967
Miami, Fla. lat. 25.47°					
Average temperature	66.2	66.2	69.8	73.4	77.0
Degree days	74	56	19	0	0
Slope 0°	1,263	1,531	1,808	2,003	2,032
30°	1,748	1,913	1,990	1,933	1,784
60°	1,848	1,879	1,753	1,487	1,237
90°	1,539	1,444	1,167	801	594
Nashville, Tenn. lat. 36.07°					
Average temperature	37.4	41.0	48.2	59.0	68.0
Degree days	828	672	524	176	45
Slope 0°	600	883	1,211	1,657	1,903
30°	858	1,157	1,404	1,702	1,780
60°	941	1,195	1,316	1,421	1,353
90°	827	987	975	896	757
New York, N.Y. lat. 40.46°					
Average temperature	32.0	32.0	39.2	50.0	60.8
Degree days	973	879	750	414	124
Slope 0°	537	773	1,148	1,392	1,675
30°	837	1,061	1,383	1,456	1,602
60°	959	1,129	1,337	1,249	1,263
90°	873	962	1,025	833	759
Phoenix, Ariz. lat. 33.26°					
Average temperature	50.0	55.4	59.0	66.2	75.2
Degree days	474	328	217	75	0
Slope 0°	1,093	1,502	1,918	2,367	2,666
30°	1,706	2,092	2,295	2,430	2,436
60°	1,928	2,203	2,157	1,976	1,747
90°	1,703	1,809	1,548	1,140	827

June	July	Aug.	Sept.	Oct.	Nov.	Dec.
66.2	69.8	68.0	59.0	50.0	33.8	23.0
102	25	40	174	474	930	1,330
2,031	2,046	1,740	1,443	993	555	495
1,886	1,938	1,789	1,710	1,398	885	899
1,444	1,507	1,503	1,617	1,499	1,024	1,101
830	878	964	1,195	1,273	937	1,048
64.4	71.6	69.8	64.4	53.6	42.8	37.8
78	0	0	78	372	678	871
2,404	2,573	2,216	1,653	1,023	559	338
2,218	2,425	2,297	1,975	1,428	870	516
1,665	1,845	1,916	1,870	1,522	996	590
909	1,003	1,183	1,369	1,284	904	542
80.6	80.6	82.4	80.6	77.0	71.6	68.0
0	0	0	0	0	0	65
1,955	1,977	1,870	1,646	1,432	1,303	1,174
1,651	1,698	1,733	1,705	1,690	1,751	1,672
1,101	1,152	1,282	1,426	1,596	1,816	1,800
534	553	666	888	1,180	1,483	1,527
75.2	78.8	77.0	71.6	60.8	48.2	41.0
0	0	0	10	180	498	763
2,087	2,036	1,819	1,576	1,204	799	592
1,869	1,858	1,795	1,764	1,569	1,170	898
1,355	1,374	1,438	1,589	1,599	1,290	1,015
714	739	854	1,101	1,287	1,128	912
69.8	75.2	73.4	68.0	57.2	46.4	33.8
6	0	0	27	223	528	887
1,936	1,907	1,811	1,329	964	589	471
1,777	1,783	1,836	1,520	1,290	885	761
1,340	1,367	1,575	1,404	1,345	995	888
758	786	943	1,016	1,115	891	821
84.2	89.6	87.8	82.4	71.6	59.0	51.8
0	0	0	0	22	234	415
2,725	2,400	2,253	2,091	1,664	1,248	1,031
2,364	2,143	2,195	2,355	2,217	1,916	1,683
1,601	1,518	1,705	2,094	2,261	2,140	1,946
704	738	934	1,386	1,790	1,864	1,753

Table 31. Continued

		Jan.	Feb.	Mar.	Apr.	May
Philadelphia, Pa. lat. 39.53°						
Average temperature		32.0	33.8	41.0	51.8	62.6
Degree days		1,014	871	716	367	122
Slope	0°	645	892	1,279	1,566	1,817
	30°	1,031	1,241	1,547	1,641	1,731
	60°	1,191	1,327	1,495	1,402	1,351
	90°	1,085	1,129	1,139	918	793
Portland, Me. lat. 43.39°						
Average temperature		23.0	24.8	32.0	41.0	51.8
Degree days		1,339	1,182	1,042	675	372
Slope	0°	578	872	1,321	1,495	1,889
	30°	1,015	1,308	1,684	1,602	1,836
	60°	1,223	1,456	1,684	1,403	1,468
	90°	1,149	1,279	1,326	953	889
Salt Lake City, Utah lat. 40.46°						
Average temperature		28.4	32.0	39.2	48.2	57.2
Degree days		1,172	910	763	459	233
Slope	0°	648	964	1,347	1,826	2,191
	30°	1,066	1,390	1,660	1,945	2,099
	60°	1,248	1,512	1,621	1,674	1,634
	90°	1,147	1,300	1,245	1,092	932
San Diego, Cal. lat. 32.44°						
Average temperature		53.6	55.4	57.2	59.0	62.6
Degree days		314	237	219	144	79
Slope	0°	976	1,264	1,577	1,710	1,817
	30°	1,455	1,676	1,822	1,719	1,667
	60°	1,612	1,785	1,684	1,400	1,240
	90°	1,408	1,399	1,205	848	674
Seattle, Wash. lat. 47.27°						
Average temperature		41.0	44.6	44.6	50.0	55.4
Degree days		738	599	577	396	242
Slope	0°	287	500	972	1,458	1,844
	30°	457	711	1,240	1,605	1,829
	60°	535	779	1,254	1,440	1,500
	90°	500	688	1,013	1,012	946
Washington, D.C. lat. 38.51°						
Average temperature		35.6	37.4	44.6	55.4	64.4
Degree days		871	762	626	288	74
Slope	0°	585	846	1,178	1,484	1,646
	30°	884	1,144	1,394	1,539	1,559
	60°	997	1,205	1,329	1,306	1,216
	90°	895	1,014	1,004	852	720

June	July	Aug.	Sept.	Oct.	Nov.	Dec.
71.6	75.2	73.4	68.0	57.2	46.4	35.6
0	0	0	38	249	564	924
2,042	1,983	1,714	1,430	1,080	704	560
1,863	1,844	1,724	1,635	1,454	1,084	926
1,390	1,402	1,415	1,504	1,516	1,229	1,089
768	790	879	1,078	1,252	1,101	1,008
60.8	68.0	66.2	59.0	48.2	37.4	28.4
111	12	53	195	508	807	1,015
1,992	2,065	1,774	1,410	1,005	578	508
1,853	1,959	1,830	1,870	1,427	941	941
1,423	1,526	1,541	1,582	1,537	1,099	1,160
824	890	989	1,172	1,309	1,010	1,109
68.0	77.0	75.2	64.4	51.8	39.2	32.0
84	0	0	81	419	849	1,082
2,540	2,342	2,084	1,671	1,233	780	567
2,317	2,185	2,125	1,963	1,732	1,265	971
1,705	1,652	1,750	1,833	1,843	1,466	1,159
890	902	1,069	1,320	1,542	1,332	1,083
64.4	68.0	69.8	69.8	64.4	59.0	55.4
52	6	0	16	43	140	257
1,880	2,016	1,839	1,644	1,330	1,046	903
1,657	1,803	1,777	1,773	1,680	1,513	1,395
1,182	1,297	1,386	1,575	1,670	1,646	1,577
619	669	789	1,052	1,307	1,413	1,402
60.8	64.4	64.4	60.8	53.6	46.4	42.8
117	50	47	129	329	543	657
1,918	2,087	1,749	1,207	696	390	235
1,817	2,020	1,848	1,461	983	641	386
1,433	1,615	1,597	1,414	1,067	756	459
869	980	1,064	1,082	925	706	435
73.4	77.0	75.2	69.8	59.0	48.2	37.4
0	0	0	33	217	519	834
2,054	1,947	1,701	1,351	1,034	777	541
1,864	1,802	1,700	1,521	1,360	1,195	857
1,379	1,362	1,386	1,387	1,400	1,352	989
752	762	853	987	1,145	1,206	904

Table 31. Continued

		Jan.	Feb.	Mar.	Apr.	May
Montreal, Quebec lat. 45.30°						
Average temperature		15.8	19.4	28.4	41.0	53.6
Degree days		1,566	1,381	1,175	684	316
Slope	0°	405	736	1,178	1,473	1,730
	30°	680	1,108	1,512	1,599	1,696
	60°	810	1,241	1,525	1,417	1,376
	90°	760	1,100	1,217	979	859
Toronto, Ont. lat. 43.40°						
Average temperature		26.6	26.6	32.0	42.8	53.6
Degree days		1,233	1,119	1,013	616	298
Slope	0°	445	681	1,075	1,369	1,760
	30°	719	962	1,326	1,458	1,709
	60°	841	1,044	1,307	1,275	1,370
	90°	778	906	1,025	871	839
St. Johns, N.F. lat. 47.31°						
Average temperature		24.8	24.8	28.4	33.8	41.0
Degree days		1,262	1,170	1,187	927	710
Slope	0°	294	552	883	1,176	1,473
	30°	475	809	1,108	1,272	1,451
	60°	559	899	1,112	1,134	1,195
	90°	525	799	896	803	774
Ottawa, Ont. lat. 45.27°						
Average temperature		14.0	14.0	26.6	41.0	53.6
Degree days		1,624	1,441	1,231	708	341
Slope	0°	530	839	1,233	1,484	1,830
	30°	974	1,304	1,594	1,611	1,795
	60°	1,198	1,478	1,613	1,428	1,454
	90°	1,142	1,319	1,289	986	901

exchange rate, is appropriate only to low-intensity, low-humidity growing.

AIR MOVEMENT

In calculating R values we found that the surfaces of the house had associated R values due to trapped adjacent air layers. These surfaces weren't even hairy, and so it is obvious that plant surfaces are surrounded by even thicker dead-air layers. In the natural environment the wind ventilates leaf surfaces with the CO_2 necessary for plant growth; in the greenhouse, plant growth is inhibited without air movement. Thus, the fans and blowers in the designs serve more than one purpose.

CARBON DIOXIDE, CO_2

Plants are just the opposite of people in their respiration habits; they inhale carbon dioxide and exhale oxygen. In fact, scientists believe that plants are responsible for all of the oxygen presently in the earth's atmosphere. While plants thrive in the normal percentage of CO_2 found in the atmosphere, they grow even better with higher levels. If the plants in our greenhouse were to use up all of the CO_2, they would simply stop growing. This poses no problem in a conventional greenhouse, since inside and outside air exchange almost at will through the hundreds of glazing joints. Overheating is solved simply by venting hot air at the top, to be replaced by

June	July	Aug.	Sept.	·Oct.	Nov.	Dec.
62.6	64.4	62.6	59.0	46.4	33.8	21.2
69	9	43	165	521	882	1,392
1,804	1,878	1,620	1,141	736	368	294
1,694	1,797	1,683	1,341	1,013	548	484
1,325	1,424	1,434	1,274	1,081	619	573
797	862	945	959	923	563	540
62.6	64.4	62.6	59.0	50.0	39.2	30.2
62	7	18	151	439	760	1,111
1,914	1,940	1,598	1,266	824	452	349
1,782	1,840	1,639	1,480	1,123	682	566
1,372	1,438	1,380	1,394	1,188	772	665
801	849	895	1,034	1,004	699	622
50.0	59.0	59.0	51.8	42.8	35.6	30.2
432	186	180	342	651	831	1,113
1,583	1,620	1,251	1,031	625	294	257
1,499	1,562	1,295	1,219	861	431	443
1,194	1,260	1,114	1,166	923	486	536
747	793	760	893	796	443	512
60.8	62.6	60.8	57.2	46.4	32.0	17.6
90	25	81	222	567	936	1,469
2,054	2,014	1,727	1,307	813	452	401
1,928	1,928	1,800	1,564	1,145	727	746
1,496	1,523	1,534	1,497	1,234	847	925
879	911	1,005	1,127	1,059	782	890

fresh air from the outside. Our greenhouse, however, has the prime purpose of generating a maximum amount of heated air, and so another solution must be found. The solution is simply to exchange air with the adjacent living space, providing the plants with CO_2 and the house with O_2.

SUNSHINE

Plants require both minimal intensities and durations of radiation for growth and for reproduction (flowering). The radiation intensity in a greenhouse is sufficient for nearly any plant, but the photoperiod (duration) is insufficient in the winter months for many. Seek advice from local commercial growers on the photoperiod requirements of the plants you would like to grow. A problem unique to the solar greenhouse with its insulated north, east, and west walls and often dark-colored north wall is heliotropism, or growing toward the sun. Two of the designs below have white-painted north walls to reflect sunlight to the backside of the plants and thus promote more even growth. A very uniform growth is obtained at the expense of some efficiency, since a portion of the light is thereby bounced right out of the greenhouse.

The Basic Structure

The greenhouse consists of: (1) an insulated concrete perimeter wall extending below the surface either three feet or to below the local frost depth, whichever is greater, (2) a south wall of 46″ × 76″ tempered insulated glass panels supported by 4 × 8 framing members 48″ on-center, (3) insulated east and west end-walls of ordinary wood frame construction, and (4) rigid 44″ × 76″ insulating panels that slide on tracks between the framing to cover the glazing at night. Differences among the three designs shown are related only to the handling of excess heat.

The perimeter wall foundation must extend below the frost depth in order that it not, in some unoccupied winter, heave and cause a destructive differential movement between the greenhouse and the house. Sinking the greenhouse into the ground ("pit greenhouse") has two advantages: headroom is gained in the lean-to structure which is necessary when the height of the structure is limited by the height of the existing wall; the ground below the frost depth runs at a year-round temperature of approximately 90° F-latitude in degrees. At low latitudes the ground may thus be considered a source of heat. At high latitudes, while it cannot be considered a source of heat (to be a *source* it must be higher in temperature than the greenhouse average temperature), it certainly reduces conductive heat losses. The perimeter wall is insulated down to the footing with 1″ or 2″ rigid Styrofoam or urethane panels. Installation of the foam is greatly simplified by pouring the concrete with the foam panels in the form. Simply sharpen the ends of the "snap-ties" on a grinder and skewer the foam when placing the ties. The foam is later protected from physical and solar abuse by coating with a vinyl-acrylic latex product such as Childers Products Company's CP-10 Vi-Cryl. Cement-asbestos board may also be used.

If you choose to store the excess heat in a gravel bed under the floor, it would be worthwhile to pour the gravel on top of similar rigid foam panels protected by some inexpensive rigid material.

Since you are building a potential swimming pool in the ground, in other than well-drained sandy soils, provide for drainage either with a perimeter drainage tile at footing level or, better still, drill a hole through the house foundation and grout in a 2″ PVC drainpipe similar in operation to a washing machine standpipe.

The framing of the lean-to wall is controlled by the size of the glass panels. You'll find that the least expensive way to buy insulated glass is in the form of tempered glass sliding glass door replacement units. Millions of these units are manufactured each year. The largest glass dealers pay less than two dollars per square foot (1978) for a unit. If you shop around, you should be able to come close to that figure. If you have trouble, try to get a group order together; perhaps a local builder would be interested in buying a large number for fixed windows. The owner-builder students at Cornerstones pay $2.00 per square foot through the Cornerstones building materials co-op.

The panels come in three sizes: *exactly* 28″ × 76″, 34″ × 76″, and 46″ × 76″. I have chosen the 46″ panel because it allows conventional 48″ on-center framing, which looks the best and results in the least solar obstruction.

While it is not critical that the glazing be perfectly sealed, the structure will last longer and have smaller infiltration losses if the glass panels are bedded in silicone or butyl caulk, as shown in Illustration 104. All wood framing members should be thoroughly treated with either clear or white Cuprinal preservative to prevent dry rot and ugly water stains. Cuprinal is the only commercial wood preservative not toxic to plants.

The glazed wall is firmly attached at the bottom by foundation anchor bolts 48″ on-center cast into the concrete and penetrating the 2″ × 8″ treated wood sill. Before attaching the sill to the foundation lay a strip of 1″ × 6″ fiberglass sill-sealer or a bead of Polycel One foam to prevent infiltration. The top of the glazed wall is attached to the existing structure by removing a

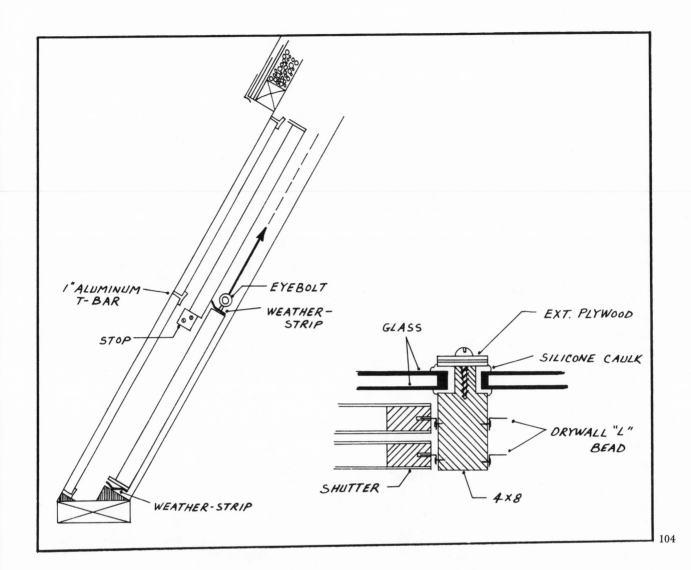

1" ALUMINUM T-BAR

EYEBOLT

STOP

WEATHER-STRIP

WEATHER-STRIP

GLASS

EXT. PLYWOOD

SILICONE CAULK

DRYWALL "L" BEAD

SHUTTER

4×8

104

few courses of siding and lag-bolting a 2″ × 10″ top plate to the building studs. The lean-to members are then nailed to the plate, using metal framing angles.

The insulating shutters are made exactly as in Chapter 13, of Thermoply and wood, except that they slide on tracks inside the framing spaces instead of swinging on hinges. Each shutter slides on a pair of simple metal tracks, such as drywall L-bead, screwed to the inside faces of the 4″ × 8″s. The metal tracks project into saw kerfs made in the shutter edges by a table saw. Wax the metal to make operation easier. The shutters are stored during the day at the top of their tracks behind the opaque roof, which serves also to protect the glazing from ice falling from the adjacent roof. Two or more overlapping shutters are used in each glazing bay in order to maintain a high glass-to-opaque-surface ratio on the south wall. Illustration 104 shows how the top and bottom projecting lips of the shutters allow sealing of the air space and raising of the shutter assembly with one rope and pulley.

Three Systems

I have named the first system (Illustration 105) *symbiotic exchange,* since the house and green-

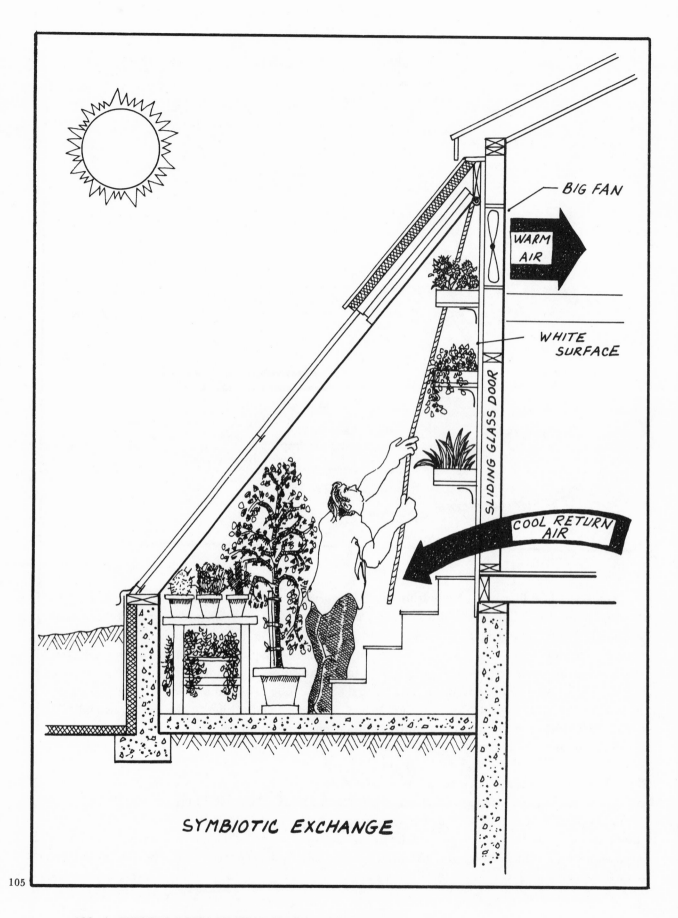

BIG FAN

WARM
AIR

WHITE
SURFACE

SLIDING GLASS DOOR

COOL RETURN
AIR

SYMBIOTIC EXCHANGE

105

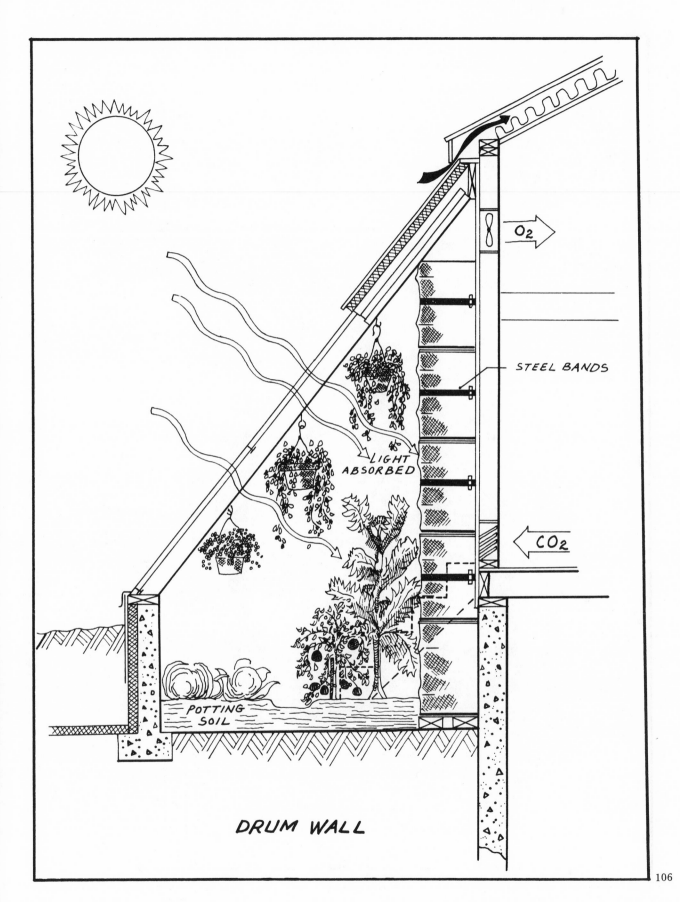

O₂

STEEL BANDS

LIGHT
ABSORBED

CO₂

POTTING
SOIL

DRUM WALL

106

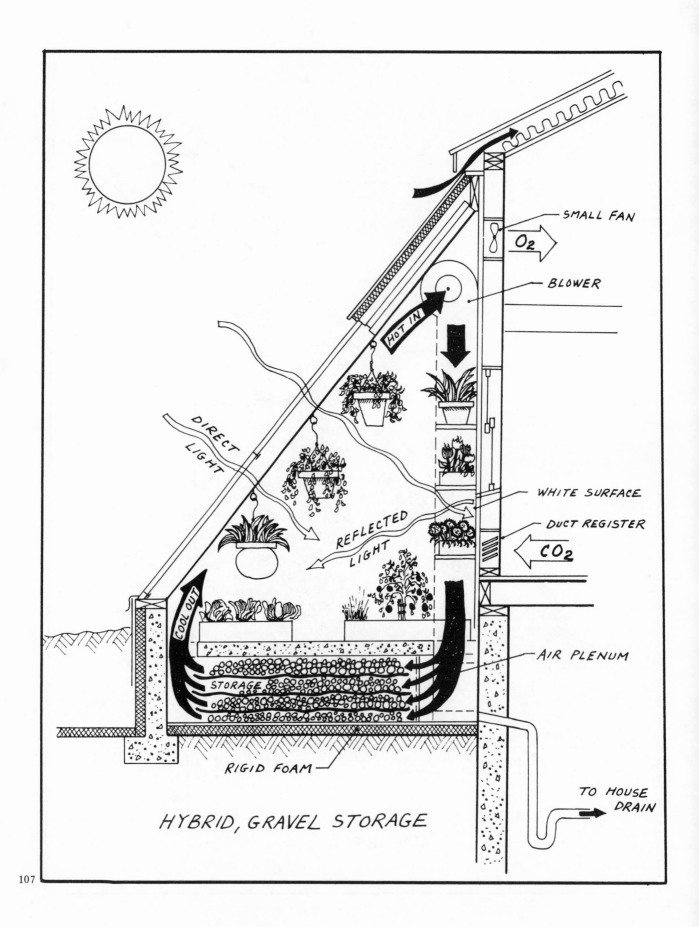

SMALL FAN

O₂

BLOWER

HOT IN

DIRECT LIGHT

REFLECTED LIGHT

WHITE SURFACE

DUCT REGISTER

CO₂

AIR PLENUM

COOL OUT

STORAGE

RIGID FOAM

TO HOUSE DRAIN

HYBRID, GRAVEL STORAGE

107

house rely upon each other for heat and for exchange of respiration gases. The amount of air that must be moved to keep the greenhouse from overheating is large. As a rule of thumb, the fan shown must move 10 cubic feet of air per minute per square foot of glazing in order to keep the temperature difference between the heated air and the cool return air to 10 Fahrenheit degrees on a clear winter day. Calculate the number of square feet of south glass, multiply by 10, and consult a W. W. Grainger catalogue (most hardware stores have them) for a multispeed window fan of the appropriate size.

The symbiotic exchange system is the most effective in lowering the fuel bill of the adjacent structure, since it has no storage losses. The entire winter clear-day heating load of an average building in the northern U.S. can be supplied by a greenhouse with glazing of 10 to 20 percent of the floor area of the adjacent structure.

The weak point of this system is the inability to maintain relative humidities in excess of 20 percent for fear of excess humidity in the adjoining living space. The structure would be better described as a sun space than a production greenhouse.

The second system (Illustration 106), the *drumwall,* is intended to serve primarily as a self-heating, self-regulating greenhouse. Heat gained by the attached structure is minor compared to the heat gain of the previously described symbiotic system.

The drumwall, popularized by Steve Baer, gets its name from the stack of 55-gallon drums completely covering the back wall. The drums are 90 percent filled with a mixture of ethylene glycol antifreeze and water and topped off with a quart of motor oil. The antifreeze prevents freezing and inhibits rusting of the barrels; the floating oil membrane retards evaporation and allows the use of recycled drums.

The key to the success of the drumwall system lies in the unique properties of water: the ability to absorb the greatest amount of heat per pound per $F°$ temperature rise of any natural substance,

and the ability rapidly to convect heat gained away from the metal surface. One water-filled drum absorbs roughly 400 Btu for each $1F°$ temperature rise and returns the identical amount in cooling. Fifty drums stacked five high and ten wide will rise and fall in temperature only $10F°$ in absorbing and returning 200,000 Btu—the equivalent of burning 2 gallons of fuel oil or 200 cubic feet of gas! If the drums are painted a dark color and not shaded by plants, they will absorb sufficient sunlight directly to prevent overheating of the greenhouse air. The dark surface serves as an effective radiator at night, reemitting the radiation absorbed during the day.

As a rule of thumb, provide one 55-gallon drum for each 6 square feet of glazing to limit the temperature rise of the drums to $10F°$ on a clear winter day.

The high small fan and low return louvers (which can also be a window or door) serve to heat one adjacent room and exchange just enough air to maintain the CO_2 level of the greenhouse. Both plant growth and drum heat exchange would benefit from a circulating fan within the greenhouse.

Strong points of the drumwall include economy and passivity. The weak points are the minimal heat contributed to the adjacent structure and the tendency toward plant heliotropism.

The third system (Illustration 107), the *hybrid rock storage,* is very similar in operation to an active solar system. It is called hybrid because it is neither a pure passive nor a pure active system. It has all of the elements of the active system, but the storage is within the collector and the collector is the heated space itself.

Sunlight strikes the vegetation and other interior surfaces of the greenhouse, raising their temperatures. The warm surfaces, in turn, warm the greenhouse air; when the greenhouse air reaches a predetermined upper limit a thermostat turns on the blower, which then forces the warm air down through a rock storage bed. Because of the great surface area of the rocks, the emerging air is always within a few degrees of the rock temperature; the air is thus "purified" of its excess heat.

At night the greenhouse air temperature drops; when it reaches a predetermined lower limit, a second thermostat turns the blower on again; the emerging air is again roughly the temperature of the rocks, but this time warmer than the greenhouse. Heat stored during the day is thus recovered at night. Operation of the blower at night is also desirable to prevent the formation of cold air pockets.

The rock storage is in the form of round riverbed stone or crushed and screened stone of 2" to 3" in diameter. The stone is installed in 6" layers between continuous sheets of 6 mil polyethylene. The top layer of polyethylene allows a 4" reinforced concrete slab to be poured as a floor over the stone. Polyethylene sheets are installed between the 6" layers of stone to prevent the warm buoyant air from rising and thus avoiding heat exchange with the bottom of the rock bed.

In order to distribute the air throughout the rock bed, the air collected from a single point at the top of the greenhouse is forced down through a vertical duct of the same cross-section as the blower outlet (roughly 2 square feet) and diverted at the bottom in both east and west horizontal directions by a curved vane in the plenum. The plenum is formed by a short framed wall covered with 1" wire mesh and braced about 18" out from the existing foundation wall. The air outlet at the opposite end is effected by simply terminating the poly sheets 6" from the wall and allowing the return air to flow out of slots or holes cast into the slab at regular intervals. The total area of the outlets should be twice the area of the duct cross-section and the on-center spacing no more than 24".

As rules of thumb allow:

2-1/2 cubic feet of 2" to 3" diameter stone for each square foot of glass, in order to hold the temperature cycle to 10 to 15F° on a clear winter day;

one 1/3-horsepower hot-air furnace blower for each 200 square feet of glazing. The operating pressure for the blower will be about 1/4" static pressure. Find the appropriate blower in the W. W. Grainger catalogue.

The strong point of the hybrid system is thermostatic control. The drawback is the noise of the blower. Typical electrical consumption for a 1/3-horsepower blower operating 50 percent of the time will amount to about $5 per month.

Solar Domestic Water Heaters (Illustration 108)

It is likely that you are spending more per unit of heat delivered for water heating than for space heating. Unless you also heat electrically, you are probably charged more than what the utilities call the "trailing-step" (the lowest rate of all). Even if you do heat electrically, you do so only about six months of the year. If you heat both your house and domestic water with oil, the same problem occurs each summer; the oil furnace runs at a very low efficiency in the summer just to heat water.

For this reason the solar domestic water heater (which is just a miniature version of the active solar system I previously maligned) can easily pay for itself.

Here is a step-by-step procedure by which you can determine whether the Super-Sunshine Solar Company's collector will pay for itself on your roof.

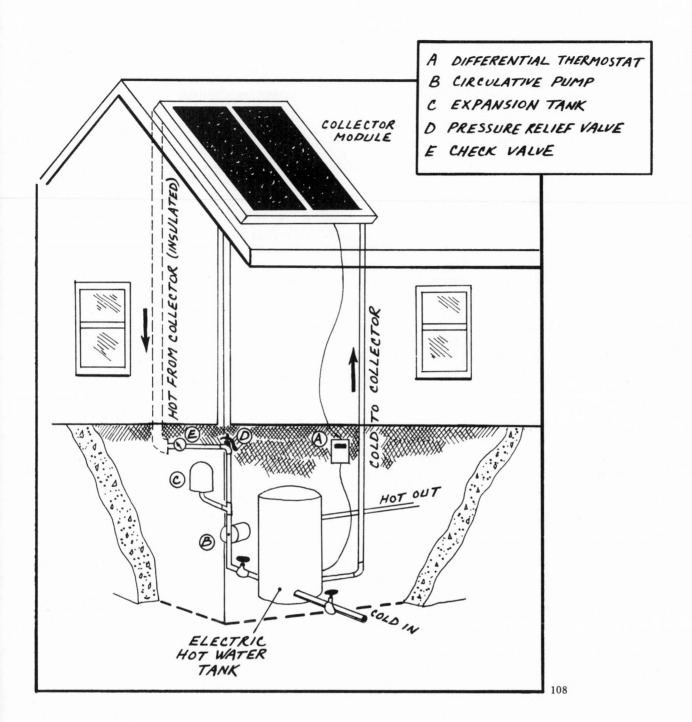

A DIFFERENTIAL THERMOSTAT
B CIRCULATIVE PUMP
C EXPANSION TANK
D PRESSURE RELIEF VALVE
E CHECK VALVE

COLLECTOR
MODULE

HOT FROM COLLECTOR (INSULATED)

COLD TO COLLECTOR

HOT OUT

COLD IN

ELECTRIC
HOT WATER
TANK

108

Example: A Boston family of four presently heats their house with oil and their hot water by electricity. After checking with the Boston Edison Co., they find that they are paying about 5¢ per kwh for the electricity used in the water heater. (The trailing-step is only 3.3¢, but their consumption doesn't reach that level.) The Super-Sunshine Solar Company has a university report demonstrating that their collector is 40 percent efficient at converting solar radiation to hot water on an annual basis *in the Boston area*. The company will install a 36-square-foot collector complete with storage tank and controls for a guaranteed $1,500. Will the solar collector pay for itself within the estimated twenty-year life?

procedure	*example*
1. Calculate the gallons of hot water used per year. Assume 15 gallons per day per person.	1. 4 people $\times$ 15 gal./day $\times$ 365 days = 21,900 gal.
2. Calculate the number of therms (10^5 Btu) required to heat the water from the ground water temperature (roughly 90°-lat.) to 140°F.	2. 21,900 gal./year $\times$ 8.3 lb./gal. $\times$ (140 – 90 + latitude) = 167 therms/year
3. Determine the cost per therm of heat delivered. Find the cost per unit of fuel and then consult Illustration 59 for the cost per therm.	3. 5¢/kwh = $1.46/therm
4. Find the total number of Btu's per year falling on one square foot of roof tilted at approximately the latitude angle for the site from Table 32.	4. For Boston at 30° tilt (nearest to 42° latitude): 15,458 Btu/sq. ft. $\times$ 30 days = 463,740 Btu or 4.64 therms/sq. ft. yr.
5. Calculate the number of therms collected by the collector by multiplying by the area of the collector and its efficiency.	5. 4.64 therms/sq. ft. $\times$ 36 sq. ft. $\times$ 0.40 = 66.8 therms
6. Calculate the first year savings: cost/therm $\times$ therms collected	6. $1.46/therm $\times$ 66.8 therms = $97.50
7. Calculate lifetime savings by multiplying by the 20-year Present Worth Factor, Table 1.	7. Assuming electric rates will increase at inflation plus 2%/year PWF = 24.3 life savings = 97.50 $\times$ 24.3 = $2,370
8. Calculate the percentage of hot water solar-heated.	8. $\dfrac{66.8 \text{ therms}}{167 \text{ therms}}$ = 40%

Our conclusion is that this particular collector in Boston will return approximately $2,400 on a $1,500 investment (a benefit/cost ratio of 1.58). We note from Step 8 that the fraction of water solar-heated is only 40 percent. It is very likely that the payback period and benefit/cost ratio would be improved by adding enough collector to the same storage and controls to bring the solar fraction up to 50 percent.

Is the above example realistic? The solar water heating industry is presently in its infancy. True, solar water heaters have been used extensively around the world for at least fifty years, but it is only recently that they have been widely used in climates as severe as those of the northern U.S. In 1976 the Massachusetts Electric Company installed 100 solar water heaters made by as many manufacturers. Of the 100 units, 69 experienced some form of difficulty, 30 units froze, 27 saved less than 10 percent of the electric water heating bill, and the cost averaged $2,200. However, if we judged the auto industry by its performance in the similar shakedown period, few of us would own automobiles today.

Considering seven of the top systems (on the

theory that the bugs will be worked out and the worst companies will go out of business), we find the following statistics:

Average Performance of Seven Systems

electric rate	system cost	1st-year saving	lifetime saving (pwf = 24.3)	benefit/ cost	payback years
@ 3¢/ kwh	$2,207	$ 79	$1,914	0.9	more than 20 yrs.
@ 5¢/ kwh	$2,207	$126	$3,062	1.4	15 yrs.

An efficiency of 40 percent seems to be the average of the best systems. Beware of claims exceeding 50 percent; ask for documentation; remember that assumptions are different from tests, and laboratory tests (à la EPA mileage tests) are different from field tests.

The average wholesale equipment cost for a complete system is about $1,000. Obviously there is a lot of money to be saved by the person handy with plumbing tools. Be sure, if you attempt installation yourself, however, to get complete instructions from the retailer. The majority of the problems encountered in the Massachusetts test were simple plumbing errors!

16.

Burning Wooden

Introduction

Try as we may, we can never quite achieve the no-heat house referred to in Chapter 9. The first big step was *conservation:* insulation, caulking, weatherstripping, and sharing the shower with a friend. The next most economical step was *solar:* shuttering the passive solar window, eliminating north windows, installing a solar domestic water heater, and building a solar greenhouse-collector. That about empties the bag of retrofit tricks. Unless we are willing at this point to don the thermal underwear, the nightcap and bunny suit, and let nature do her thing, we are probably left with an annual fuel bill of at least 3 cords of wood, 500 gallons of oil, or 10,000 kwh of electricity.

Heating *efficiency* is defined as the amount of heat you *get* divided by the amount of heat you *paid for.* What we need has already been minimized. The only way to minimize further what we pay for is to increase our heating efficiency; that is what this chapter is all about. First we will consider what can be done to the present heating system. Second, we will consider heating with wood, which, while not more efficient, is certainly cheaper in rural areas and a lot more secure (unless you sell your woodlot to an Arab).

Things to Do with Your Present System

SETTING BACK THE THERMOSTAT

The human comfort zone is defined by heating and ventilating engineers as that range of temperature and humidity over which lightly clothed sedentary adults feel comfortable. The zone has been defined experimentally by observing the rate of production of widgets and gizmos by lightly clad factory workers, the theory being that production falls off at both high and low temperature limits once the workers expend more energy complaining than producing. I don't question the results of the experiment, but I do question the assumption that we should all be lightly clad all of the time.

Ever since Honeywell started selling thermostats we have been raising generations of Americans who feel that the maintenance of $72 \pm 2°$ F is a birthright. Not only people, however; cats and dogs too. I have a nasty short-haired cat with dandruff who pounces on my bed every time the fire goes out in "her wood stove." Meanwhile her cousin, owned by some obviously more intelligent person, is daily seen about the woodpile on winter days wearing her version of a natural raccoon coat.

I teach energy-efficient solar house building to bankers and builders on cold winter nights down at the Cornerstones barn. Some nights the classroom is maintained at between 55°F and 60°F only through the valiant labors of the undersized wood stove and some diligent poking and feeding. The relative meaninglessness of the human comfort zone is struck home as the builders progressively shed layer upon layer of clothing while the bankers do just the opposite.

Scientific studies show the comfort zone to be variable with season and climate. Is it not a fact that 50°F seems frigid in July but absolutely balmy in January? The point I'm trying to make is that there is nothing absolute about the human comfort zone. Nor should the thermostat on the wall be regarded as an authority. It took an acquaintance of mine, after moving into an electrically heated house, nearly a year to get up the courage to disobey the thermostats. Every room of the house, you see, had a little round thermostat labeled simply "COLD—COMFORT ZONE—HOT"!

Permanent Setback: Let's see how much fuel is saved by running the house at a constant lower temperature. As you recall, the amount of fuel annually consumed in a house is directly proportional to the number of degree days at the site. Degree days, base 65°F, is defined as the accumulated number $(65°F - T_{ave})$ for all of the days in the heating season. The figure 65°F is used on the assumption that we desire to run our house at this temperature. Degree days can be based upon any temperature we wish, however. If we were to reduce our operating temperature permanently by 1 degree Fahrenheit down to 64°F, we would then reduce the number of degree days by 1 for every day of the heating season. At a site with 280 heating days in the heating season (280 days when T_{ave} is less than 65°F) then we would have reduced the number of degree days by exactly 280. If the normal number of degree days, base 65°F, were 7,500, then the 1-degree thermostat

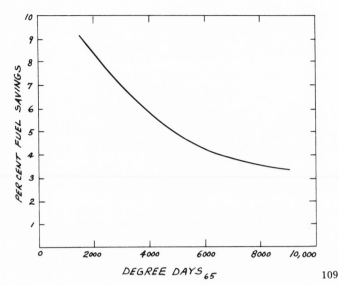

109

setback would have reduced the number of degree days (and therefore the annual fuel bill) by 280/7,500 or 3.7 percent. As we continue to drop the thermostat, the number of heating days decreases also, and so the percentage reduction in the annual fuel bill drops. Illustration 109 shows the annual fuel savings you can expect from each degree F of permanent thermostat setback as a function of the base-65°F degree days. At first glance it would appear that thermostat setback is not as important in colder climates. Do not be fooled; the *percentage* saving may be less with more degree days, but the total dollar saving is greater!

Temporary Setbacks: Do the same percentage savings accrue from setbacks of a few hours? That is, if the saving from a 1-degree permanent setback is 3 percent, is the saving from a 1-degree eight-hour setback exactly 1/3 as much, or 1 percent? I remember a number of years ago reading a message from Reddy Kilowatt which accompanied my monthly electric bill. It stated that the amount of heat required to raise the temperature of household furnishings that had cooled overnight equaled the amount of heat that would have otherwise been required to keep the house at a constant temperature. In other words, "Don't turn off the electric heat overnight."

Neither case is true. The fallacy of the utility

company's argument can be demonstrated by extending the setback period farther and farther. Suppose, for example, that your electric heating bill amounts to 5,000 kwh per month. Using Illustration 109, we discover that in a climate of 4,900 degree days we would save 5 percent, or 150 kwh, by permanently setting the thermostat back from 65°F to 64°F. If we accept the utility's argument as absolute, then we would consume 150 kwh in less than 1 hour in raising the house temperature 1 degree F at the end of the month. Obviously, the message is not completely accurate.

On the other hand, furnishings and the building itself do store heat. Upon our turning the thermostat down, the house temperature doesn't drop instantaneously to the new lower setting. Temporarily the heat loss through the exterior skin of the building is supplied by the heat content of the physical components of the house. The heat storage capacity of a house is called its *thermal mass*, the number of Btu's stored per F° change in temperature. The thermal mass of a typical light wood-frame house is of the order 10,000 Btu's per Fahrenheit degree. The rate at which heat is lost by the structure as a function of ΔT (the differential temperature) is called the *heat-loss coefficient*, measured in Btu's per Fahrenheit degree per hour. A good analogy to heat loss in a house is provided by a leaky water bucket. The size of the bucket corresponds to the size of the thermal mass; the size of the hole in the bucket has the same effect as the size of the heat-loss coefficient. A small bucket with a large hole empties rapidly; similarly, a small house with a large heat-loss coefficient cools rapidly. The length of time required for the temperature of the house to drop by 63 percent of the original ΔT ($T_{in} - T_{out}$) is called the *thermal time constant*. Mathematically, the time constant is the thermal mass divided by the heat-loss coefficient.

So in a temporary thermostat setback, two things are going on: (1) a certain amount of heat has been given up by the mass of the house in dropping a degree. Precisely the same amount, neither less nor more, must be replaced upon

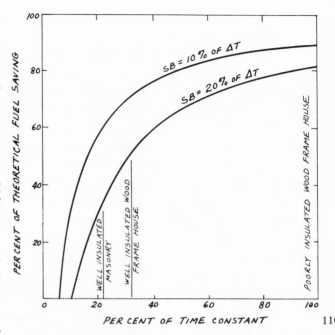

restoring the original temperature. (2) Since the temperature of the house is less than before, the ΔT is smaller and the heat loss to the outside is smaller. In sum, the amount of heat lost to the outside is less than it would have been at a steady temperature, but more than the thermostat indicates, since the thermal mass of the house keeps the house temperature from falling instantaneously. Illustration 110 shows the percentage of the maximum thermostat-indicated savings realized by setbacks of 10 percent and 20 percent of the original ΔT as a function of the thermal time constant of the house.

Example. Our site has 1,240 degree days in December. The average daily ΔT is therefore 1,240 DD per 31 days =40F°. Our house has a thermal time constant typical of well-insulated wood-frame construction, about twenty hours. An 8F° eight-hour overnight setback represents a ΔT setback of 20 percent for 40 percent of the time constant. Illustration 110 predicts that the energy savings is therefore only 60 percent of the savings predicted by the simple constant temperature model. A 4F° setback (10 percent of ΔT) would have saved 77 percent of the predicted savings.

In summary, large setbacks of short duration are not as effective in saving fuel as smaller permanent setbacks. This is particularly true of massive, well-insulated houses.

Matching the Burner to the Load

In the late departed era of cheap fuel, it was customary to oversize the house heating system. The fuel oil and electric companies discovered that warm customers were happy customers. Who could complain about a furnace that easily handled the worst winter could offer? Now that fuel prices are on the rise, however, there are a growing number of bankrupt, unhappy customers.

The last time you had your furnace tuned up, the serviceman probably happily reported that your furnace was now 80 percent efficient. That meant 80 percent of the heat value in the fuel was going into the house and 20 percent up the chimney, right? Wrong! It meant that 20 percent was going up the chimney *as long as the burner ran continuously,* as during his test. When the furnace is not running, however, some of the burner heat is still going up the chimney. If you doubt this, go up on the roof and feel the warm air coming out of the chimney even while the furnace is off. The net result of this continuous loss of heat up the chimney is a decrease of overall efficiency.

In Chapter 9, we learned to calculate the maximum hourly heat loss of a house in Btu's per hour. Oil burners and other heating systems are rated in Btu's per hour. If the furnace rated output were the same as the maximum hourly heat loss of the house, the furnace would run continuously at the coldest time of the year. During warmer periods it would run only a fraction of the time. Additionally, if the furnace were larger than need be in the first place, the fraction of running time would be even smaller. Over the entire heating season the ratio of length of running time to the length of the heating season or, alternatively, the ratio of heat produced to the maximum heat production possible is referred to as the part-load-fraction (PLF). Illustration 111

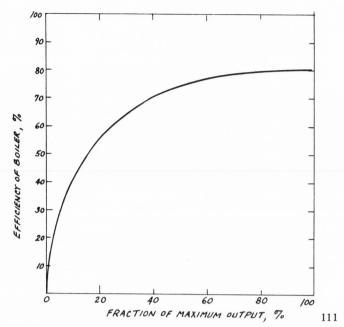

111

shows how the efficiency of an oil heat system drops with decreasing PLF.

The Cornerstones staff does energy audits. One of the numbers we always compute is the PLF. Over a full heating season it is impossible to achieve a PLF higher than 35 percent and a resulting heating-season burner efficiency of roughly 70 percent. Many of the houses we've audited, however, have a PLF of only 5 percent (seasonal burner efficiency therefore of about 30 percent). But there is that tag signed by a serviceman certifying a tested efficiency of 80 percent!

There are two steps we can take to increase the seasonal efficiency and decrease the fuel bill: (1) modify the burner to match the house better; (2) install an automatic flue damper.

MODIFY THE BURNER

You can calculate how well your present burner is matched to your house very simply. First calculate the maximum hourly heat loss at the coldest temperature of the year, as in the example at the end of Chapter 9. Then read the nozzle size rating from your burner nameplate in gallons per hour. One gallon per hour is roughly equivalent to 100,000 Btu's per hour heat output. A less mathematical but even more accurate way is simply timing the percentage of burner on-time during the coldest night of the year. If the burner capacity is more than the maximum heat loss rate your burner nozzle is oversized. Most furnaces and boilers are designed to operate over a range of nozzle sizes and burning rates. Call your burner serviceman to see if your burner's nozzle size can be reduced.

If your burner is both mismatched and old, it may pay to install a new "flame retention burner," which will boost the efficiency from 5 to 30 percentage points. Remember, however, that you are matching the burner to the house, not the house to the burner. Install the new burner or nozzle only *after* determining the new lower heat loss produced by your other energy conservation actions.

AUTOMATIC FLUE DAMPER

As we have seen, even the perfectly matched burner rates a PLF of only about 35 percent over the entire heating season. An automatic flue damper is a disk in the flue pipe, which, when closed, reduces the leakage of warm furnace air up the chimney. It is wired to the furnace controls so that it opens to allow the passage of the products of combustion and then closes when the furnace stops. These devices cost less than $200 installed and typically pay for themselves within very few heating seasons. Illustration 112 shows where the automatic flue damper is installed.

Heating with Wood

The first reason for heating with wood is psychological. Fire has played such an important role in human existence for so long that I wouldn't be at all surprised if it were necessary for mental health. Universally, people are overjoyed upon discovering the delights of wood heat. I have discovered, moreover, that the euphoria experienced is independent of the burning apparatus; glowing reports are heard on the one hand of the

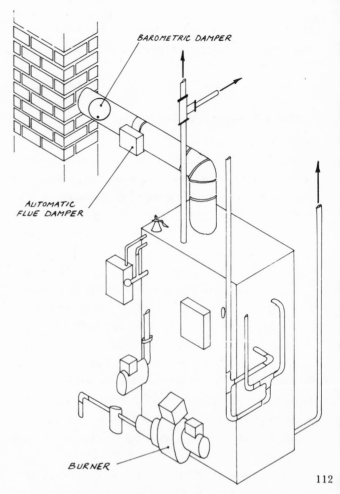

BAROMETRIC DAMPER

AUTOMATIC FLUE DAMPER

BURNER

112

unequaled performance of this European masterpiece and on the other of that American trash burner. One of the most common questions I am asked is "Which stove do you recommend?" My answer: "It don't make no difference." I don't mean to exclude myself. I have on occasion been found staring vacuously into an oil burner.

Seriously, though, there are a number of reasons to consider taking up with a wood stove:

> there is just nothing like it in the whole world;
> it keeps you busy through the winter;
> the Arabs don't own the trees—yet;
> it *may* save you money.

The Fuel Content of Wood

Saving money may be your last reason for burning wood instead of oil, gas, or electricity; I can think of no other explanation for city folks' burning wood at $2.97 per five-stick bundle in the fireplace. However, it is instructive to compare the value of wood as a fuel to the price of conventional fuels. First of all, wood is sold by the cord. In the country, a cord means a pile of wood 4′ wide by 4′ high by 8′ long. In the city, however, it often means how little wood can be made to look like a lot. In a stacked 128-cubic-foot cord of wood there is about 80 cubic feet of solid wood. The chemical makeup of the various species of wood is similar, i.e., *wood is wood;* primarily, the density is what differs. A pound of one species of wood will yield the same amount of heat as a pound of any other species. Since a cord of dry white oak weighs twice as much as a cord of dry white pine, the oak will produce twice as much heat when burned.

Table 32 lists the fuel contents of 23 different species of wood. The first column lists the maximum amount of heat released upon burning a cord of "air-dried" wood of 20 percent moisture content. This is the amount of heat that would be produced in the house if you burned the wood in your wastebasket (not recommended). With the more common and recommended practice of venting the products of combustion, about 60 percent of the maximum heat ends up in the house, with the other 40 percent going up the chimney as heat and unburned by-products. The second column gives the amount of heat realized in the proper operation of a good wood stove. The units are therms (10^5 Btu), which may also be roughly interpreted as gallons of fuel oil or 100 cubic feet of gas each. The third column further translates the heat units into kilowatt hours (kwh) of electricity. If you have a wood stove and an oil furnace, Table 33 will tell you which fuel is the better buy. For example, since the fuel equivalent of red oak burned at 60 percent efficiency is the same as 146 gallons of oil burned at 70 percent efficiency, red oak is a better buy than fifty-cent-per-gallon oil at up to $73 per cord of wood. As a second example, if you now pay 5¢ per kwh for electric heat, you would save money by burning ash wood costing up to $205 per cord.

Table 32. Fuel Value of Wood

wood species	maximum therms (10^5 Btu) per cord at 20% moisture content	therms at 60% efficiency (= gal. oil or 100 cu. ft. gas)	kwh electricity equivalent
Alder	159	95	2,800
Ash, white	233	140	4,100
Beech	248	149	4,360
Birch, white	213	128	3,750
Birch, yellow	241	145	4,240
Cedar, Eastern red	182	109	3,200
Cedar, Northern white	120	72	2,110
Chestnut	167	100	2,940
Elm, American	194	116	3,410
Fir, Douglas	186	112	3,270
Fir, balsam	140	84	2,460
Hemlock, Eastern	155	93	2,720
Hickory, shagbark	279	167	4,900
Maple, sugar	244	146	4,290
Maple, red	210	126	3,690
Maple, silver	182	109	3,200
Oak, white	264	158	4,640
Oak, red	244	146	4,290
Pine, white	136	82	2,390
Pine, lodgepole	159	95	2,800
Pine, Southern	229	137	4,030
Poplar	164	98	2,870
Spruce	155	93	2,720

It Don't Make No Difference

There are at least a hundred models of stoves to choose from, each one claimed to be unique and superior to all of the others. There is no point in listing all of them; Shelton and Shapiro's *Woodburners Encyclopedia* cannot be improved upon. Just to demonstrate the variety, I have shown in Illustration 113 the one import by which all others must be judged, the Norwegian Jøtul 118, and an example of that never-to-be-discounted Yankee ingenuity, the Tempwood. The Scandinavians, cursed with long, hard winters and a shortage of firewood, long ago developed wood stoves far superior to any pre-1975 Amer-

113a

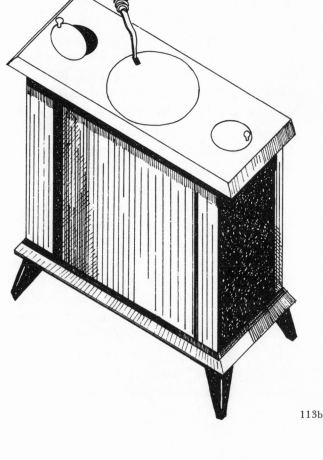

113b

ican models. To the Scandinavians, wood heating was not something limited to the hunting camp or the family room. The wood stove occupied a central position in the social areas of the house and thus had to be attractive. With a price of wood at least twice what we are accustomed to paying, efficiency was equally important. As a result, the Scandinavians have developed stoves of efficiency and beauty that have so far proven impossible to beat, at least in both regards simultaneously. Many American manufacturers have simply started reproducing the Scandinavian designs at a lower price.

Aside from the Scandinavian imitations, the American stoves are a diverse lot. If you subscribe to the aesthetic theory that equates function and beauty, some American stoves would move you to tears. I've learned to keep my mouth shut around people who proudly display what, to me,

has a lot of promise as a boat anchor. But beauty is in the eye of the beholder and I think I'll leave it there.

What about performance? Here the Americans seem to hold their own. There are chunk burners, stick burners, top-loaders, side-loaders, and end-loaders; enigmatic black boxes sporting springs and chains, Franklins with eagles and folding doors, even a few with Pyrex pie plates through which the flame may be viewed. And guess what? It doesn't make any difference. As far as I can tell, they all get about the same amount of heat out of a cord of wood.

There are several important differences to which the prospective stove owner should be alerted, however. A wood stove should *never* be *larger than required* since that bane of the wood-burner, creosote, is maximally produced by slow smoldering fires. Better to throw on another quilt or wear your longies to bed on that coldest night than to have to clean your chimney of a 2″ deposit of creosote halfway through the heating season. Buy a small stove and burn wood at a good rate and your creosote problems are largely solved.

The second difference is the weight of the stove. Regardless of whether the stove is fabricated of plate steel or cast iron, the total weight of the stove gives it thermal mass. Lightweight stoves typified by the Tempwood have a small thermal mass or heat storage capacity. They therefore begin to give off heat to the surroundings almost immediately upon firing. A very short time after the fire dies, however, they are stone cold. A 400-pound cast-iron model, on the other hand, may require a half-hour before any perceptible heat is given off; but heat is still felt several hours after the burn. If you plan to heat a space only occasionally, such as a workshop, consider the instant-heat steel stove. The cast-iron stove is one that you light in the fall, poke all winter, and let die in the spring.

Wood burning is a dirty business. The third difference, rarely mentioned, is ease of cleaning. Toward the end of the great American wood-burning era, the best American wood stoves had porcelain enamel finishes; gas and electric kitchen ranges still do for good reason. Try to wipe wood ash off a flat black stove and you'll have a flat-black-and-gray stove. Try washing it off, and the next day you'll have flat gray and rust. The only alternatives are: (1) ignore this object that more and more resembles an old engine block, (2) spray-paint it every few months with "Hibachi Black" high-temperature paint, or (3) periodically black the stove with stove polish. Enameled stoves, at an extra cost, require only wiping off with a damp rag to restore their original beauty, Enameled finishes are rare in American stoves because the enameling process requires a capital investment few manufacturers have yet been able to afford.

Getting Heat around the House

The flow of heat is a subtle thing. It's no trick to warm a single room by installing a wood stove. But heating an entire house evenly with one wood stove is an art. There are basically two options: open up the spaces and position the stove so that the heat naturally flows to wherever you want it, or keep the traditional closed-door approach and mechanically pump heat into all of the little rooms. Any damn fool can pump heat; your furnace or boiler is doing that right now. If you favor a lot of small rooms, consider adding a wood-burning furnace or boiler in parallel with your present system.

I'm personally in favor of working with natural forces rather than against them. Getting heat to flow naturally is like making love. Good lovers simply provide the proper conditions and then flow with the changing situation; bad ones come on like gang-busters and insist on getting their way. Letting nature do her thing is illustrated by the examples of Illustration 114A.

The basic law of natural heat convection is:

"HOT AIR RISES—COLD AIR FALLS."

Hot air is generated by the surface of the stove. This air is typically 30F° warmer than the surrounding air and therefore rises buoyantly. At the same time, air in contact with the outside surfaces of the house is continually losing heat and therefore falling. A convection pattern is thus established that naturally transports heat from the stove to the extremes of the space. If you were to observe the smoke from a cigarette in a stove-heated room, you would see that this convection occurs *entirely within about one foot of the ceiling and one foot of the floor!* If a solid wall were placed between you and a stove and you expected to be heated, you would be severely disappointed. No convection, no heat. Furthermore, if you opened a door between the rooms you would remain largely disappointed because air will not convect effectively without both a way in *and* a way out. Surprisingly, if you provide a vent at the very top and very bottom

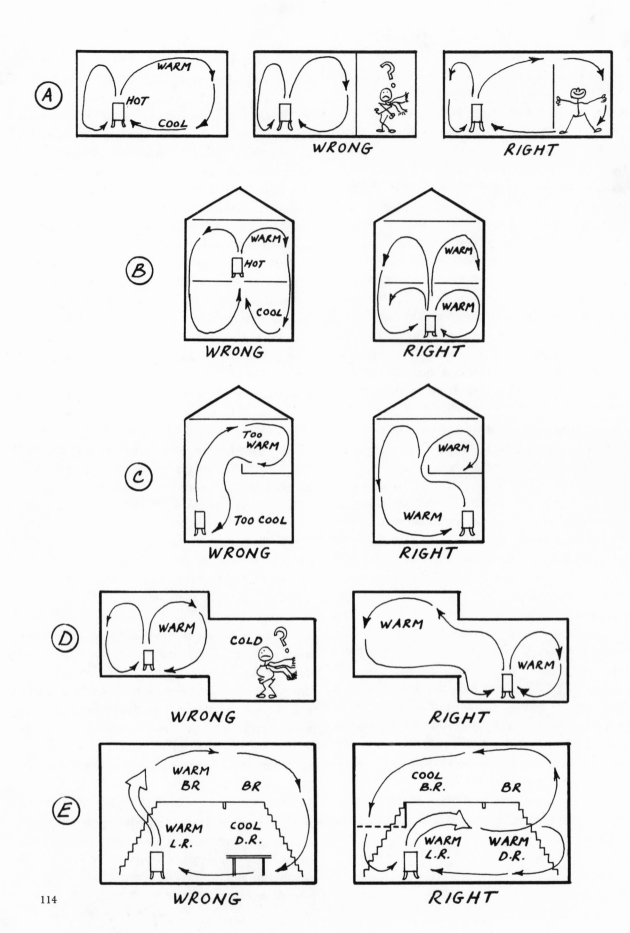

114

of the wall, the room will heat as if the wall were nonexistent.

In heating a two-story house with a single stove, the stove must be on the first floor (Illustration 114B). Although a convection pattern is established with the stove on the second story and vents in the floor, the first floor will be very cool, since the air descends into the first level space only after giving up its heat to the outside walls and windows.

Structures with high cathedral ceilings are notoriously hard to heat with wood stoves. If, as in Illustration 114C, the wood stove is located below a high open space, the 30F° ΔT air ascends like a hot air balloon, returning only after giving up its heat. With a typical 30F° difference between the ceiling and first floor, it is impossible to find a comfortable level. It's too hot in the loft and too cold on the floor at the same time! If the stove were moved to a position under the loft, however, the hot air would first have to escape from the space under the loft before rising to the second floor. In such a case the loft and the space under the loft will run at nearly identical temperatures.

All of these examples are from my own experience. If we learn only from our mistakes, I've got one of the better educations. My most recent lesson was that the split-level house in Illustration 114D is not much different from the two-story house in B. The wood stove in my house is located as in D, about three feet higher than the other end of the house. To descend that three feet is like being slowly lowered into the Maine ocean. One night the washing machine froze down there while the upper level was at 50° F. We have subsequently installed a second stove on the lower level and find (surprise!) that when it alone operates there is no cold pond of air at the upper level. In general, always place the wood stove at the lowest possible point. Heat will travel upward three or more stories (through suitable vents) and horizontal distances of fifty feet or more, particularly if accompanied by vertical displacement.

Illustration 114E demonstrates just how subtle air flow can be. A wood stove is located in the first-floor living room in a two-story house. Adjacent to the living room is the dining room, separated by only a very large wall opening, the top of which is one foot below the ceiling. Open stairways rise to the second floor from both ends. Hot air rises from the stove and forms a pond of hot air at ceiling level. Where is the outlet of this upside-down pond? The stairwell to the left, because the one-foot section of wall over the living room–dining room doorway represents a dam to the hot air. The hot air flows up the left stairwell, making the upstairs as warm as the downstairs. The air flowing up the left stairwell is replaced by cool air flowing down the right stairwell, through the dining room, and back to the stove. The net result is distressing: a too-warm upstairs bedroom and a cold, drafty dining room in sight of the stove! A solution was found in dropping a skirt around the left stairwell, forming a second hot-air dam one foot deeper than the one between the living room and dining room. The air flow now completely reverses; the dining room is warm and the upstairs bedroom cool.

Remember when installing a wood stove:

HOT AIR RISES!

Sizing the Wood Stove or Furnace

I stressed before the importance of the proper size of wood stove. Bigger is not better; it just costs more. The smallest wood stove is capable of producing heat at a substantial 30,000 Btu's per hour when burned wide open. After proper insulation, weatherstripping, and caulking, the heat demand of the average house on the coldest night is usually within this range. Picking the proper size of stove then does not relate to the maximum hourly heat production as much as to the total amount of heat (heat per hour × number of hours) produced in an overnight burn. Stove manufacturers and retailers are in the unfortunate habit of citing a stove's heating capacity in terms

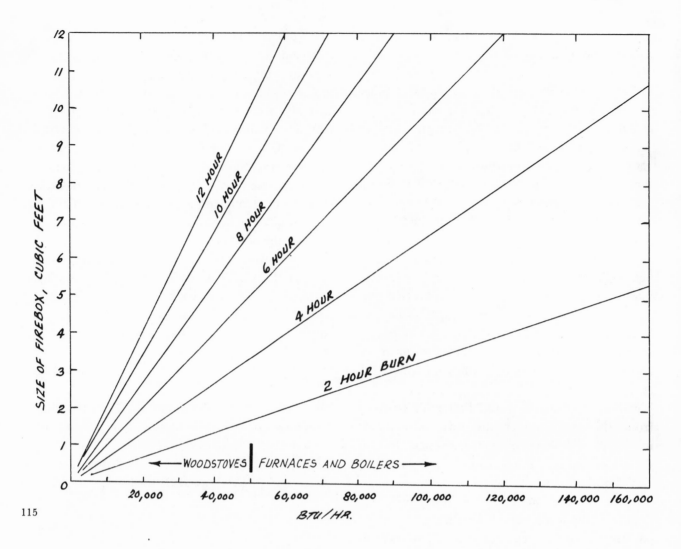

115

of cubic feet of space heated. Now we know that the heat loss of a building has less to do with its volume than with the degree to which it is insulated, weatherstripped, and caulked, its surface area, and the climate in which it is situated. If a stove dealer can't tell you anything better than the number of cubic feet heated, he should be a used car dealer.

Illustration 115 shows how to size a wood stove or furnace to your house and your habits. It is based upon the measured total Btu output of various stoves when fully loaded with air-dried red oak. The average result of dividing the total number of Btu's produced by the capacity of the firebox (and therefore the volume of wood consumed in a full stoking) is 60,000 Btu per cu. ft. This number can be converted from red oak to other species of wood by using Table 32. Simply

dividing the Btu content of wood listed in Table 33 by 128 cubic feet per cord would have predicted a figure in excess of 100,000 Btu per cu. ft. The discrepancy is explained by the fact that one does not pack wood into a firebox nearly as efficiently as in a stack of wood.

To use the chart, first calculate the maximum heat loss of the house at the lowest temperature of the year, as in the example of Chapter 9. Second, decide how long you wish the stove to burn on one load. Enter the chart with the Btu per hour rate at the bottom; rise to the diagonal line corresponding to the length of burn in hours; from the intersection read across on the left-hand scale the required cubic footage of the firebox.

Example. In order to minimize creosote buildup, I choose to pick a stove on the basis of the average January overnight temperature. Using the difference between my desired inside temperature, 60° F, and the average January minimum temperature, 10° F, I obtain a ΔT of 50F° with which to calculate the hourly heat loss. Using the heat loss form of Chapter 9, I find that the average overnight hourly heat loss is 15,000 Btu per hour. Now, I like my sleep: seven hours for health and one for beauty. I enter Illustration 115 on the bottom scale at 15,000 Btu/hr., rise up to the intersection with the eight-hour diagonal line, and read across on the left-hand scale the required firebox capacity: 2.0 cubic feet.

Installing a Wood Stove

Fires are not caused by wood stoves; they are caused by the people who operate wood stoves. Probably fewer than 1 percent of the house fires attributed to the burning of wood are caused by the failure of the wood stoves. The other 99 percent are caused by carelessness, improper installation of the stove or pipe, and creosote fires in unsafe chimneys.

There are two concerns in the installation of the stove itself: clearance from combustibles and provision for falling embers. Illustration 116 shows the clearances that must be maintained from the ordinary wood stoves. The surface temperature of such a stove is likely at some time to rise to over 1,000° F. You may stoke the stove fully some morning, open the draft up wide in order to heat the cold house rapidly, and then go off to work with your mind occupied by a problem. On a cold day the draft of the chimney may be sufficient to suck air like a blast furnace, and the stove will turn red hot. It's scary to witness such a hot stove in the dark; it's dangerous to

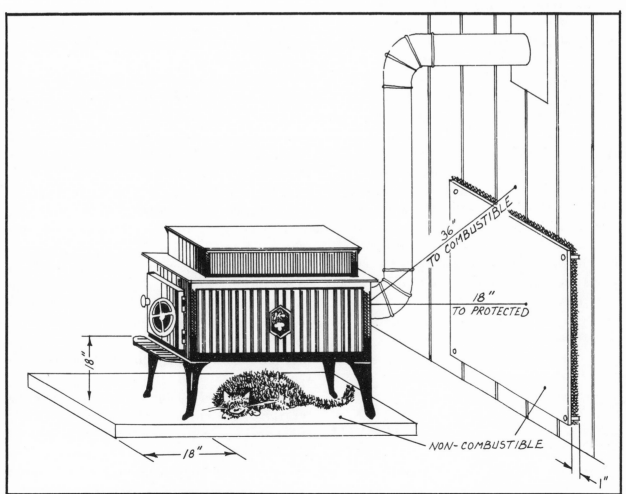

116

leave unattended. The spontaneous ignition temperature of wood is about 600° F. After many years of exposure to a hot stove, the surface of an adjacent wood wall may turn dark because of the loss of its volatile elements. The darker it becomes, the closer it approaches charcoal, which is nothing more than wood from which all but the carbon and minerals have been driven. The spontaneous ignition temperature of charcoal is around 300° F. For this reason the National Fire Protection Association specifies that a clearance of 36″ be maintained between the sides and top of a wood stove and any adjacent combustible material. If a noncombustible sheet of material, such as 24-gauge aluminum or asbestos board, is mounted over the combustible material with a 1″ minimum airspace between and below, the clearance may be reduced to 18″. Without the 1″ airspace, no reduction is allowed, regardless of the material. Clearance under the stove is not as critical, since the usual bed of ashes or sand is highly insulative. A clearance of 18″ is recommended—just enough for your wet sneakers.

The second critical item is a noncombustible floor covering extending 18″ from the stove loading door. Don't underestimate this one; I'll bet 10 to 1 that your floor has several little black burn marks if you've heated a full season without floor protection in front of the loading door!

Illustration 117 shows an attractive and simple-to-build stove base. The base need be no wider than the stove itself but 18″ longer according to the above rule. Regular construction two-by-fours form the perimeter. Dado and glue or screw the corners together as shown. Strips of 3/4″ wood

nailed to the two-by-fours form a ledge upon which rests a panel of 5/8″ plywood. The noncombustible material may be a number of decorative tiles arranged in a geometric pattern, or a layer of white marble chips. Decorative ceramic tiles may be obtained through companies specializing in tile installation and floor coverings. Marble chips are sold by garden supply retailers.

Many houses have existing fireplaces. Provided the chimney is in good condition, wood stoves can be installed for the winter and removed for the rest of the year, allowing normal operation of the fireplace. How to install the wood stove easily and attractively is the question. One option is provided by the Better'n Ben's stove—a wood stove whose backside is simply a steel plate large enough to cover the fireplace opening. All of the necessary hardware comes with the stove. A second option allowing the installation of any wood stove is shown in Illustration 118. Install a glass fireplace screen, available through Sears, Roebuck or most glass dealers. The glass screen doubles the efficiency of the fireplace by reducing the amount of excess air rushing up the chimney. When the fire dies down at night, you can close off the draft almost completely without risk of carbon monoxide or smoke that might result from closing the chimney damper. As soon as the serious heating season arrives, remove the glass doors and insert the homemade plate with thimble into the glass door slot in the frame. The plate consists of two sheets of 24-gauge aluminum with one inch of fiberglass blanket sandwiched between. The chimney thimble is screwed to the outer plate with sheet metal screws and receives the stovepipe just as in a chimney. A single aluminum plate could be used, but the double-plate sandwich fills the slot better. Tape over the fire screen draft slots as they tend to be very leaky.

This installation is more efficient than inserting the stove into the fireplace because the stove radiates to the room on three sides and the radiation from the rear surface is reflected back into the room by the aluminum plate.

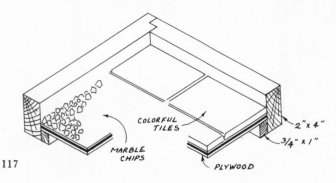

117

MARBLE CHIPS

COLORFUL TILES

2″ x 4″

3/4″ x 1″

PLYWOOD

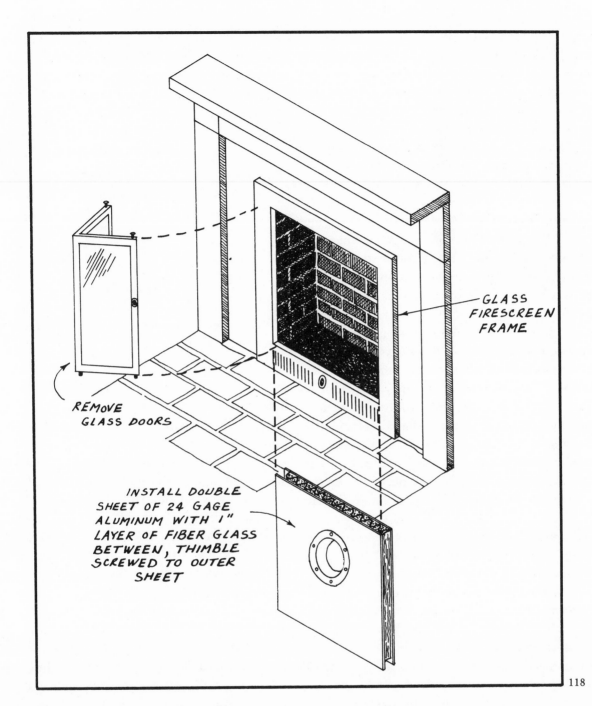

GLASS FIRESCREEN FRAME

REMOVE GLASS DOORS

INSTALL DOUBLE SHEET OF 24 GAGE ALUMINUM WITH 1" LAYER OF FIBER GLASS BETWEEN, THIMBLE SCREWED TO OUTER SHEET

118

Stovepipe and Chimney

After enduring all the salesmen's pitches, deliberating, finding the proper thimble, stovepipe, and elbows, cutting the stovepipe and your thumb in the process, lugging the 400-pound stove with no handles home and finally paying the bill, you may feel it's time for you and the old lady to have an old-fashioned highball around the new woodburner. But it's not.

I remember once paying $500 for a stereo system, lugging it home, tearing open the cartons and, for lack of a knife, biting the insulation off the wires, which I then connected (using a nail file) to a likely-looking set of four screws at the rear of the chassis. My heart racing with anticipation, my trembling fingers groped at the controls like a teenaged boy encountering his first bra. Finally—there was the ON/OFF control!

. . . Nothing . . . NOTHING! Nothing but the faint odor of burned wire insulation. As they say, if all else fails, read the instructions.

Hooking up a wood stove is like that, only the consequences may be far more serious. When things get dull around here I go down to the local fire station. Lately, things have been quite lively. Recently the station received a call from a motorist who, passing by, noticed smoke emanating from the gable vents of a house in town. When the chief arrived, sure enough, it appeared that a fire was in progress in the attic. The firemen were about to chop a hole in the roof and extinguish the blaze when the proprietor stopped them. It seemed that the owner had discovered a principle that promised to revolutionize the heating industry. The deteriorating chimney had been removed fifty years ago down to attic floor level and the remainder left as a harmless relic. The owner had heard that half of the fuel value of wood is lost up the chimney and he theorized (correctly, I might add) that he could recover some of his losses by discharging the smoke into the attic!

About a month later the fire department arrived at another house that was engulfed in flames. After the fire had burned itself out, there stood a wood stove, but where was the chimney? This puzzled both the owner and the chief until the owner allowed as how he didn't recall ever seeing a chimney on his house anyway! Apparently there had once been a chimney, subsequently removed. The space formerly occupied by the chimney had been converted to a closet, but the metal thimble in the plaster wall had never been removed. The owner, in anticipation of the joys of woodburning, had simply hooked the stove up to the closet and kindled a roaring blaze.

Don't be one of those who will ultimately force the insurance companies to raise their rates for woodburning homes. Before you kindle the fire, call in the local fire department to check your installation.

There are three basic chimney options: the present chimney is safe; the present chimney needs lining; there is no chimney.

IS THE PRESENT CHIMNEY SAFE?

Chimney sweeps are reappearing in every area of the country where woodburning is popular. Your stove dealer should have the names of a few; if not, try the Yellow Pages or the fire department. A good chimney sweep should have the equipment to check the condition of a chimney. The test consists of closing off the top of the chimney and then introducing smoke into the flue. An unsafe chimney will leak smoke from cracks and loose mortar joints.

LINING THE CHIMNEY

An unlined chimney may possibly be lined by a mason by lowering clay tile of the appropriate size from above. A rope is looped through the tile and then withdrawn by pulling on one end after the tile is in place. A carbide masonry drill is then used to cut an opening for the stovepipe thimble. Opinions differ as to the effectiveness of this procedure, even among masons. A large percentage feel it's a waste of their time and your money since the joints between the flue tiles cannot be effectively sealed.

A very effective but less used method is to line the chimney with a stainless steel smoke pipe. Type 316 stainless steel smoke pipe (resistant to the acetic acid in creosote) can be fabricated in six-foot lengths by any large sheet metal shop. Measure the distance from the thimble to the chimney outlet and the inside dimensions of the chimney and show the sheet metal shop a sketch of your installation. They can then fabricate the exact lengths of pipe required, as well as a stainless elbow at the bottom and a top plate that will seal off the opening between the pipe and the chimney and support the weight of the pipe. An oversized hole will have to be temporarily created in the masonry at the bottom in order to insert the elbow and connect the pipe lowered from above. Fasten the sections of pipe together before lowering from the top, using stainless steel screws. Some heat will be gained and stored by the masonry from the flue gas if the masonry is exposed to the living space. If the chimney is enclosed, however, little heat is gained by the house; in that case the chimney will draw better and accumulate less creosote if the cavity between the pipe and the masonry is filled from above with fireproof vermiculite insulation.

NEW CHIMNEYS

Two popular forms of new chimney are concrete block and prefabricated metal pipe. Both cost about the same per linear foot. The concrete block chimney has a large thermal mass and, if exposed to the interior of the house, will extract and radiate heat from the flue gases and thereby increase the overall efficiency of a wood stove by 5 to 10 percent. Installed outside the house, however, it is a total disaster. The large

ΔT between the flue gas and the outdoor air results in excessive heat loss of the flue gas and a guaranteed creosote buildup. Never build a masonry chimney on the outside of a building!

Prefabricated metal chimneys are sold under a variety of trade names, the most widely recognized being Metalbestos. In spite of the name, the insulating material between the two stainless steel pipes is not asbestos, but a cement–fiberglass mixture. Illustration 119 shows the three common prefabricated pipe installations. All of the manufacturers of this type of chimney make complete lines of fittings, supports, and terminations, but the products are not interchangeable. The chimneys are easily installed by the home handyman, provided he doesn't mind working on the roof. The pipe comes in a variety of diameters. The inside diameter must be at least as great as that of the stove outlet. Two or more stoves may be installed on the same chimney using tee-fittings as long as: (1) the entry points are separated vertically by a few feet, and (2) the cross-sectional area of the pipe is at least as great as the sum of the areas of the stove outlets.

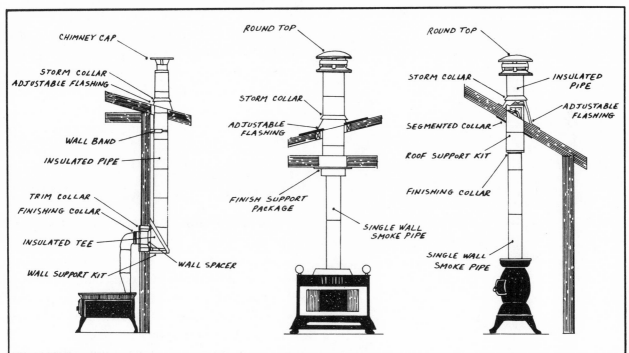

119

Stovepipe and Chimney Clearance

Illustration 120 shows the critical dimensions for stovepipes and chimneys. Starting at the stove outlet, the smokepipe must be of a diameter equal to or larger than the stove outlet; it should change direction by no more than a total of 180° before entering the chimney; the horizontal run should not exceed three-quarters of the height of the chimney above the entry point; and the smokepipe (which may at times be hotter than the stove) must be no closer than 18″ to any combustible material. In case of a fire in the smokepipe, the pipe is subject to violent forces and should therefore be cemented into the thimble, supported every six feet horizontally, and screwed together at every joint, using three sheet-metal screws. The chimney itself must extend in height at least three feet above the roof at the point of exit and two feet above any other point within a horizontal distance of ten feet. The latter rule requires a chimney height of nine feet above a 45° roof! At such a height, the prefabricated metal chimney must be braced against the wind. While a single-wall stovepipe must maintain a clearance of 18″ from combustibles, the masonry and prefabricated chimneys require only 2″ clearance.

Start the prefabricated chimney at just below ceiling level, whether in conventional construction or with a high cathedral ceiling. A significant amount of heat can be extracted from the single-wall pipe before it enters the insulated pipe, raising the overall efficiency of the installation again by 5 to 10 percent.

Creosote

No discussion of woodburning would be complete without a few words about creosote. Creosote is a general term for the products of incomplete combustion deposited on the walls of the stovepipe and chimney. It is the bane of woodburners because: (1) it smells bad, (2) it looks bad, (3) it can in extreme cases completely block the chimney within a heating season, and (4) if it ignites, it can burn like a jet engine with a stuck throttle, reducing an unsound chimney and the surrounding house to a smoldering rubble. Creosote is like bad breath: everyone has it sooner or later to varying degrees. But, like bad breath, it can be reduced to a harmless level by brushing and restricting what you feed your stove. Creosote accumulation in the chimney is minimized by:

burning dry wood with a maximum moisture content of 20 percent

having the right size stove to eliminate the need for long-smoldering burns

feeding the fire small loads more often and burning at a moderate rate

using only inside masonry or insulated metal chimneys.

If you have obeyed all of these rules and still have a too-rapid creosote accumulation, change from enameled or blue steel to chrome-plated or stainless steel smokepipe. The latter two will lose less heat because of lower surface emissivity.

Finally, in case of fire, your best defense is a

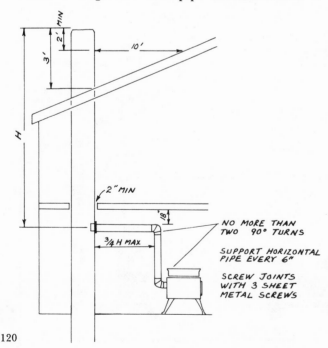

120

NO MORE THAN TWO 90° TURNS

SUPPORT HORIZONTAL PIPE EVERY 6″

SCREW JOINTS WITH 3 SHEET METAL SCREWS

sound chimney and a tight stove. The ability to deprive a chimney of the oxygen necessary to sustain a chimney fire is one of the best arguments for an airtight stove. Spraying water into the chimney is very harmful to the masonry as well as to your oriental rugs.

Symbols Used in the Text

A	area of surface	PV	present value, dollars
a_o	fixed cost of insulation operation, dollars per square foot	PWF	present worth factor
a_1	cost of insulation material, dollars per board foot	p	rate of fuel price increase, percent per year
a_2	cost of framing a space, dollars per board foot	psf	pounds per square foot
a_3	value of living space, dollars per board foot	psi	pounds per square inch
BCR	benefit-cost ratio	Q	air infiltration, cubic feet per hour
Btu	British thermal unit	q	fossil fuel initially available
b	breadth of board, inches	R	thermal resistance, square foot, °F per Btu
c	compressive stress, pounds per square inch	R_o	thermal resistance of uninsulated construction
c‖	compression parallel to grain, pounds per square inch	RGH	rough sawed
D	depth of insulation, inches	S	section modulus, inches cubed (in.^{3})
DD	degree days	SC	shading coefficient
d	depth of board, inches	SF	solar factor
E	modulus of elasticity, pounds per square inch	S4S	surfaced-four-sides
FV	future value, dollars	T	temperature, °F
f	extreme fiber stress in bending, pounds per square inch	t	time, years
H	heat flow, Btu's per unit of time	t‖	tension parallel to grain, pounds per square inch
HD	heating days	W	total weight, pounds
h	horizontal shear stress, pounds per square inch	w	uniformly distributed load, pounds per square foot
I	moment of inertia, inches to the fourth power (in.^{4})	Y	solar radiation climatic factor
i	interest rate, percent per year	α	absorptivity of surface
L	clearspan of a beam, feet	Δ	difference
LCC	life-cycle cost	ΔT	temperature difference, °F
l	length of a post, inches	ϵ	emissivity of surface
l/d	slenderness ratio of a post, inches per inch	σ	Stefan-Boltzmann constant
M	bending moment, inch pounds	<	less than
MC	marginal cost	≤	less than or equal to
MS	marginal saving	>	greater than
o.c.	on-center spacing, inches	≥	greater than or equal to

Glossary

AIR-DRIED: wood seasoned by exposure to atmosphere with no artificial heat.

ALTERATION: any building change that does not alter the total volume.

ANCHOR BOLT: a bolt cast into concrete foundation to anchor a wood sill.

BALLOON FRAME: a frame in which the studs are uninterrupted from sill to rafter.

BASEMENT: the lowest story of a house, if below ground.

BEAM: any wood structural member that carries a load in bending.

BEARING WALL: a wall that supports a load in addition to its own weight.

BLOCKING: short pieces nailed between major framing members to act as fire-stops or provide a nailing surface.

BOARD: lumber less than nominally two inches thick.

BOARD FOOT: the equivalent volume of one square foot, one inch thick.

BRACE: a diagonal framing member fastened to major horizontal and vertical members to provide a triangle resisting racking forces.

BRIDGING: diagonal members that transfer vertical loads from a floor joist to its neighbors.

BTU (BRITISH THERMAL UNIT): the amount of heat energy required to raise the temperature of one pound of water by $1F^{\circ}$.

CASEMENT: a window hinged at a vertical edge to swing out.

CAULK: to seal a joint in a building.

COLLAR BEAM: a horizontal member connecting rafters near the ridge.

COLUMN: a vertical free-standing load-carrying member.

CORNER BRACES: diagonal members at building corners to resist racking.

CORNICE: decorative trim at the meeting of roof and wall.

DEAD LOAD: the weight of the building itself.

DEGREE DAY: the difference between a base temperature and the average temperature of a day. The base is usually $65^{\circ}F$.

DIMENSION LUMBER: lumber 2 to 5 inches thick and up to 12 inches wide.

DORMER: a structure projecting from a roof, usually containing a window.

DRY ROT: a fungus that decays wood in the presence of moisture and warm conditions.

DRYWALL: wall covering material not requiring mixing.

EAVE: the overhanging portion of a roof.

FASCIA: the vertical surfaces of the eave.

FENESTRATION: the area and arrangement of glazing.

FLASHING: sheet materials used to prevent water penetration at building joints.

FLUE: an individual passage in a chimney.

FOOTING: the base of the foundation, usually wider than the portion above.

FOUNDATION: the structure below the first floor, usually masonry.

FRAMING: the skeleton of the building.

GABLE: the portion of wall above the lowest point of the roof.

GIRDER: a large beam supporting floor joists at the same level as the sills.

GIRT: a large horizontal beam supporting the ends of upper-story floor joists between posts.

HEADER: a member that receives a set of repetitive members at right angles.

HEAT TRANSMISSION COEFFICIENT: number of Btu's lost through an area of one square foot when the temperature on the opposite sides differs by $1F^{\circ}$.

HUMIDITY: the amount of water vapor in air in pounds per pound of air.

INTERIOR TRIM: all the interior woodwork designed to conceal joints.

INSULATION: a material which resists heat flow.

JOIST: repetitive horizontal members supporting the floor or ceiling load.

KILN-DRIED: wood seasoned using artificial heat.

KNOT: portion of branch embedded in tree.

LATH: any material fastened to framing to receive plaster.

LEADER: portion of gutter designed to carry water away from building.

LEDGER: a strip nailed to the side of one member to support another member from below.

LINEAR FOOT: a length of one foot, independent of area or volume.

LIVE LOAD: the weight due to occupancy of a building.

LUMBER: wood which has been sawed and planed only.

MANSARD ROOF: a double-pitched roof with the lower section containing dormers.

MASONRY: stone, concrete, or brick bonded together with mortar.

MATCHED: lumber milled with matching tongue-and-groove edges.

MODULAR BUILDING: the dimensioning of a building to use materials based on a common measurement.

MOISTURE CONTENT: the amount of water in wood expressed as a percentage of the oven-dry weight of wood.

MOLDING: a narrow piece of shaped wood used to decorate or conceal a joint.

NOMINAL SIZE: the rough size of a member before planing.

NONBEARING WALL: a wall that supports only its own weight.

ON-CENTER: the distance from the center of one member to the center of the next.

PENNY: the size of a nail, usually written "d."

PERMEABILITY: a measure of the ease with which water vapor passes through a material.

PIER: a masonry column.

PITCH: the slope of anything expressed as the rise divided by the run or span.

PLAN: a drawing representing the horizontal arrangement of a building.

PLATE: member connecting the ends of the studs and posts.

PLATFORM FRAME: a house frame in which the floor joists of one story rest on the top plate of the wall below.

POST: the vertical wall members at the corners and wall intersections.

PURLIN: members at right angles to rafters serving to break up the roofboard span.

RABBET: a rectangular section cut along the edge of a board.

RAFTER: the main load-carrying members of the roof, usually running up and down the slope.

RELATIVE HUMIDITY: the humidity expressed as a percentage of the maximum possible humidity at that temperature.

RIBBON or RIBBAND: a board let in to the studs to support the bottom of upper story joists.

RIDGE or RIDGEPOLE: the member at the peak of the roof to receive the rafter ends.

RISER: the vertical board between steps.

ROOFERS: roofboards nailed to rafters or purlins.

ROUGH LUMBER: lumber that has been sawn but not planed.

ROUGH OPENING: the opening in the framing to receive windows and doors.

SASH: the wood frame of a window, which holds the glass.

SECTION: a drawing of a building in the vertical plane.

SHADE COEFFICIENT: the amount of sunlight penetrating a window compared to an unshaded single-glazed window at 1.0.

SHEATHING: the material covering the house frame.

SHEETING: any material applied in large sheets, usually polyethylene.

SHIPLAP: lumber that has been rabbeted to match edges.

SIDING: the material covering the outside of a building.

SILL: the bottommost piece of wood; interfaces wood frame with foundation.

SLEEPERS: wood strips over concrete to fasten a wooden floor.

SOFFIT: the horizontal part of the eave.

SPAN: the distance between supports.

SQUARE: forming a 90° angle; also 100-square-foot area.

STORY: the space between a floor and a ceiling.

STUDS: vertical framing members between the posts used to support vertical loads and provide nailing surfaces for interior and exterior sheathing.

SUBFLOOR: the first layer of flooring over joists.

SURFACED LUMBER: lumber that has been planed after sawing.

THERMOSTAT: any device that controls a heating or cooling device by responding to changes in temperature.

TIE BEAM: a beam connecting the base of rafter pairs to prevent outward thrust.

TIMBERS: wood framing members whose smallest dimension is five inches.

TREAD: the horizontal surface of a stair.

TRIM: wood used to decorate or conceal building joints.

TRUSS: rafters, ceiling joists, and ties assembled in such a way as to span a greater distance than the rafter alone.

VAPOR BARRIER: any material that forms a membrane resistant to the passage of water vapor.

VENTILATION: the provision for moving air, either mechanically or naturally.

WEATHERSTRIP: materials used to seal the joints between fixed and movable parts of a building.

Bibliography

Part I

Fitch, James Marston. *American Building: The Historical Forces That Shaped It*. New York: Schocken Books, 1974.
Greater Portland Landmarks, Inc. *Living With Old Houses*. Portland, Maine: Great Portland Landmarks, Inc., 1975.
Grow, Lawrence. *The Old House Catalogue*. New York: Main Street Press, 1976.
Historic-Salem, Inc. *The Salem Handbook. A Restoration Guide for Homeowners*. Salem, Mass.: Historic-Salem, Inc., 1977.
Lovins, Amory B. *Soft Energy Paths*. Cambridge, Mass.: Ballinger Publishing Company, 1977.
Meadows, Donella, and D. L. Meadows. *Limits to Growth*. New York: Basic Books, Inc., 1974.
Scher, Les. *Finding and Buying Your Place in the Country*. New York: Collier, 1974.
Stanforth, Deirdre, and Martha Stamm. *Buying and Renovating a House in the City*. New York: Alfred A. Knopf, Inc., 1974.
Stephen, George. *Remodeling Old Houses*. New York: Alfred A. Knopf, Inc., 1973.
Whiffen, Marcus. *American Architecture since 1780: A Guide to the Style*. Cambridge, Mass.: The M.I.T. Press, 1969.
Williams, Henry L., and Ottalie K. Williams. *A Guide to Old American Houses, 1700–1900*. New York: Barnet, 1967.
Williams, Henry L., and Ottalie K. Williams. *Old American Houses: How to Restore, Remodel and Reproduce Them*. New York: Crown Publishers, Inc., 1957.

Part II

Browne, J. S. C. *Basic Theory of Structures*. London: Pergamon Press, Inc., 1966.
Construction Guides for Exposed Wood Decks. Forest Service, USDA, Sup. of Doc. Stock No. 001-000-02577-5, 1972.
Dietz, Albert G. *Dwelling House Construction*. Cambridge, Mass.: The M.I.T. Press, 1946.
National Design Specification for Stress-Grade Lumber and Its Fastenings. Washington, D.C.: National Forest Products Association, 1973.
Parker, Harry. *Simplified Engineering for Architects and Builders*, 5th ed. New York: John Wiley & Sons, Inc., 1975.
Weidhaas, Ernest R. *Architectural Drafting and Design*, 2nd ed. Boston: Allyn & Bacon, Inc., 1972.
Wood Handbook. Agriculture Handbook Number 72, Forest Products Laboratory. Washington, D.C.: Sup. of Doc. Stock No. 0100-03200, 1974.

Part III

Climates of the States. NOAA. Washington, D.C.: Sup. of Doc. No. 003-017-00211-0, 1973.
Condensation Problems in Your House: Prevention and Solutions. Forest Service, USDA. Washington, D.C.: Sup. of Doc. Stock No. 001-000-03318-2, 1974.
Consumer Guide. *Energy Saver's Catalogue*. New York: G. P. Putnam's Sons, 1977.
In the Bank—Or up the Chimney? HUD. Washington, D.C.: Sup. of Doc. Stock No. 023-000-00297-3, 1975.
Portola Institute. *Energy Primer*. Menlo Park, Cal.: Portola Institute, 1974.
Principles for Protecting Wood Buildings from Decay. Forest Products Laboratory. Washington, D.C.: Sup. of Doc. Stock No. 001-001-00362-0, 1973.
Window Design Strategies to Conserve Energy. National Bureau of Standards. Washington, D.C.: Sup. of Doc. Stock No. 003-003-01794-9, 1977.

Part IV

Campbell, Stu, and Doug Taff. *Build Your Own Solar Water Heater.* Charlotte, Vt.: Garden Way, 1978.
Fisher, Rich, and B. Yanda. *Solar Greenhouse.* Santa Fe, N.M.: John Muir Publications, 1976.
Gay, Larry. *The Complete Book of Heating with Wood.* Charlotte, Vt.: Garden Way, 1974.
McCullagh, James, ed. *Solar Greenhouse Book.* Emmaus, Pa.: Rodale Press, 1978.
Nearing, Helen and Scott Nearing. *Building and Using Our Sun-Heated Greenhouse.* Charlotte, Vt.: Garden Way, 1977.
Passive Design Ideas for the Energy Conscious Architect. Rockville, Md.: National Solar Heating and Cooling Information Center, 1977.
Shelton, Jay, and Andrew B. Shapiro. *The Woodburners Encyclopedia.* Waitsfield, Vt.: Vermont Crossroads Press, 1976.
Taylor, Kathryn S., and Edith W. Gregg. *Winter Flowers in Greenhouse and Sun-Heated Pit.* New York: Charles Scribner's Sons, 1969.

Fix-It

DeCristoforo, R.J. *Handtool Handbook for Woodworking.* Tucson, Ariz.: H. P. Books, 1977.
Reader's Digest. *Complete Do-It-Yourself Manual.* Pleasantville, N.Y.: Reader's Digest, 1973.
Reader's Digest. *Fix-It-Yourself Manual.* Pleasantville, N.Y.: Reader's Digest, 1977.
Richter, H. P. *Wiring Simplified,* 32nd ed. St. Paul, Minn.: Park Publishing, 1977.
Time-Life Books. *Basic Wiring.* Alexandria, Va.: Time-Life, 1976.
Time-Life Books. *Plumbing.* Alexandria, Va.: Time-Life, 1976.
Simplified Electrical Wiring. Sears, Roebuck & Co., 1969.

Carpentry and Building

Cole, John N., and Charles G. Wing. *From the Ground Up.* Boston, Mass.: Atlantic–Little, Brown, 1976.
Concrete Masonry and Brickwork. U.S. Department of the Army. New York: Dover Publications, Inc. 1975.
Low Cost Wood Homes for Rural America—Construction Manual. Agriculture Handbook Number 364, Forest Service, USDA, Washington, D.C., 1969.
McCormick, Dale. *Against the Grain: A Carpentry Manual for Women.* Iowa City, Iowa: Iowa City Women's Press, 1977.
Reschke, Robert C. *How to Build Your Own Home.* Farmington, Mich.: Structures Publishing, 1976.
Roberts, Rex. *Your Engineered House.* New York: M. Evans & Co., Inc., 1964.
Wagner, Willis. *Modern Carpentry.* South Holland, Ill.: Goodheart-Wilcox, 1976.

Associations and Preservation Agencies

American Association for State and Local History
1315 Eighth Avenue, South
Nashville, Tenn. 37203

Association for Preservation Technology
1706 Prince of Wales Drive
Ottawa 5, Canada

National Trust for Historic Preservation
740-748 Jackson Place, N.W.
Washington, D.C. 20006

Office of Archeology and Historic Preservation
National Park Service
U.S. Department of the Interior
Washington, D.C. 20240

Journals

Old House Journal
199 Berkeley Place
Brooklyn, New York 11217

Technology and Conservation
1 Emerson Place
Boston, Mass. 02114

121

A Word about Cornerstones

Cornerstones' avowed purpose is the education of owner-builders; the end result is much larger. Owner-builders often find that the design and construction of their own low-cost energy-efficient shelter is just the beginning of a new life-style — a life-style of self-awareness and surety in an unsure world. We chose the name Cornerstones because we hoped people would find here the cornerstones of new, more rewarding lives.

Every summer, from May through October, people of all ages and from all walks of life join us in Maine for intensive three-week courses. The summer program consists of morning classroom instruction on the principles and particulars of design, followed by afternoon hands-on carpentry classes. Evenings are spent either socializing or in drafting class. In the hands-on program, each three-week class builds a small but complete house from the ground up.

Designing and building one's own house often requires more than we can give a student in the allotted three weeks. For those desiring continued help through the design and construction phase, a correspondence design seminar allows the remote student to work with his/her teacher until completion of the project.

Charlie and Susan Wing
Cornerstones
54 Cumberland St.
Brunswick, Me. 04011

Index

98; high vapor permeability, 97; masonry construction and, 138; R values, 97; shrinkage, 97, 100–101, 135, 138; temperature/humidity sensitivity, 97; water resistance, 98; walls, xii
Urethane foam insulation, 94, 98–99, 129, 138, 184; aerosol cans, 161; sprayed, 138
U-thane insulation. *See* Urethane foam insulation

Value, assessing for house, 19
Vapor barrier, 118, 127, 215; effects of lack of, 3, 112, 134, 141; loosening outside surfaces and, 121–122; new construction, 119; plywood as, 119, 121, 126; polyethylene as, xii, 71, 118–120, 122, 130, 135, 137, 140, 141, 142; UF foam and, 97; wallpaper as, 120, 135
Vapor pressure, concept of, 114
Velcro strips, 151
Ventilation, 127, 135, 215; attic, 122, 142, 145; cathedral ceiling, 141, 142; ceiling light fixtures, 122, 141; exterior sheathing, 121; household odors, 156; minimum requirement, 156–157 (*see also* Air exchange rate); passive solar house, 168–169, 189; soffit, 97, 122, 140, 142, 145; through walls for heat flow, 201–203; windows in summer, 158
Verandas, 7
Vermiculite insulation, 140
Vertical loads, 28; and bending, 34, 38–41; and compression, 33, 35, 36; and tension, 33–34, 37
Victorian styles, 7–10
Vinyl siding. *See* Siding
Vinyl weatherstrip, 158, 159

Wallpaper: above chair rail, 5; vinyl as vapor barrier, 119, 135
Walls: cavities in (*see* Stud cavities); in

compression, 33; curved, 20–21; insulating, xii, 99–100, 135–140; kneed, 144–145; load-bearing, 54, 66, 67, 214; making thicker, 137; non-load-bearing, 66, 69, 215; rafters joined to, 52; removal of, 66, 67, 69; unfinished and insulation, 137
Wall sheathing. *See* Sheathing, wall
Water: drum wall heat storage system, 169, 189; heat absorption by, 189; resistance of insulation to, 95, 97, 98, 127; solar heating of, 165, 190–193, 194; states of, 110; temperature scales and states of, 75–76; wasted hot, 86
Water vapor, 110; basement, 130; forced into house cavities, 113–117; reducing in home, 117–126; sources of, 117, 156
Weatherstrip, 157–160, 194, 215; aluminum, V-type, xii; brass, 157; doors, 92, 157, 159–160; and infiltration, xii; of insulating shutters, 153; spring metal, xii, 157, 158; types, 158; when to install, 155; windows, xii, 92, 158–159
"Well-water temperature," 132
West-facing windows, 69, 92, 158
Wind: and infiltration, xii, 114; lateral force of, 28, 34, 38, 41, 69 (*see also* Wind pressure)
Wind load, 29–30, 41, 51
Window ratio, 92
Windows: eliminating, 67, 69, 70, 158, 194; heat gain, 86–88, 147; heat loss, xii, 86, 147; infiltration through, xii, 154, 157, 158; north-facing, 69, 92, 157–158, 194; sash area, 86; shuttered, 147; single-/double-glazed, xii, 147, 148, 156; as solar collectors, 146–150; south-facing, 69, 86, 92, 146–150; top sash caulked, xii, 158, 159; types, 157, 159; weatherstripping, xii, 92, 157, 158–159
Window styles: bay, 7, 8; dormer, 7, 8, 9, 10, 11; double-hung, xii, 20–21; even

spacing of, 20–21; large, 6; round-top, 20–21; small paned, 20–21; stained glass, 10
Wind pressure, water vapor forced into house cavities by, 114–115
Wind rose map, 115
Wiremold, vapor barrier and, 119, 137
Wiring: costs, 67; insulating around, 134, 137, 140; vapor barrier and surface, 119, 137
Wood (*see also* Lumber; Plywood); internal forces on, 32–33; moisture content, 215; pressure-treated, 130; properties of, 35–36; resistance to bending, 38; R value, 100; spontaneous ignition of, 206; strength of, 34
Wood, heating with, xii, 67, 71, 92, 107, 117, 157, 165, 198–211 (*see also* Wood stoves); and creosote, 200–201, 205, 209, 210–211; disadvantages of, 201; dried, 199, 210; fires in homes and, 205, 208; fuel content, 198–199; and heat flow, 201–203; reasons for, 198
Woodburners Encyclopedia, The (Shelton and Shapiro), 199
Wood stoves, xii, 56, 71, 92; base for, 206; cast iron/plate steel, 201; clearance needed, 205–206, 210; efficiency of, 155, 200; enamel finishes, 201; firebox size, 203–204; in fireplace, 206; high temperature paint for, 201; installation of, 203, 205–210; length of burn, 203, 204; model differences, 199–201; with Pyrex doors, 156, 200; radiative transfer, 79, 206; size, 200–201, 203, 310; tightness, 211
Woodwork, interior: fancy, 5, 20–21; vapor barrier and caulking around, 120, 135
W. W. Grainger catalogue, 189, 190

Zero-energy houses, 85, 93
Zonolite, 140